With bes[illegible]

from

Rajendra & [illegible]

The Process of Financial Liberalization in India

The Process of Financial Liberalization in India

KUNAL SEN
RAJENDRA R. VAIDYA

DELHI
OXFORD UNIVERSITY PRESS
CALCUTTA CHENNAI MUMBAI
1997

Oxford University Press, Great Clarendon Street, Oxford OX2 6DP

Oxford New York
Athens Auckland Bangkok Calcutta
Cape Town Chennai Dar es Salaam Delhi
Florence Hong Kong Istanbul Karachi
Kuala Lumpur Madrid Melbourne Mexico City
Mumbai Nairobi Paris Singapore
Taipei Tokyo Toronto

and associates in
Berlin Ibadan

ISBN 0 19 564260 0

Typeset by Sheel Arts, Delhi 110 092
Printed at Pauls Press, New Delhi 110 020
and published by Manzar Khan, Oxford University Press
YMCA Library Building, Jai Singh Road, New Delhi 110 001

To Our Parents

Foreword

Financial liberalization is an essential element of economic reforms and structural adjustment. India has a very well-developed financial system and a long tradition of financial intermediation by private firms. However, the major banks were nationalized in the sixties. Insurance firms were nationalized earlier. Thus the nationalized public sector institutions dominate the financial system. With regulated interest rates, directed and often subsidized credit, financial markets are far from competitive. Thus financial liberalization can be quite beneficial to the Indian economy. The process of financial liberalization, however, raises a number of questions:

i) What are the links between financial liberalization and the general macroeconomic environment within which it occurs?
ii) What kind of legal infrastructure, market transparency and regulatory regimes pertaining to the financial sector are needed?
iii) What would be the impact of financial liberalization on the money demand and money supply process?
iv) What should be the role of the central bank as the regulator of the financial sector during an era of increasing central bank independence?

Kunal Sen and Rajendra R. Vaidya address these issues in this book. They first undertake a detailed examination of the changes in each sector (banks, development finance institutions, etc.) and market (money, credit, capital, etc.) since the reforms of mid–1991 and hypothesize on the possible path that different constituents of the Indian financial system may take in the future. The book then analyses four specific issues in the reform process: first, the regulatory regime pertaining to banks and development finance institutions; second, the interaction between financial and real sector reforms and the consequence of financial sector reforms on the financing of industry and agriculture; third, the link between the financial liberalization process and the general macroeconomic environment within which it occurs; and finally, the implications of financial liberalization for the conduct of monetary policy.

The book highlights the importance of initial conditions and the gradualist approach followed in avoiding a major disruption of economic activity in India, as has been observed in several other developing countries that have undergone financial liberalization. However, the authors argue that the successful completion of the reform process will depend critically on the appropriate sequencing of microeconomic and macroeconomic reforms and real sector and financial sector reforms. For example the development of treasury bills markets is a precondition for effective management of foreign capital inflows, and the formulation of exit procedures and bankruptcy codes compatible with a truly efficient financial system.

This book is part of a project on Financial Liberalization in Developing Countries, initiated and partly funded by the International Development Research Centre, Canada. The general objective of the project was to analyse financial liberalization and regulation in five developing countries, namely Argentina, India, Nigeria, Turkey and Uruguay. As a result, this study on India has benefited from a deeper understanding that the authors obtained through exchange of experiences, understanding and ideas with other participants of the project.

Kirit S. Parikh
Director
Indira Gandhi Institute of Development Research
Mumbai
May 1997

Acknowledgements

This book originated while we were working on a project titled 'Financial Liberalization in Developing Countries' at the Indira Gandhi Institute of Development Research (IGIDR), Mumbai. The project was initiated by the International Development Research Centre (IDRC), Canada, at a meeting held in Ottawa in September 1994. IDRC and Centro de Estudios de Estado y Sociedad (CEDES), Buenos Aires, hosted a workshop in Buenos Aires during May-June 1995, where we had detailed discussions with other participants in the project regarding a common conceptual framework within which the financial liberalization process in developing countries could be analysed. We thank Professor Varouj Aivazian of the University of Toronto and the faculty of CEDES for a set of wonderfully clear lectures on the micro- and macro-theoretic literature on financial markets.

Parts of the study were presented in workshops at the IGIDR and Bilkent University, Ankara, during February–March 1996 and December 1996, and June 1996 respectively. We gratefully acknowledge the comments of the seminar participants at these workshops, in particular Dr Melvin Ayogu of the University of Jos, Dr Erol Cakmak of Bilkent University, Dr Jayati Sarkar of IGIDR, Dr Charles Soludo of the University of Nigeria and Dr Romar Correa of the University of Mumbai. We would also like to thank Dr Jose Maria Fanelli of CEDES, Dr Rohinton Medhora of IDRC and Dr A. Vasudevan of the Reserve Bank of India, Mumbai for incisive comments on an earlier draft.

The book was completed while Kunal Sen was a post-doctoral Fellow at the Australia South Asia Research Centre (ASARC) in the Department of Economics, The Australian National University, Canberra, during 1995–6. He is grateful to ASARC and the Department of Economics for providing excellent research facilities during his stay. He would, in particular, like to thank Dr Ric Shand, Executive Director of ASARC for his constant encouragement and support. Advice and help from Dr Chandra Athukorala, Dr K.P. Kalirajan and Dr Govinda Rao, all faculty at ASARC, are gratefully acknowledged. His spouse, Shilpi, provided valuable research assistance at a critical juncture of the project and tolerated long absences from home, for which he is thankful.

Rajendra R. Vaidya would like to thank Professor Kirit S. Parikh, Director of IGIDR, for encouragement and support. He benefited a great deal from discussions with Dr Subir Gokarn and Dr Veena Mishra, both members of the faculty at IGIDR. He is grateful to ASARC for providing research facilities during his visit to Canberra in August 1996. He would like to thank his wife, Jayshree, for putting up with the stresses and strains which are an integral part of an endeavour such as this.

The authors would also like to thank Manjushri Basu for her able assistance with the editing of the manuscript.

This work was carried out with the aid of a grant from the International Development Research Centre, Ottawa, Canada, for which we are grateful.

The views expressed by the authors do not reflect those of the institutions to which they belong. The authors alone are responsible for any errors and omissions in the study.

Contents

Tables

Figures

1

Introduction

The liberalization of financial markets remains one of the most controversial issues in the literature on economic reform. Perhaps more than in any other area of structural adjustment, financial markets and their reform have occassioned the broadest swings in economic thought. Till the 1960s, the dominant view in the literature was the neo-Keynesian perspective which argued that interest rates should be kept low, in order to promote capital accumulation. Also, during this period, the guiding philosophy of governments in several less developed economies was one of economic planning with directed credit programmes and interest rate controls. These became popular as a means of allocating scarce resources to 'preferred sectors' at low cost. In the 1970s, following the growing disillusionment with the policies of 'command and control', and the realization that 'government failure' is a pervasive feature of planned economies (Krueger 1995), the neo-liberal view on financial markets gained ascendancy. The most well-known proponents of this view were McKinnon (1973) and Shaw (1973) who argued that, in the context of a typical developing country, financial repression—a combination of heavy taxation, interest rate controls and government participation in the credit-allocation process—would lead to both a decrease in the depth of the financial system and a loss of the efficiency with which savings are intermediated. Therefore, the McKinnon–Shaw paradigm of financial repression implied that the complete liberalization of the financial sector was an essential pre-condition to successful economic development.

In recent years, however, there has been a re-assessment of the neo-liberal view of financial markets. First, new theoretical developments—in particular, the application of the theories of 'asymmetric information' and 'incomplete contracts' to financial markets—suggest that financial markets are different from other markets (such as commodity markets) in that 'market failures' are more pervasive in financial markets than in other markets in the economy. This indicates that there exist 'forms of government intervention that will not only make (financial) markets function better but will also improve the performance of the economy' (Stiglitz 1993, p. 20). Secondly, the rather dismal experience with financial liberalization in those countries which underwent a significant reform of financial markets—in particular, the Southern Cone countries in the 1970s and the 1980s—along with the successful growth performance of countries which had 'repressed' their financial sector such as Japan, Korea and Taiwan indicates that financial liberalization, under certain conditions, may lead to undesirable macroeconomic outcomes, and that some amount of financial repression in other cases may, in fact, have a beneficial effect on the economy's growth performance. Country experiences with financial liberalization also indicate that the proper conduct of the monetary policy can be a vital pre-condition for the success of the reforms. Moreover, country experiences with financial liberalization also suggest that path dependency is an important attribute of the process of financial liberalization—in other words, initial conditions (i.e., the state and level of development of the financial sector and the macroeconomic environment) determine in great part the success or failure of financial sector reforms in a developing country.

In this chapter, we briefly review theories of asymmetric information and incomplete contracts, and examine their application to financial markets while emphasizing the implications of these theories in analysing the process of financial liberalization in developing countries. We also discuss in brief such lessons as can be drawn from recent country experiences with financial liberalization and financial repression. Finally, we present the outline of our study.

I. Recent Developments in Theory

A financial system contributes to growth and development by mobilizing savings and then efficiently allocating these savings across investment projects and also by providing insurance to risk-averse savers and investors. The neo-liberal perspective on financial liberalization takes a *laissez-faire* financial system to be the desirable goal of public policy and argues that the optimal policy for the government is to withdraw from all financial markets completely. Gertler and Rose (1994) provide a succinct description of the neo-liberal view:

> Suppose that perfect competition exists, that information is freely available and that individuals can credibly commit to honouring all agreements. The financial

system performs flawlessly in this environment. The absence of informational frictions and the ability of contracting parties to make credible promises implies that everyone is able to lend and borrow freely at risk-corrected rates of interest. Market forces consequently allocate income efficiently between consumption and saving, and then in turn allocate saving efficiently across investment projects. Each individual adjusts his saving to equalize the marginal utility of a unit of foregone consumption with the expected marginal benefit—the expected product of the gross return on saving and the discounted marginal utility of future consumption. The total funds furnished from saving flow to equalize risk-corrected marginal returns across investment projects. Competitive forces ensure that lending and borrowing rates adjust to clear markets and that no one earns extra-normal profits. And the entire process is costless; the flow of funds from savers to borrowers does not absorb any resources (p. 15).

Three important implications follow from the neo-liberal approach to financial markets. Firstly, as the private market outcome is fully efficient, any public intervention in financial markets can only be counter-productive. Secondly, the neo-liberal view takes financial structure to be irrelevant and indeterminate, in keeping with the predictions of the Modigliani-Miller theorem. In other words, financial factors do not matter in determining investment and growth, which depend only on real factors—these being mainly, changes in technology and the supply of productive inputs. Thirdly, there is no role for financial intermediaries in the neo-liberal paradigm. As it is costless to obtain information and enforce contracts, therefore individuals can enter into financial relationships without the aid of institutions.

In recent years, two assumptions of the neo-liberal paradigm have come increasingly under scrutiny. The first is the assumption of perfect information which implies that all relevant information is freely available to all agents in the market. However, in reality, most financial markets are characterized by asymmetries of information that exist between providers of capital and those seeking capital. For instance, insiders (the firm's managers and controlling shareholders) almost inevitably have more information concerning the firm's prospects than outsiders (the firm's creditors and small shareholders).

The second assumption of the neo-liberal approach that has been questioned in the literature is the supposition that individuals and firms may costlessly write and enforce richly detailed financial contracts. However, 'this "completeness" of financial markets may not be a reasonable approximation of reality if either information or the ability to enforce contracts is severely limited' (Gertler and Rose 1994, p. 20). In the real world, complete contracts are the exception rather than the rule as it is prohibitively expensive for parties to write a contract that anticipates the many things that may happen. Instead, parties will write a contract that is incomplete, and that will be revised and renegotiated as the future unfolds. The theories of asymmetric information and incomplete contracts have implications for financial markets that are significantly different from those of the neo-liberal paradigm. We discuss each of these theories in turn.

Asymmetric Information

As Greenwald and Stiglitz (1992) have argued, financial markets differ from other markets where goods are traded contemporaneously, in that where financial markets are concerned, money is exchanged today, for a promise of returns in the future. While there are several models that have examined the implications of asymmetric information for financial markets, perhaps the most well- known is the Stiglitz-Weiss (1983) model of credit rationing. In this model, there are two sets of borrowers—'good' and 'bad'. The expected return to the bank depends on the probability of repayment, so that the bank would like to be able to identify borrowers who are more likely to repay. It is difficult to identify 'good' borrowers and to do this, the bank uses a variety of screening devices. The interest rate is one such screening device: those who are willing to pay high interest rates may, on an average, be investing in riskier projects. They are willing to borrow at high interest rates because they perceive their probability of repaying the loan to be low. Therefore, as the interest rate rises, the average 'riskiness' of those who borrow increases, possibly lowering the bank's profits. Also, as the interest rate rises, it induces the borrowing firms to undertake projects with lower probabilities of success but higher pay-offs when successful. The key prediction of the model is that the profit-maximizing or equilibrium interest rate may be lower than the market-clearing rate—that is to say, there will be potential borrowers who will be unable to obtain credit even if they indicated a willingness to pay more than the market rate.

The above model implies that 'market failures' can be quite endemic to credit markets (which are in general characterized by imperfect information).[1] Therefore, an important implication of the presence of asymmetric information is that there may exist government interventions that take into account the costs of information as well as the establishing of markets that can make all individuals better off (Stiglitz 1993). Also, the theory of asymmetric information provides a

[1] Similar types of 'market failures' have been shown to exist in equity markets too (see Myers and Majuf 1984; Greenwald, Stiglitz and Weiss 1984; Cho 1986).

clear reason why financial factors are important in a firm's investment decisions. As credit and equity rationing prevails in financial markets for certain types of firms (possibly those young in age or small in size), these firms cannot costlessly substitute between internal and external finance. Consequently, the availability of internal funds will be a key determinant of the firm's investment practices. The theory of asymmetric information can also explain why, contrary to the prediction of the neo-liberal model, we see the existence of financial intermediaries in most modern economies. With the presence of information asymmetries in the financial market, it would be costly for each individual investor to evaluate the quality and performance of the borrowers. By avoiding duplication in verification, financial intermediaries can thus exploit economies of scale in information provision and thereby, reduce the cost of finance (that is to say, information provision is a natural monopoly). Therefore, it is optimal for the investor to 'delegate' the screening and monitoring of prospective borrowers to the financial intermediary (Diamond 1984).

It can be argued that problems of imperfect information may be more acute in developing countries which are characterized by segmented markets, firms with a short history of operations and an absence of information-gathering institutions (such as credit rating agencies). Moreover, the significant presence of small firms imply a greater difficulty in the collection, evaluation and dissemination of information.

INCOMPLETE CONTRACTS

The theory of incomplete contracts provides an additional perspective on why financial structure matters in a market economy. This theory argues that in a world of incomplete contracts, the *ex post* allocation of power (or control) matters (for a recent exposition, see Hart 1995). To be specific, take two forms of external finance—debt and equity. Debt finance yields a fixed return to its suppliers in states when the firm is not bankrupt (that is, the firm has sufficient funds to make the fixed payment), while in states when the firm is bankrupt the suppliers of debt finance receive such funds as are available to the firm and also the right to make decisions about the firm's subsequent operation. Equity finance on the other hand gives its suppliers the right to the firm's residual returns after payments to the suppliers of debt finance, and in addition the right to vote on decisions concerning the firm's operations in states when the firm is not bankrupt. In states when the firm goes bankrupt, the limited liability provisions mean that suppliers of equity may receive nothing. Although suppliers of equity finance have the right to the firm's residual returns in non-bankruptcy states, they do not have right to receive a fixed payment in every period: those of the firm's returns which belong to the suppliers of equity may be retained by the firm's managers to finance further investment (Edwards and Fischer 1994).

Clearly, debt and equity have different control rights attached to them which enable the suppliers of these forms of finance to remove control of the firm from the incumbent managers in different circumstances. The theory of incomplete contracts provides two important insights into the process of financial liberalization. Firstly, it predicts that the design of financial arrangements in the economy can have a strong influence on growth. More specifically, 'bank-based' financial systems (such as those in Germany and Japan) may have a more favourable effect on economic performance than 'market-based' systems (such as those in the UK and the US). A 'bank-based' system which is characterized by a close involvement of banks in corporate activities—for example, bank representation in corporate boards, bank holdings of corporate equity, etc.—may lead to superior results. The bank's role as monitors of management will not only enable the control rights of equity to be exercised effectively but also do the same for debt's control rights (since banks in this system are both suppliers of equity and debt finance for the firm). In contrast, market-based systems which have a high degree of dispersion of equity ownership suffer from a 'free-rider' problem—no single shareholder has any incentive to devote resources to the monitoring of incumbent management as there is a cost in obtaining the relevant information and hardly any benefit.

Secondly, the theory of incomplete contracts argues that the legal infrastructure—in particular, property rights, contract enforceability and bankruptcy procedures—has an important role to play in determining the success of financial sector reform (Modigliani and Perotti 1991). For example, high costs in penalizing loan defaulters, or in the recovery of collateral, can act as serious impediments to financial intermediation. Also, a poorly designed bankruptcy procedure that does not sufficiently penalize managers of firms in the bankruptcy state will weaken the strong disciplining role that debt has on managerial performance.

In summary, theories of asymmetric information and incomplete contracts provide a vision of the financial system that is markedly different from that of the neo-liberal model. These theories also provide a role for the government to rectify 'market failures' that may exist in financial markets. However, it should be pointed out that these theories do not provide a rationale for the kinds and magnitude of financial repression observed in several developing countries. These theories recognize that a decentralized financial market is vastly superior to a system of publicly managed credit flows and administered interest rates, and to flourish, a private financial market requires an efficient system of contract enforcement, regulatory safeguards, macroeconomic stability and the removal of distortions in the real sector. Therefore, public policy should be directed specifically towards these objectives rather than tinkering with credit flows or interest rates.

II. Recent Experiences with Financial Liberalization and Repression

In the 1970s and 1980s, several countries in Latin America followed the neo-liberal prescription in undertaking comprehensive and far-reaching financial reforms. However, in these countries, the reforms did not yield the expected efficiency gains and in some cases, had significant real costs to the economy with wide-spread bankruptcies, sustained periods of high real interest rates, and high inflation. As a consequence, governments re-intervened in the domestic financial sectors of these economies in some cases the degree of government intervention even exceeding that of the pre- repression period. In Chile, for example, the period was one of increasing domestic and external indebtedness, high real interest rates and financial crises (1982–3), ultimately requiring massive bail-outs of a large portion of the domestic banking system.[2]

The Southern Cone experiences provide three lessons for other developing countries contemplating financial reform. Firstly, macro-economic stability is an essential pre-condition for successful reforms—the Southern Cone countries undertook reforms in a situation of high macroeconomic instability. Secondly, adequate bank supervision is an essential component of reforms—liberalization of the financial sector must be accompanied by the setting up of an appropriate regulatory framework. Thirdly, financial sector reforms must also be accompanied by real sector reforms (such as trade liberalization and the reduction in barriers to entry to firms in the industrial sector)—liberalizing the financial sector in the presence of severe distortions in the real sector can be a recipe for disaster.

[2] For a description of the reforms and their consequences, see Diaz-Alejandro (1985).

The experiences of the East Asian countries (such as Korea and Taiwan) who achieved rapid economic growth with relatively under-developed or 'repressed' financial systems also called for a re-assessment of the neo-liberal view. An influential study on the comparative experiences of these countries—the World Bank (1993)—finds that a 'mild' financial repression may have been an important contributing factor in this region's superior economic performance—for example, Korea's directed credit programmes that allowed its exporters to obtain funds at relatively low cost may have helped in the country's manufacturing export drive. Also, the suppression of interest rates of bank loans below market rates in several of the countries in this region resulted in an excess demand for credit, permitting governments to take an active role in credit rationing. This in turn 'gave governments strong leverage with which to influence the behaviour of firms' (World Bank 1993, p. 356).

However, the relative success of the East Asian experience with financial repression should be interpreted with caution. Firstly, in no East Asian country did the policy-makers follow the forms and degree of repression that is evident in other developing countries (for example, in the East Asian countries, deposit rates were kept more or less positive in real terms, and the governments of these countries did not persistently use the financial sector for their seigniorage needs, as is the case with other developing countries). Secondly, directed credit given to firms in countries like Korea and Japan were conditional on export performance—if the firm could not export, it did not receive further directed credit (Nam and Lee 1995; Park and Patrick 1994). Thirdly, in some of these countries, such as Taiwan, the presence of a vibrant informal sector which had historically played an important role in the intermediation of funds to small and medium-sized firms meant that these economies never faced the full negative effect of the policies of financial repression (Chou 1995).[3]

An issue that has received relatively little attention in the literature has been the implications of financial liberalization for monetary policy. As several country studies show, the conduct of monetary policy becomes increasingly complex in a deregulated environment (Tseng and Corker 1991; Frowen and Kath 1992; Caprio et al. 1994).

[3] Empirical studies that have investigated the relationship between financial development and economic growth for a large number of countries using cross-sectional data (e.g., King and Levine 1993) also support the hypothesis that while mild financial repression may be preferred to a completely *laissez-faire* system, severe financial repression is disastrous for financial intermediation and growth.

In a liberalized environment, it becomes necessary to abandon the use of direct instruments of monetary control such as required reserve ratios and administered interest rates on government securities. At the same time, innovations in the payments technology and the liberalization of asset markets may cause instability in money demand. Financial liberalization, therefore, can have a significant impact on the conduct of monetary policy both by altering the process of money supply creation and by leading to fundamental changes in the relationship between money demand, incomes and interest rates.

III. Financial Sector Reforms in India

In 1991, the Indian government initiated a comprehensive market-oriented reform programme. At the core of the programme was a phased deregulation of the financial sector along with reform of the trade and industrial policies. Important elements of the financial liberalization programme were a lifting of several interest rate ceilings in both the credit and bond markets, an easing of the requirements that had made it mandatory for banks to hold a part of their portfolio in non-interest bearing reserves and low yielding government securities, a partial dismantling of barriers to entry into the banking sector and greater freedom given to banks to close unviable branches in rural and semi-urban areas. Along with the liberalization measures there was a move to introduce a regulatory mechanism that could ensure the safety and solvency of the financial sector in the deregulated environment.

The recent attempts of the Government of India to reform financial markets need to be looked at within the context of (a) the historical evolution of financial sector policies in India, (b) issues relating to the regulation of banks and other financial institutions, (c) the interactions between the real and financial sectors, (d) the macroeconomic environment and (e) issues relating to the conduct of monetary policy in a deregulated environment.

IV. Outline of the Study

Chapter 2 provides a brief history of the evolution of the financial sector policies in India in the post-independence period. It also discusses the motivation for the reforms and describes the key steps taken therein. An analysis of the flow of funds is undertaken in Chapter 3 with a view to identifying 'stylized facts' of the financial intermediation process during the period 1971–92. This chapter also examines the changes that the process of financial liberalization has brought about in the key financial institutions—commercial banks, development finance institutions, and other financial institutions—and financial markets—money, credit, government securities and capital.[4] Chapter 4 studies the regulatory regime pertaining to banks and development finance institutions. In this chapter, we address issues such as deposit insurance, policies regarding new entry of banks and market structure, the supervision system and capital adequacy norms. The interactions between the real and financial sectors is the focus of Chapter 5. In particular we deal with two issues; (a) the real sector reforms—reduction of legal barriers to entry, streamlining of exit procedures and bankruptcy laws and privatization of public enterprises—and their relationship with financial sector reforms, and (b) implications of financial sector reforms on the modes of financing of industry and agriculture and the changes therein. Chapter 6 traces the evolution of the macroeconomic environment since the beginning of the reform process and analyses the consequences of financial liberalization with respect to macroeconomic variables such as inflation, interest rates, and savings and investment. The conduct of monetary policy in a liberalized environment is the subject of Chapter 7. We estimate the impact of financial liberalization on the money demand and money supply process. We also discuss issues pertaining to the choice of an appropriate 'instrument' and 'target' for the central bank and the independence of the central bank in the context of financial sector reforms. Chapter 8 presents the conclusions.

V. Data Sources

In a study of this nature the question of data consistency and reliability are of critical importance. We have used the most recent data available from the three main sources of macroeconomic and financial data in India, namely: *Report on Currency and Finance; Reserve Bank of India Bulletin;* and the *National Accounts Statistics*. The first two are published by the Reserve Bank of India and the third is published by the Central Statistical Organization, Government of India.

[4] We restrict our analysis to the *formal* sector including the non-bank financial intermediaries.

2

Repression and Reform in the Indian Financial Sector, 1947–1995

The evolution of the Indian financial sector in the post-independence era can be divided into three distinct periods. The first period, 1947-68, saw the consolidation of the Reserve Bank of India in its role as the agency in charge of the supervision and control of banks. In this period, the Indian banking sector operated in a fairly liberal environment. The nationalization of 14 commercial banks in 1969 was a turning point in the evolution of financial sector policies in India. The Reserve Bank of India now began to play a more direct and active role with banking policies re-oriented to act 'as an active instrument of growth' (RBI 1983, p. 7) and to meet social objectives such as the reduction in inequalities of income and the concentration of economic power. As a consequence, policies of financial repression—interest rate controls, directed credit programmes, etc.—increased in magnitude during this period. In the late eighties, initial attempts were made by policy-makers to deregulate and develop key financial markets (such as money and T bills markets). However, a more comprehensive liberalization of the financial sector had to wait till the initiation of a structural adjustment cum stabilization programme by the Indian government in 1991.

In this chapter, we provide an overview of the evolution of financial sector policies in India in the post-independence era. In Section I, we describe in brief the financial sector policies followed prior to the reforms. Section II discusses the motivation for the reforms and the key steps implemented in the reform process.

I. Background to the Reforms

Developments in the Pre-nationalization Period

The Reserve Bank of India (RBI) was established on 1 April 1935 with the passing of the Reserve Bank of India Act (1934). Initially the bank was not completely state owned. It was only after India attained independence that the bank was nationalized on 1 January 1949. The main objectives of the bank set forth in the preamble to the Reserve Bank of India Act were 'to regulate the issue of bank notes and the keeping of reserves with a view to securing monetary stability in India and generally to operate the currency and credit system of the country to its advantage'.

In the years just after independence banks did not need to borrow heavily from RBI mainly because they were able to meet their liquidity needs by selling government securities to the RBI. The first major step to stop this practice was initiated in November 1951 when RBI announced an increase in the bank rate from 3 to 3.5 per cent and simultaneously stopped buying goverment securities (except in exceptional circumstances). Instead the bank introduced a system of making advances to banks against government securities at the bank rate. This put an end to automatic monetization of the public debt and the banks were forced to turn to RBI for funds. Over the years various changes have been made both in the operation of this system of rediscounting government securities and in the bank rate.

At the time of the establishment of RBI, all scheduled banks were required by the RBI Act to maintain a minimum cash reserve of 5 per cent of their demand liabilities and 2 per cent of their time liabilities on a daily basis. In addition banks had to maintain liquid assets in cash, gold or government securities amounting to not less than 20 per cent of demand and time liabilities. This was referred to as the Statutory Liquidity Ratio (SLR). In 1962 the RBI was empowered to vary the Cash Reserve Requirement (CRR) between 3 per cent and 15 per cent of total demand and time liabilities. In order to prevent banks from selling government securities in the process of adjusting to changes in the CRR, banks were required from 1962 onwards to maintain a minimum amount of liquid assets in cash, gold and government securities that amounted to at least 25 per cent of their demand and time liabilities over and above the CRR. This ratio has been increased over the years.

RBI was also empowered to stipulate minimum lending rates and ceiling rates on various types of advances. As regards interest payable on deposits, these were governed by a voluntary agreement reached among the important banks operating in India prior to 1964. RBI has directly regulated the interest payable on various types of deposits since 1964.

Apart from the standard functions of the central bank, RBI was also entrusted with the task of developing a sound banking structure on modern lines keeping in view the fragmented and chaotic structure of banks at the time of independence. To undertake this task effectively RBI acquired extensive powers of supervision and control of commercial banks over the years. The most important empowering legislation was the Banking Companies Act, 1949. Under this Act, RBI was empowered to i) control opening of new banks and bank branches, ii) inspect books of accounts of a banking company, and iii) prevent voluntary winding up of a licensed banking company. The later amendments to this Act, i.e. the amendments of 1950, 1953 and 1956, aimed at providing greater control of the liquidation of banks. This was of utmost importance because bank failures were a major problem between 1937 and 1947 during which time 647 banks though they were all small banks had failed. Between 1947 and 1951 the number of bank failures were reduced to 242. These failures again were of relatively small banks. After 1951 the scenario changed dramatically due to the above mentioned legislation. Nevertheless, though with less frequency, bank failures continued to be a problem.

In 1960 two relatively large banks—Laxmi Bank and Palai Central Bank—were liquidated and several small banks experienced serious financial difficulties including bank runs. In the light of these developments, a new section was added to the Act which empowered the Government of India, on the recommendation of RBI, to compulsorily merge weak banks with relatively stronger ones. As a consequence of these measures the number of scheduled and non-scheduled banks fell from 566 in 1951, to 85 in 1969. A deposit insurance scheme was introduced in 1962 with the establishment of the Deposit Insurance Corporation.

Right from its inception, it was envisaged that the RBI would play a promotional role especially with respect to agricultural credit. In the late forties and fifties banks by and large existed only in urban areas. The All India Rural Credit Survey Committee appointed in 1951 reported that out of the total borrowings of farmers in 1951–2, which was estimated to be Rs 750 crores, commercial banks provided only 0.9 per cent while agriculturalist money-lenders and professional money-lenders provided 24.9 and 44.8 per cent respectively. In spite of the branch licensing policy operational in the sixties which emphasized the spread of branches to rural and semi-urban areas, little was actually achieved. After the establishment of the State Bank of India (SBI) in 1955,[1] there were distinct efforts on its part to expand rural branches though there was no explicit statutory requirement to this effect.

[1] SBI was created by nationalizing the Imperial Bank of India and in 1959, eight major state associated banks were made its subsidiaries.

In the period between 1951 and 1968 the main features of the allocation of bank credit were (for details see Gupta 1988, especially Chapter 6):
i) There was a distinct increase in the share of credit going to industry which rose from 34 per cent in 1951 to 67.5 per cent in 1968. A large portion of this was cornered by the corporate sector (about 80 per cent) and the small-scale sector got the rest.
ii) A distinctive feature of credit provided to the industrial sector was its excessively skewed size distribution in favour of large borrowers.
iii) Over this period the agricultural sector got a little over 2 per cent of total bank credit.

These features of bank credit were not consistent with the goal of achieving an equitable allocation of credit and the relative priorities set out in the Five Year Plans. To correct these shortcomings the Government of India introduced a bill in parliament in December 1967 which provided for extensive social control over banks and banking policy. In order to exercise social control over banks the Government of India established the National Credit Council in February 1968. The council was entrusted with the following important tasks (among others):
i) to assess the demand for bank credit from various sectors and;
ii) to determine priorities for the allocation of credit, keeping in mind the available resources and the special needs of the priority sectors comprising of agriculture, the small-scale industry and exports.

The first meeting of the council was held in February 1968 and the council recommended that commercial banks should allocate in 1968–9 additional amounts of Rs 35 to 40 crores, and Rs 60 to 70 crores to agriculture and the small-scale industry respectively. These targets set were in fact achieved by the commercial banks in March 1969.

Bank Nationalization and Beyond

In July 1969, 14 of the largest Indian scheduled commercial banks were nationalized. The nationalization of these 14 banks when combined with the SBI and its associate banks meant that 22 of the largest banks accounting for 86 per cent of the deposits had become public sector banks (Krishnaswamy, Krishnamurthy and Sharma 1987). In April 1980, six more banks were nationalized bringing the share of public sector banks' deposits to 92 per cent. The ostensible objective of the nationalization was the need for the Government of India to 'control the heights of the economy and to meet progressively ... the needs of development of the economy in conformity with national policy and objectives'.[2] With resource mobilization being a key objective of the

[2] Preamble to the 'Banking Companies (Acquisition and Transfer of Undertakings) Act', August 1969.

Indian planning process, the newly nationalized banks were 'asked' to mobilize deposits on a massive scale by setting up branches in rural and semi-urban areas. At the same time, with the adoption of the Fourth Five Year Plan in 1969, a strategy for agrarian development which laid considerable emphasis on technological modernization, was initiated (Chakravarty 1987). One important element in the above strategy was the provision of adequate credit to the agricultural sector. Furthermore, there was a renewed emphasis on poverty alleviation and employment generation in the planning process during this period. This led to an exercise of intense pressure on the public sector banks by the Government of India to lend to the priority sectors (covering agriculture and allied activities, small-scale industry, retail trade, transport operators, professionals, and craftsmen). By March 1979, the 'priority sector lending requirements' (as they came to be known) stipulated that 33 per cent of each bank's total credit should be advanced to the priority sector with not less than 16 per cent going to agriculture. This was later raised to 40 per cent with a further stipulation that one-half of advances to the agricultural sector should consist of loans to small and marginal farmers. The priority sector lending requirements have remained ever since at 40 per cent of total bank credit.

The other financial institutions have had a longer history of public ownership with existing insurance companies being nationalized in 1956 to form the Life Insurance Corporation of India (LIC). Financial institutions such as the Unit Trust of India (UTI, which is a publicly owned mutual fund) and the Industrial Development Bank of India (IDBI) were set up by the RBI[3] in collaboration with other financial institutions with specific objectives in mind. Thus, the UTI would promote the stock market (since its goal was to invest savings mobilized from households in corporate stocks and bonds), and the IDBI would provide direct and indirect long-term finance to firms in industrial sector. Term loans to the industrial sector were also provided by the Industrial Finance Corporation of India (IFCI) and the Industrial Credit and Investment Corporation of Inda (ICICI).

It should be noted that the policies of financial repression began in the Indian context with the nationalization of banks in 1969. However, while the need for social control of the banking sector provided the initial rationale for these policies, the subsequent intensification in the latter over the seventies and eighties, was largely due to the government's increasing need to use the banking sector for financing its own deficits. The fiscal deficit to GDP ratio increased steadily

[3] IDBI was taken over by the government in 1975 and converted into a separate organization.

during this period from 3.56 per cent in 1971–2 to 1975–6 to 8.29 per cent in 1986–7 to 1990–1 (Table 2.1). The government used the banking sector as a captive source of funds by means of the statutory liquidity ratio (SLR). The SLR is the proportion of net demand and time deposits that banks have to maintain in India in cash, gold and unencumbered approved securities. The latter are mostly central and state government securities and bonds issued by term-lending institutions like IDBI, IFCI and the State Finance Corporations. As we have noted before, the SLR requirement was originally intended as an instrument of monetary policy so as to prevent banks from offsetting the effects of variable reserve requirements by liquidating their holdings of government securities. However, over the years, the SLR 'has provided an expanding captive market for government securities and hence served as a means of allocating a larger share of banks' resources to government' (RBI 1985, p. 254). The SLR also performed another important role of allocating cheap funds to development finance institutions. The SLR requirement which was 28 per cent in 1970–1 was gradually increased until it stood at 38.5 per cent in 1989–90 (Table 2.2).

Table 2.1

Trends in the Fiscal and Budget Deficits, 1971–2 to 1989–90
(as a percentage of GDP)

Variable	1971–2 to 1975–6	1976–7 to 1980–1	1981–2 to 1985–6	1986–7 to 1990–1
Fiscal Deficit	3.56	5.07	6.84	8.29
Budget Deficit	0.96	1.34	1.33	2.09

Source: Indian Economic Statistics—Public Finance, Ministry of Finance, various issues.

Table 2.2

Changes in the Statutory Liquidity Ratio (SLR)

Year	SLR
1964–5	25
1970–1	28
1972–3	30
1973–4	32
1974–5	33
1978–9	34
1981–2	35
1984–5	36
1985–6	37
1987–8	38
1990–1	38.5

Source: Report on Currency and Finance, RBI, various issues.

Another consequence of the ever-widening deficits of the central government in the seventies and eighties was the increasing monetization of the deficit during this period—the budget deficit to GDP ratio increased from 0.96 per cent in 1971–2 to 1975–6 to 2.09 per cent in 1986–7 to 1990–1. To partially neutralize the effects of the increase in the monetary base brought about by deficit financing on monetary growth, the policy-makers steadily increased the Cash Reserve Ratio (CRR) from 7 per cent in 1973–4 to 15 per cent in 1989–90 (Table 2.3). This meant a larger proportion of bank funds were locked into non-interest bearing bank reserves. At the same time, to keep the cost of borrowing low for itself, the government systematically suppressed the government securities markets (and money) markets during this period. As a result, open market operations, which were an important instrument of monetary policy in the pre-repression period, lost their effectiveness as policy tools.

Table 2.3

Changes in the Cash Reserve Ratio (CRR)

Year	SLR
1962–3	3
1973–4	7
1974–5	4
1976–7	6
1981–2	7.5
1982–3	7
1983–4	8.5
1984–5	9
1987–8	10
1988–9	11
1989–90	15

Source: Report on Currency and Finance, RBI, various issues.

The effects of financial repression policies quite clearly had a negative effect on the financial sector: markets were heavily segmented and underdeveloped secondary markets inhibited the competitive pricing of assets (Rangarajan 1994); the presence of non-price allocation mechanisms led to an inefficient use of credit; the several restrictions on banks' uses of funds and the imposition of branch licensing requirements had a significant negative impact on bank profitability; and the restrictions on bank entry and the dominance of the public sector banks greatly inhibited competition and efficiency in the banking sector.

II. The Strategy of Financial Sector Reform

The initial impetus to reforms in the financial sector came with the submission of two influential committee reports to the RBI—the Chakravarty Committee in 1985 and the Vaghul Committee in 1987. The first committee was set up by the RBI to 'undertake a review of the working of the monetary system and suggest measures for improving the effectiveness of monetary policy' (RBI 1985, p. 1). Its main recommendations to the RBI were: i) to develop Treasury Bills (T Bills) as a monetary instrument so that open market operations could gradually become the dominant instrument of monetary policy; ii) to revise upwards the yield structure of government securities so as to create a demand for public debt outside of the RBI and hence, limit the degree of monetization of the debt; and iii) to adopt monetary targeting as an important monetary policy tool with price stability being the ultimate objective of monetary policy. The second committee was set up to study the money market. It recommended a phased decontrol and development of money markets and the gradual integration of these markets with other key short-term markets such as the treasury bills market.

Since the mid-eighties, RBI has implemented in a phased manner several of the key recommendations of the two committees. In the government securities markets, a scheme for T bills of 182 days was introduced in November 1986. This was initially on a monthly auction basis and without any rediscounting facilities with the RBI. The RBI also took several steps to develop the money markets. In April 1988, the RBI instituted the Discount and Finance House of India (DFHI), to provide liquidity to the money markets. In May 1989, as a further step towards the liberalization of the money markets, the ceiling on the call money rate was withdrawn. In 1988–9, the RBI also introduced Commercial Paper and Certificates of Deposit as new short-term instruments in the Indian financial market. By the late eighties, there was significant deregulation and development of the short-term segment of the financial markets in India, with little progress in the deregulation of credit and capital markets.

More radical reforms had to wait till the adoption of the structural adjustment cum stabilization programme by the Indian government in 1991. With the adoption of the reform package, two important pre-conditions for the financial sector reform were fulfilled. Firstly, with a sharp reduction in the central government's fiscal deficit in the first year of the reforms, there was less of a need to use the banking sector as a captive source of funds. Secondly, the implementation of far-reaching reforms in trade and industrial policies meant that the allocation of resources were increasingly market-driven. This implied that for the reforms in the real sector to succeed, trade and industrial policy reforms had to be supported by reforms in the financial sector, so that scarce investible funds could be drawn to the most productive uses.

In November 1991, a committee set up by the Government to study the working of the financial system—the Narasimham Committee (MOF, 1991)—submitted its report. The main recommendations of the Committee were: a) to bring down the SLR in a phased manner to 25 per cent over five years; b) to use the CRR as an instrument of monetary policy and not as a means of controlling the secondary expansion of credit brought about by monetization of the fiscal deficit; c) to phase out directed credit programmes and to reduce the requirement to lend to 'priority sectors' down to 10 per cent of aggregate credit; d) to bring the interest rate on government borrowing in line with other market-determined interest rates and to phase out concessional interest rates; e) that banks and financial institutions achieve a minimum 4 per cent capital adequacy ratio in relation to risk weighted assets by March 1993; f) that the more profitable public sector banks be permitted to issue fresh capital to the public through the capital market; g) that banks and financial institutions adopt uniform accounting practices in regard to income recognition and provisioning for non-performing loans; h) that branch licensing be abolished and the matter of opening and closing of branches be left to the commmercial judgement of individual banks; i) to liberalize policies towards foreign banks with regard to the opening of offices as branches or subsidiaries; j) that a quasi-autonomous body under the aegis of the RBI be set up to supervise banks and finanical institutions; k) to phase out the privileged access of development finance institutions to concessional finance; and l) in the capital market, freedom be given to issuers of capital to decide on the nature of the instrument, its terms and its pricing. The recommendations of the committee provided the blueprint of the reforms that followed in the financial sector.

In Tables 2.4 and 2.5, we summarize the key steps taken with financial sector reforms in the period 1991–2 to 1995–6. As is clear from the tables, there has been significant progress with regard to financial liberalization since 1991–2. Most of the major recommendations of the Narasimham Committee have been implemented. We

Table 2.4

Progress of Financial Sector Reforms, Banking, 1991–2 to 1995–6[a]

Reforms	1991–2	1992–3	1993–4	1994–5	1995–6
Reserve Requirements:					
CRR	---	---	Average CRR reduced from 15 per cent to 14.5 per cent.	CRR increased to 15 per cent.	CRR reduced to 14 per cent.
SLR	...	...	SLR reduced from 38.5 per cent to 37.25 per cent.	SLR reduced to 31.5 per cent.	...
Interest Rates					
Structure	---	Lending rates rationalized from six to four categories.	Further rationalization to three categories.	---	---
Lending Rates	...	Minimum Lending Rate (MLR) for credit limit of over Rs 2 lakhs reduced from 20 per cent to 17 per cent.	MLR on credit limits of Rs 2 lakhs reduced to 14 per cent.	MLR on credit limits of Rs 2 lakhs abolished.	...
Internal Debt Management Policies	---	Auctions of 364- days and 91-days T bills and dated securities introduced.	---	Agreement between RBI and the Government on pre-determined limit on net issue of *ad hoc* T bills.	---

Reforms	1991–2	1992–3	1993–4	1994–5	1995–6
Regulatory Issues	A risk-asset ratio system for banks introduced as a capital adequacy measure. A system of income recognition and provisioning for non-performing loans introduced.	---	---	The Board of Financial Supervision (BFS) set up under the Chairmanship of Governor of RBI to ensure implementation in asset classification, income recognition, and capital adequacy.	---
Competition Policies	---	Approval given by RBI 'in principle' for establishment of new banks in the private sector. Branch licensing policy considerably liberalized.	The 'State Bank of India Act' of 1955 amended to enhance scope of the provision for partial private shareholding.	'Banking Companies Acts' of 1970–80 amended to permit banks to raise capital up to 49 per cent from the public.	---

Note: [a] The coverage for 1995–6 is until end-December 1995.
Source: Report on Trend and Progress in Banking and *Report on Currency and Finance,* RBI, various issues.

Table 2.5

Progress of Financial Sector Reforms, Other Financial Institutions and the Capital Market, 1991–2 to 1995–6[a]

Reforms	1991–2	1992–3	1993–4	1994–5	1995–6
Other Financial Institutions	Interest rate deregulation.	...	...	...	BFS takes up supervisory responsibility of all-India development banks and non-banking financial companies.
The Capital Market	Private sector involvement in mutual funds permitted. SEBI granted statutory powers. Functions of Controller of Capital Issues transferred to SEBI.	Restrictions on pricing and issues of capital removed.	...	...	...

Note: [a] The coverage for 1995–6 is until end-December 1995.
Source: Report on Currency and Finance, RBI, various issues.

present a detailed assessment of the reforms in the financial sector and the changes that they have brought about in Indian financial markets in Chapter 3.

III. Concluding Remarks

It should be noted that reforms in certain financial markets (money and treasury bills markets) had been initiated well before the reform package adopted in 1991. Also, prior to the 1991 reforms, on the government's initiative, a wide range of financial institutions had been set up. This, as we shall see, greatly facilitated the various sectors of the economy to deal with the changes brought about by the comprehensive reform process initiated in 1991.

3

Structure and Evolution of the Financial System

Since the early 1970s, there has been a significant widening and deepening of the Indian financial sector. Commercial banks which were previously confined to the metropolitan and urban areas have gradually moved out to rural and semi-urban areas, allowing easy access to banking facilities for a greater number of people. Other financial intermediaries such as the development finance institutions which were set up with the objective of financing the investment activities of the industrial sector have seen an impressive growth in their assets. In fact, since the eighties, institutions such as the Industrial Credit and Investment Corporation of India (ICICI), Industrial Development Bank of India (IDBI) and the Unit Trust of India (UTI), have been playing a role equal in importance to that of commercial banks in the intermediation of funds. In the financial markets too, there has been a considerable growth and development with new financial instruments and services appearing on the scene in the money and capital markets.

Our purpose in this chapter is threefold. Firstly, in Section I we analyse the flow of funds database published by the Reserve Bank of India (RBI) for the period 1971–2 to 1991–2 (and where data is available, till 1992–3) with a view to identifying salient features of the financial intermediation process in India during the pre-reform period and the years immediately following the reforms. In our analysis, we assess the relative importance of the three non-financial sectors—the government, the private corporate sector and households—in the sources and uses of funds, and the two main sets of financial intermediaries in India—commercial banks and public financial institutions—in the intermediation of funds from ultimate lenders to ultimate borrowers. This analysis sets the stage for a detailed examination of the major changes that have occurred in the Indian financial sector as a consequence of financial liberalization. In Section II, we focus our attention on the key players in the financial system, i.e., commercial banks and large financial bodies such as the term-lending institutions, the insurance companies and the Unit Trust of India. In Section III, we trace the evolution of major financial markets: these being money, credit and capital markets. In this section, we also examine two other sets of institutions that have become increasingly important in the new milieu: the firms in the non-bank corporate sector (e.g., non-financial companies, hire purchase companies, leasing companies and investment companies), and the credit rating agencies.

I. An Overview of the Financial Intermediation Process

We begin this section by providing a brief overview of the level of financial development in the Indian economy since independence. Several indicators are available in the literature to assess the financial development of an economy (see Goldsmith 1969). These are : i) the Finance Ratio; ii) the Financial Inter-Relations Ratio; iii) the New Issue Ratio and iv) the Intermediation Ratio. The Finance Ratio is the ratio of total financial claims issued during the year to national income and is an indicator of the rate of financial development in rotation with the rate of economic growth. The Financial Inter-Relations Ratio is the ratio of total volume of financial assets at any point of time to the stock of physical assets at that time. It thus indicates the relationship between the economy's financial structure and real asset structure. The New Issue Ratio is the ratio of primary issues to net physical capital formation, primary issues being defined as financial claims issued by the non-financial sector. It is an indicator of the extent to which the non-financial sector has financed its investment through external funds. Finally, the Intermediation Ratio is the ratio of the volume of financial instruments issued by financial institutions to the volume of primary issues by non-financial units. It measures the importance of financial institutions relative to non-financial units in raising resources to finance investment.

As we see in Table 3.1, all four indicators show a steady increase over the period 1950–1 to 1991–2. There are, however, differences in the behaviour of these ratios over the different time-periods, with the Finance Ratio showing the sharpest increase in the 1970s. The New Issue ratio, on the other hand, witnesses the largest increase in the 1980s. This may indicate the different patterns of growth of the banking sector and capital markets in different periods of time, with the former showing the most significant growth in the seventies while the latter does so in the eighties.

Table 3.1

Indicators of Financial Development

Indicators	1951–2	1960–1	1970–1	1980–1	1985–6	1991–2
Finance Ratio	0.75	9.45	17.15	33.03	35.1	41.3
Financial Inter-relations Ratio	0.08	0.69	1.18	1.49	2.15	2.29
New Issue Ratio	0.17	0.56	0.71	0.85	1.25	1.28
Intermediation Ratio	N.A.	0.24	0.66	0.76	0.73	0.79

Source: Flow of Funds Accounts, *RBI Bulletin,* various issues.

The two surplus sectors (net lenders) have been the household and the rest of the world, and the two deficit sectors (net borrowers) have been the government and the private corporate sector (Table 3.2). It should be noted here that the government sector as defined in the flow of funds database includes public sector enterprises. The surpluses of the household and the rest of the world sectors have increased steadily over time and so have the deficits of the government and private corporate sector. There has been some indication of a change in this trend since 1991–2 with the government sector reducing its dependence on external funds.

Table 3.2

Financial Surplus or Deficit by Sector Percentage of GDP

Surplus (+)/ Deficit (–) as per cent of GDP	1971–2 to 1975–6	1976–7 to 1980–1	1981–2 to 1985–6	1986–7 to 1990–1	1991–2	1992–3
Private Corporate Business	– 0.9	–1.4	– 2.4	– 2.2	– 2.7	– 5.3
Government	– 4.0	– 5.8	– 8.5	– 9.9	– 8.3	– 6.5
Household	4.3	6.1	6.9	8.0	9.2	7.8
Rest of the World	0.2	0.6	1.5	2.6	0.4	1.9

Source: Flow of Funds Accounts, *RBI Bulletin,* various issues.

Among the three non-financial sectors, the government has been the largest borrower as indicated by its share in total sources of funds (Table 3.3). Again, there is an indication of a reversal of this trend since the 1991 reforms. Not surprisingly, government securities has been the second most important financial instrument in total sources (after loans and advances) though the importance of corporate securities has been steadily increasing. The role of trade credit in mobilizing funds has decreased steadily over the years. Though the household sector has been the single largest lender of funds, its share in total uses of funds has shown a surprising downturn in the first two years of the nineties (Table 3.4). While currency and deposits are the most preferred financial investments by the non-financial sector, the share of corporate and other financial institutions' (OFI) securities in total uses of funds by this sector have been increasing steadily over the years. Here, OFI comprises all non-bank financial institutions including term-lending institutions, insurance funds and mutual funds.

Table 3.3

Non-financial Sectors' Sources of External Funds (per cent)

Sectors/Instruments	1971–2 to 1975–6	1976–7 to 1980–1	1981–2 to 1985–6	1986–7 to 1990–1	1991–2	1992–3
Distribution of funds by sector raising funds:						
Private Corporate Business	17.5	16.1	21.1	17.8	31.7	37.0
Government	64.7	65.5	63.6	67.2	59.8	49.2
Household	17.8	18.4	15.3	15.0	8.5	13.7
Distribution of funds by source::						
Currency and Deposits	1.3	4.4	5.9	10.7	9.1	8.2
Government Securities	31.1	24.6	23.4	25.7	16.6	14.4
Corporate Securities	1.3	2.3	4.3	4.9	8.8	11.6
OFI Securities	0.0	0.0	0.0	0.0	0.0	0.0
Loans and Advances	41.3	40.6	37.4	35.7	37.8	46.8
Trade Debit or Credit	10.1	6.1	4.5	1.2	−0.7	−0.7
Other Liabilities	14.8	22.1	24.5	21.8	28.3	19.7

Source: Flow of Funds Accounts, *RBI Bulletin*, various issues.

Table 3.4

Uses of Funds by Non-financial Sectors (per cent)

Sectors/Instruments	1971–2 to 1975–6	1976–7 to 1980–1	1981–2 to 1985–6	1986–7 to 1990–1	1991–2	1992–3
Distribution of funds by sector investing funds:						
Private Corporate Business	5.1	5.2	7.6	7.0	17.0	9.6
Government	18.1	15.4	12.9	13.8	10.0	16.5
Household	76.8	79.5	79.5	79.1	73.0	73.9
Distribution of funds by Uses:						
Currency and Deposits	49.2	26.4	42.7	45.0	45.8	40.0
Government Securities	−1.2	− 0.1	0.4	0.3	0.5	0.6,
Corporate Securities	0.3	1.4	3.5	1.7	4.3	5.9
OFI Securities	0.6	0.6	1.9	3.7	11.9	7.6
Loans and Advances	14.6	25.5	26.9	7.7	11.4	15.1
Trade Debit or Credit	6.3	6.3	6.8	3.0	−1.1	0.3
Other Assets	30.1	39.9	17.8	38.6	27.3	30.5

Source: Flow of Funds Accounts, *RBI Bulletin*, various issues.

The household sector's saving pattern in financial assets shows considerable variation over the period 1971–2 to 1994–5 (Table 3.5). The most striking feature of the household portfolio choice in the nineties has been the shift from the assets, 'claims on government' and bank deposits, to corporate securities and mutual funds. Claims on government (of which the most important component are small savings such as National Savings Certificates and Indira Vikas Patras) are mostly savings in government bonds which confer tax benefits on the investor. The interest rate on this asset has remained more or less unchanged over the period under consideration. However, while the return on this asset is perhaps below par to other comparable assets, the risk premium is close to zero. Similarly, the risk premium on bank deposits may also be considered to be close to zero, given the prevalence of deposit insurance in the Indian banking system. On the other hand, the risk premium on corporate securities and mutual funds is arguably higher. Given the shift of households from the safe asset 'claims on government' to the more risky corporate securities and mutual funds, this may indicate an expectation of higher returns from the latter set of assets with the growth in the capital market in the nineties. This is clear from Table 3.6 where one finds that the rate of return differential between units of UTI and bank deposits increased steadily over the eighties and early nineties. On the whole, financial savings as a percentage of GDP increased steadily over the period 1971–2 to 1994–5.

Table 3.5

Savings of the Household Sector in Financial Assets (Gross) percentage distribution

Assets	1971–2 to 1975–6	1976–7 to 1980–1	1981–2 to 1985–6	1986–7 to 1990–1	1991–2 to 1994–5
Currency	13.3	13.6	11.1	12.1	11.4
Bank Deposits	46.6	49.2	42.4	35.8	34.5
Life Insurance	9.9	7.6	7.2	8.3	9.3
Provident Fund	20.0	17.4	16.7	18.5	17.8
Claims on Government	1.4	4.7	10.8	12.3	6.8
Corporate Securities	0.7	2.1	3.2	4.9	8.7
UTI and other Mutual Funds	0.4	0.4	1.4	4.1	6.7
Other Assets	7.7	5.1	7.2	4.1	4.8
Memo:					
Financial Savings/GDP (per cent)	5.5	8.5	9.2	10.6	12.2

Source: Report on Currency and Finance, RBI, various issues.

Table 3.6

Rates of Return on Financial Assets

Rates of Return[a]	*ideb-id*	*ig-id*	*uti-id*
1971–2 to 1975–6	1.1	1.8	0.9[b]
1976–7 to 1980–1	3.5	3.4	1.6
1981–2 to 1985–6	5.2	3.7	2.4
1986–7 to 1990–1	3.8	3.1	4.3
1991–2 to 1994–5	...[c]	1.0	6.4

Notes: [a] *id* is the one-year interest rate on deposits; *ideb* is the interest rate on debentures; *ig* is the interest rate on national savings certificates and *uti* is the yield rate on units of *uti.*

[b] Average refers to period 1973–4 to 1975–6.

[c] Data for 1993–4 and 1994–5 not available.

Source: Report on Currency and Finance, RBI, various issues.

Turning to the third non-financial sector, i.e. the private corporate sector, we find that its dependence on external funds has increased steadily over the period 1971–2 to 1985–6 (Table 3.7). This trend seems to have been reversed in the second half of the eighties, reflecting an improved savings performance on the part of corporate firms during this time. Among the sources of external funds, debentures have played an increasingly important role, with trade credit declining in importance. The share of OFIs in the private corporate sector's total sources of funds has increased from 4.6 per cent in 1971–2 to 1975–6 to 30.5 per cent in 1991–2 while that of banks has fallen from 13.9 per cent to 6.3 per cent in the same period. This 'stylized fact' is one of the most revealing features of the Indian flow of funds data. Clearly, any analysis of what the Indian financial sector must 'look like' in a deregulated environment must take into account the predominant role that OFIs play in the intermediation of funds to private firms. The increasing involvement of private firms in financial arbitrage is evident from Table 3.8. Investment in real assets as a proportion of total uses has decreased from 87.5 per cent in 1971–2 to 1975–6 to 68.3 per cent in 1991–2. The increase in financial investments has occurred mostly in deposits and loans and advances.

Table 3.7

Private Non-financial Sector's Sources of Funds (per cent)

Sources	1971–2 to 1975–6	1976–7 to 1980–1	1981–2 to 1985–6	1986–7 to 1990–1	1991–2
Internal[a]	56.6	46.9	33.2	36.7	40.2
External	43.4	53.1	66.8	63.3	59.8
Of Which:					
Paid-up Capital	2.7	5.4	3.0	2.0	3.7
OFI	2.0	1.5	1.5	1.6	3.0
Household	0.5	3.4	1.3	0.2	0.5
Debentures	0.7	1.0	7.5	10.8	10.6
OFI	0.3	0.8	3.1	8.0	8.7
Household	– 0.2	0.9	3.6	1.8	1.4
Fixed Deposit	0.0	0.6	0.0	2.9	2.3
Household	0.0	0.0	0.0	2.9	1.5
Borrowings	22.4	27.9	32.1	27.1	31.2
Banks	13.9	15.8	19.1	18.7	6.3
OFI	2.2	5.4	7.7	12.2	18.8
Trade Credit	7.9	4.5	2.3	– 0.3	–1.6
Memo:					
Share in Total:					
OFI	4.6	7.6	12.3	21.8	30.5
Banks	13.9	15.8	19.1	18.7	6.3
Household	0.3	4.3	4.8	4.9	3.3

Note: [a] Private Corporate Saving (in current prices).
The entries do not add up to 100 per cent as some small categories have been omitted for the sake of brevity.

Source: Flow of Funds Accounts, *RBI Bulletin* and *National Accounts Statistics*, CSO, various issues.

Table 3.8

Private Non-financial Sector's Uses of Funds (per cent)

Sources	1971–2 to 1975–6	1976–7 to 1980–1	1981–2 to 1985–6	1986–7 to 1990–1	1991–2
Real[a]	87.5	82.9	83.5	79.1	68.3
Financial	12.5	17.1	16.5	20.9	31.7
Of Which:					
Cash in Hand	2.3	1.0	0.6	0.5	0.2
Deposits	2.0	6.5	6.0	5.5	10.3
Commercial Banks	0.0	4.6	4.1	3.2	6.7
Loans and Advances	5.5	9.2	8.1	11.1	17.6
Investments	0.3	0.5	1.8	3.7	3.6
Others	2.4	– 4.6	– 4.0	– 8.4	–19.2

Note: [a] Private Corporate Gross Domestic Formation (current prices).
Source: Flow of Funds Accounts, *RBI Bulletin* and *National Accounts Statistics*, CSO, various issues.

The distribution of assets across major financial intermediaries can be examined at four different points of time (Table 3.9). It is clear from this table that the period 1971–91 can be divided into two distinct sub-periods. The first sub-period 1971–81 was the period of growth for commercial banks whose share in total assets of financial intermediaries increased sharply from 26.4 per cent in 1971 to 42.9 per cent in 1981. In the same period, co-operative banks declined significantly in importance, their share dropping from 18.7 per cent in 1971 to 2.3 per cent in 1981. The second sub-period 1981–91 is the period of growth for financial institutions whose share in total assets increased from 16 per cent in 1981 to 25.6 per cent in 1991. The most noticeable growth was that of the term-lending institutions whose share in total assets increased from 5.9 per cent in 1981 to 10.9 per cent in 1991. Interestingly, in the period 1991–3, the share of commercial banks in total assets has fallen by two percentage points. On the other hand, the share of financial institutions has increased by 1.3 percentage points in the same period. In particular, the share of UTI has increased significantly since 1991 from 4.8 per cent in that year to 6.2 per cent in 1993.

Table 3.9

Distribution of Assets, Banking and Financial Institutions (per cent)

Assets (as at end-March)	1971	1981	1991	1993
Banking	66.0	84.0	74.4	73.1
Of which:				
RBI	21.0	24.4	25.8	26.8
Commercial Banks	26.4	42.9	46.5	44.3
Co-operative Banks	18.7	2.3	2.1	2.0
Financial Institutions	34.0	16.0	25.6	26.9
Of which:				
Term-lending:	n/a	5.9	10.9	11.0
IDBI	n/a	3.0	4.7	4.6
ICICI	n/a	0.7	1.5	1.8
IFCI	n/a	0.6	1.2	1.4
IRBI	n/a	0.1	0.2	0.2
Exim Bank	n/a	0.0	0.4	0.4
NABARD	n/a	1.6	2.6	2.3
NHB	n/a	0.0	0.2	0.4
State Financial Institutions:	n/a	1.7	2.1	1.9
SFC	n/a	1.0	1.3	1.2
SIDC	n/a	0.7	0.8	0.6
Investment Institutions:	n/a	8.2	12.2	13.6
LIC	n/a	6.5	6.1	6.2
GIC and Subsidiaries:	n/a	1.2	1.3	1.3
UTI	n/a	0.5	4.8	6.2
Other Institutions:	n/a	0.2	0.4	0.4
DICGC	n/a	0.2	0.4	0.4
ECGC	n/a	0.0	0.1	0.1

Source: RBI (1985) and *Report on Trend and Progress in Banking 1993–4*, RBI.

The two key sectors in the intermediation process in India are commercial banks and the OFIs. Where did these two sectors obtain their funds from and where have they invested these funds? To answer these questions, we need to consider their sources and uses of funds separately. Table 3.10 confirms our *a priori* expectation that household bank deposits have been the main source of funds for banks. Yet interestingly, this particular source of funds has been declining in importance over the years, with an increasing share of funds till the

1990–1 period coming from the private non-financial and the rest of the world sectors (most of the latter in the form of foreign currency deposits held by non-resident Indians). The share of funds obtained by borrowing from commercial banks has also increased in the second half of the eighties indicating the increasing importance of the call money market as a major source of short-term funds in recent years.

Table 3.10

Commercial Banks' Sources of Funds (per cent)

Sources	1971–2 to 1975–6	1976–7 to 1980–1	1981–2 to 1985–6	1986–7 to 1990–1	1991–2
Paid-up Capital	0.1	0.2	0.9	2.1	3.5
Deposits:	92.2	87.6	82.7	86.1	115.5
Banking[a]	1.2	1.4	0.8	1.2	3.0
OFI	6.8	2.7	1.7	1.8	9.2
Private Non-financial	0.0	2.1	2.5	4.7	15.4
Government	7.6	8.2	7.4	7.3	36.1
Rest of World	2.5	4.7	8.1	12.6	–7.8
Households	69.4	68.3	62.0	57.4	63.2
Borrowings:	3.6	2.6	6.1	9.6	– 20.5
RBI	3.3	–1.3	1.6	5.4	– 20.9
Commercial Banks	0.0	– 0.9	1.3	5.5	– 21.4
OFI	0.2	3.1	4.6	3.9	0.2
Rest of World	0.1	0.5	0.1	0.2	0.6
Other liabilities	4.2	9.6	10.4	2.2	1.6

Note: [a] Includes RBI.
Source: Flow of Funds Accounts, *RBI Bulletin,* various issues.

Two interesting points emerge from the data on commercial banks' uses of funds (Table 3.11). Firstly, an increasing share of bank funds has been held as cash and balances with the RBI or invested in government securities over the eighties. This finding is not surprising given the sharp increases in the Cash Reserve Ratio (CRR) and the Statutory Liquidity Ratio (SLR) in the late eighties as a means of financing the ever-widening fiscal deficit of the government. However, what is surprising is the second finding—that the share going to private corporate firms has remained fairly stable in the 1980s (in fact, the data shows a slight increase from 14.6 per cent in 1981–2 to 1985–6 to 16.9 per cent in 1986–7 to 1990–1).[1] Banks seem to have adjusted their portfolio by reducing lending to the government sector.

[1] It should be noted here that the 1991–2 data is difficult to interpret given the sharp fall in bank credit in that year due to austerity measures implemented by the government as a part of the stabilization programme.

Table 3.11
Commercial Banks' Uses of Funds (per cent)

Uses	1971–2 to 1975–6	1976–7 to 1980–1	1981–2 to 1985–6	1986–7 to 1990–1	1991–2
Cash and Balances with RBI	6.3	16.7	11.3	16.3	10.5
Investment:	31.1	30.0	28.7	35.8	49.8
OFI	1.4	6.0	7.3	5.5	1.4
Private Non-financial	0.5	0.1	0.1	0.4	2.5
Government	28.3	23.5	21.2	29.9	45.9
Bank Credit:	58.4	53.7	55.1	45.8	40.8
Private Non-financial	22.6	14.3	14.5	16.5	7.1
Government	16.7	10.7	11.8	1.3	3.7
Household	17.0	28.1	28.3	27.6	18.2
Other Assets	4.3	– 0.4	4.9	2.1	–1.1
Memo:					
Share going to:					
Government	45.0	34.2	32.9	31.2	49.6
Private Non-financial	23.1	14.4	14.6	16.9	9.6

Source: Flow of Funds Accounts, *RBI Bulletin,* various issues.

The data on OFIs' sources and uses of funds also reveal certain interesting patterns (Tables 3.12 and 3.13). Firstly, we find that the share of *contractual* saving institutions such as the provident and life insurance funds in total OFI sources of funds has declined over the years. Similarly, the share of funds obtained from commercial banks (mostly through mandatory investment in OFI securities via the SLR) has fallen over the eighties. Instead, there has been a shift in sources of financing to UTI and other mutual funds. This indicates the rise in prominence of *market-based* financial intermediaries who obtain most of their funds directly from households and who invest mostly in the capital market. Secondly, and following from the first finding, there has been a dramatic increase in OFI investments and lending to the private non-financial sector over the period 1971–2 to 1990–1; the share of funds going to the latter increasing from 12.9 per cent in 1971–2 to 1975–6 to 28.3 per cent in 1986–7 to 1990–1. This trend showed no signs of reversal in 1991–2. The share going to the government fell sharply from 57.8 per cent in 1971–2 to 1975–6 to 20.9 per cent in 1986–7 to 1990–1. Again, the data clearly reveals the increasing dominance of the OFI sector in the financing of corporate investment, its share in total OFI plus bank funds going to private firms increasing from 35.2 per cent in 1971–2 to 1975–6 to 60.7 per cent in 1991–2.

Table 3.12

Other Financial Institutions' Sources of Funds (per cent)

Sources	1971–2 to 1975–6	1976–7 to 1980–1	1981–2 to 1985–6	1986–7 to 1990–1	1991–2
Paid-up Capital:	1.5	1.9	4.0	2.4	1.6
Banking	0.3	0.3	0.1	0.4	0.4
Government	1.4	1.5	3.4	1.4	0.7
Household	– 0.2	0.1	0.5	0.6	0.4
Bonds and Debentures:	7.0	13.1	14.7	13.3	10.4
Commercial Banks	5.9	12.1	13.3	8.9	6.8
Private Corp. Business	0.0	0.0	0.1	1.0	–1.9
Rest of World	0.0	0.0	0.3	1.5	2.5
Household	0.3	0.1	0.2	0.5	2.8
Deposits:	0.0	0.2	4.8	5.0	4.6
Private Non-financial	0.0	0.5	0.0	0.2	0.9
Household	0.0	0.3	4.6	4.4	3.1
Borrowing:	13.2	19.3	16.3	17.3	14.2
Banking	9.0	6.7	7.5	8.3	2.3
Government	1.9	7.1	6.3	2.6	1.9
Rest of World	1.7	0.5	2.4	5.2	9.1
Household	0.6	7.6	0.0	0.0	0.0
Life Fund	30.4	20.5	17.0	14.8	14.6
Provident/Pension Fund	40.3	36.6	32.5	24.1	17.7
Unit Capital	1.5	1.6	5.7	13.2	19.6
Other Mutual Funds	0.0	0.0	0.0	3.1	6.5
Trade Debts	0.0	0.0	0.1	0.3	0.7
Other Liabilities	6.2	6.7	5.0	6.6	10.5

Note: The entries do not add up to 100 per cent as some small categories have been omitted for the sake of brevity.

Source: Flow of Funds Accounts, *RBI Bulletin,* various issues.

Table 3.13

Other Financial Institutions' Uses of Funds (per cent)

Uses	1971–2 to 1975–6	1976–7 to 1980–1	1981–2 to 1985–6	1986–7 to 1990–1	1991–2
Currency and Deposits	8.3	13.5	17.2	24.6	25.8
Loans and Advances:	31.4	43.8	42.4	43.6	27.9
Banking	4.4	7.3	11.2	11.7	– 6.3
Private Non-financial	9.1	11.9	15.4	18.4	21.2
Government	9.3	10.7	8.0	7.1	3.9
Rest of World	0.1	0.3	0.3	0.7	1.7
Household	5.2	10.3	4.9	3.5	3.6
Investment:	59.8	40.1	37.5	27.8	36.8
Private Non-financial	3.8	2.8	5.8	9.9	13.3
Shares	3.2	1.9	1.9	4.9	9.0
Debentures	0.6	1.0	3.9	5.2	4.3
Government	48.5	31.9	26.8	13.8	21.4
Rest of World	0.1	0.1	0.1	0.1	0.1
Other Assets	0.5	2.5	2.9	3.9	9.4
Memo:					
Share going to:					
Government	57.8	42.6	34.7	20.9	25.3
Private Non-financial	12.9	14.7	21.1	28.3	34.5
Share of OFIs in Total OFI and Commercial Bank Funds going to Private Non-financial Sector	35.2	38.0	40.9	47.0	60.7

Note: The entries do not add up to 100 per cent as some small categories have been omitted for the sake of brevity.

Source: Flow of Funds Accounts, *RBI Bulletin,* various issues.

To conclude, we have found that while the government and the household sectors respectively have been the largest borrower and lender in the real sector for the period 1971-91, there are indications that the relative importance of these two sectors may be declining in the sources and uses of funds with the onset of the reforms. In the case of the household sector, there is evidence to suggest a significant portfolio substitution from bank deposits and contractual savings assets to market-based assets since 1991. Perhaps our most important finding is the change in the structure of financing of corporate investment with the increasing domination of OFIs (and the marginalization of commercial banks) in the intermediation of funds to private firms. This finding has significant implications both for the design of the reform package and the effect that the reforms may have on the intermediation of funds from ultimate lenders to ultimate borrowers. In the next section, we examine in detail the state and level of development of the two groups of financial intermediaries—commercial banks and other financial institutions—at the beginning of the reform process and the implications of the reforms for the evolution of these two groups.

II. The Structure of the Indian Financial System

In Figure 3.1, we provide a stylized representation of the structure of the Indian financial system. Among the two major sets of financial institutions in the economy—the banking sector and other financial institutions—the former comprises the central bank (the Reserve Bank of India), commercial banks and co-operative banks. Commercial banks can be of two types—scheduled and non-scheduled. Scheduled commercial banks are required to maintain a minimum amount of capital and obey RBI directives regarding the CRR. The RBI permits scheduled banks to approach it for financial assistance if needed. Presently an overwhelming majority of commercial banks in India are in the scheduled category.[2] Commercial banks can be classified in terms of ownership and function into three groups—Regional Rural Banks (RRBs), public sector banks and private banks. Private banks in turn can either be Indian branches of foreign banks or domestically owned private banks. Regional rural banks are government sponsored regionally based rural oriented commercial banks established under the Regional Rural Banks Act of 1976. Given the specific role of the RRBs in financing agricultural (and allied) activities, we postpone discussion of the RRBs to Section II of Chapter 5 where we undertake a brief examination of the rural credit system in India. Our discussion of co-operative banks is also dealt within this section given the possibly important role this group of banks can play in intermediating funds to rural borrowers in a liberalized financial environment.

Other financial institutions can be classified into three groups—term-lending institutions, mutual funds and the insurance sector. Among development banks, the largest in size and influence are the IDBI and the ICICI. Among the mutual funds, by far the largest in size is the UTI (though in recent years, several new mutual funds have also arrived on the scene). Finally, the two main insurance funds are the Life Insurance Corporation of India (LIC) and the General Insurance Corporation of India (GIC). In the rest of this section, we first review developments in the commercial banking sector as a whole and then examine in turn each of the major financial institutions.

[2] In March 1995, only three of 288 commercial banks were non-scheduled and accounted for 0.02 per cent of total bank deposits.

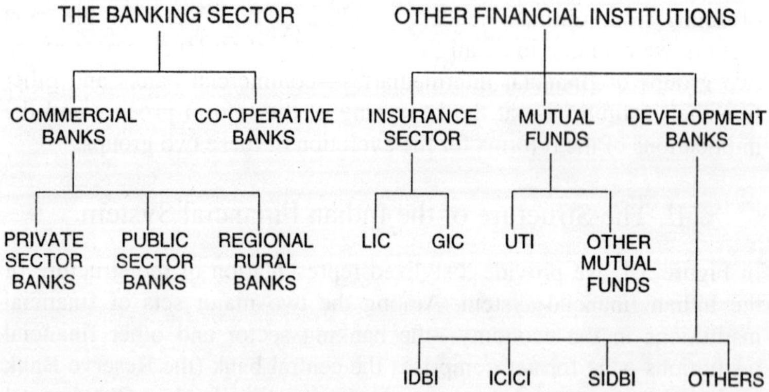

Figure 3.1 The Structure of the Financial System

COMMERCIAL BANKS

Since 1969, there has been significant growth in the commercial banking system both in geographical coverage and amount of resources mobilized. This is evident from Table 3.14. All indicators of bank progress show a distinct improvement in the period 1969–93. Perhaps the most revealing indicator of such development in India is the increase in deposits as a percentage of national income from 15.3 per cent in 1969 to 51.8 per cent in 1994. This has been arguably the key factor behind India's impressive performance in the mobilization of domestic savings. As is well known in the literature, India's savings rate is one of the highest among countries at a similar stage of economic development (Joshi and Little 1994). Also, as Figure 3.2 shows, with most of the increase in deposits being in the form of time deposits,[3] this has resulted in a spectacular increase in the M3/GDP ratio since the late sixties.

There are two reasons supporting the high levels of deposits mobilized (as a ratio of national income) by the banking sector. Firstly, there has been a phenomenal increase in geographical coverage by banks with a more than seven-fold increase in the number of bank branches. Most of the new branches have been set up in the rural areas. This has led to a sharp decline in the population per bank branch from 65,000 in 1969 to 14,000 in 1993. As a result, the rural population has increased its share in total deposits from 7.2 per cent in 1973 to 14.6 per cent in 1993 (Table 3.15). Another indicator of the increase in locational spread of banks is the tendency towards equalization in the

[3] Between 1973 and 1993, 84.5 per cent of the increase in aggregate bank deposits was in the form of time deposits. In end-March 1993, time deposits constituted 84.3 per cent of total deposits.

population per bank branch across states (Table 3.16). The standard deviation, for instance, fell from 113,000 in 1969 to 4,100 in 1994. This also indicates the rapid shrinkage in inter-state disparities with regard to access to banking facilities. The increase in geographical coverage is the result of a strictly enforced branch licensing policy followed by RBI. Under this policy, RBI restricted banks from opening branches in urban and metropolitan areas. Instead, the thrust of branch expansion was mostly to the 'under-banked' districts in rural and semi-urban areas. The branch licensing policy was itself influenced by the launching of the Lead Bank scheme in December 1969. Under this scheme, a particular public sector bank was designated as the Lead Bank for a particular district. The lead bank was then responsible for surveying the credit needs, development of branch banking, and an extension of credit facilities to the districts allotted to it (RBI 1983).

Table 3.14

Scheduled Commercial Banks—Progress since 1969

	June 1969	June 1984	March 1991	March 1994
Total Offices in India.[a]	8,262	45,332	60,220	61,803
Rural	1,833 (22.2)	25,372 (56.0)	35,206 (58.5)	35,329 (57.2)
Semi-Urban	3,342 (40.5)	9,262 (20.4)	11,344 (32.2)	11,890 (19.2)
Urban	1,584 (19.2)	5,769 (12.8)	8,046 (13.4)	8,745 (14.1)
Metropolitan	1,503 (18.2)	4,929 (10.9)	5,624 (9.3)	5,839 (9.4)
Population per office (in thousands)	65	15	14	15
Deposits as percentage of National Income	15.2	37.9	50.0	51.8
Deposits per office (in lakhs)	56	143	334	524
Credit per office (in lakhs)	44	95	202	270
Credit-Deposit Ratio (%)	77.5	67.4	60.6	51.6
Investment-Deposit Ratio (%)	29.3	36.3	37.7	41.2

Note: [a] Figures in parenthesis indicate percentage of total offices.

Source: RBI (1985), *Reports on Trend and Progress of Banking in India;* CSO, *National Accounts Statistics 1995.*

Table 3.15

Distribution of Deposits of Scheduled Commercial Banks (per cent)

Population Group	June 1973	June 1981	March 1993
Rural	7.2	13.0	14.6
Semi-Urban	23.3	23.2	19.5
Urban	25.4	24.6	23.3
Metropolitan	44.1	39.2	42.6

Source: RBI (1985); *Banking Statistics,* RBI, 1995.

Table 3.16

State-wise Population per Bank Branch (in '000)

States	June 1969	June 1994
Northern Region	46	11
Haryana	56	13
Himachal Pradesh	80	7
Jammu and Kashmir	124	10
Punjab	38	9
Rajasthan	68	14
Northern-eastern Region	203	17
Arunachal Pradesh	n/a	13
Assam	193	18
Manipur	510	22
Meghalaya	137	10
Mizoram	n/a	9
Nagaland	250	17
Tripura	300	15
Eastern Region	135	17
Bihar	200	18
Orissa	211	15
West Bengal	85	16
Central Region	115	16
Madhya Pradesh	116	15
Uttar Pradesh	114	16
Western Region	38	13
Gujarat	34	12
Maharashtra	43	14
Southern Region	44	12
Andhra Pradesh	74	14
Karnataka	37	10
Kerala	34	10
Tamil Nadu	37	13
Mean	110.7	12.4
Standard Deviation	113	4.1

Source: Report on Trend and Progress in Banking 1993–4, RBI.

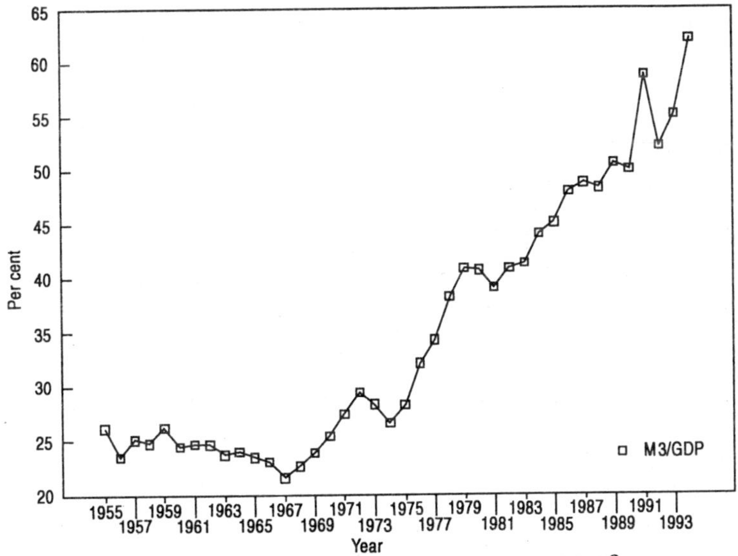

Figure 3.2 M3/GDP Ratio, 1955–6 to 1994–5[a]

Note: [a] Data refers to financial year.

Sources: Reports on Currency and Finance, RBI; *National Accounts Statistics,* CSO, various issues.

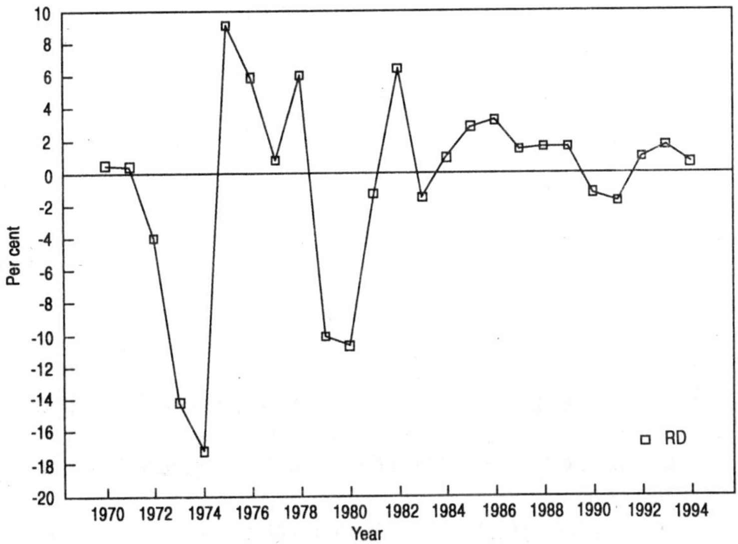

Figure 3.3 Commercial Bank Real Deposit Rate (RD)[a, b]

Notes: [a] Interest Rate on One Year Term Deposits minus the inflation rate.
[b] Data refers to financial year.

Source: Report on Currency and Finance, RBI, various issues.

The second reason behind the impressive performance in deposit mobilization has been the positive real rate of return that was available on bank term deposits (barring the oil price shocks of 1973–4 and 1979–80 and the high inflation period of 1989–91, see Figure 3.3). As Mckinnon (1973) has argued, a deposit rate that is positive in real terms is an essential prerequisite for financial deepening. In the Indian context, there are few available studies that have investigated the relationship between the bank deposit rate and financial deepening. A recent study with Indian data that uses a modern time-series perspective to examine the relationship finds a unequivocally positive relationship between the real deposit rate and financial saving (Athukorala 1995). Interestingly, the study also finds that a bank density variable (population per bank branch) has a significant positive influence on financial saving.

As we have discussed in Chapter 2, a key impetus to the current reforms in the financial sector was the conclusion that two decades of social control of banks had led to a 'decline in the productivity and efficiency and erosion of the profitability of the banking sector' (Ministry of Finance 1991, p. iii). The erosion of profitability of banks has ensued from factors influencing both income and expenditure in the banking industry. On the income side, banks have not been able to realize their potential income due to various restrictions on the use of funds. The most important of these have been the directed investment and credit programmes. Directed investment programmes have been the extremely high levels of the CRR and SLR in the late eighties. Directed credit programmes have consisted of lending requirements to designated 'priority sectors' in the economy: a feature being that the rates of return available to banks have been less than rates of return available on alternate deployment of funds. It is difficult to argue with the Narasimham Committee's contention then that such programmes have been responsible for the declining profitability of commercial banks over the seventies and eighties. As Table 3.14 indicates, there has been a steady decline in the credit-deposit ratio (matched by a corresponding increase in the investment-deposit ratio) over the period 1969–94. Since a significant portion of credit is to the private corporate sector (where banks have much more flexibility to fix their own rates of interest), this in essence implies a decline in the profitable segment of banks' use of funds.

Since 1991, however, there has been a scaling-down of the directed investment programmes, particularly with regard to the SLR. As noted in Chapter 2, there has been a gradual reduction in the SLR since the onset of the reforms, the SLR standing at 31.5 per cent in October 1994, a level that was last observed in 1972. There has been less progress in reducing the CRR mainly due to an unstable macro-economic environment (we go into this in more detail in Chapter 6). There has been little progress also in reducing the scale of the directed credit programmes. We discuss the directed credit programmes in more detail in our review of the credit market (in Section III of this chapter).

On the expenditure side, the Narasimham Committee has drawn attention to the 'over-expansion' of the banking sector due to the rigidly enforced branch licensing policy. It is pertinent to mention here that foreign banks in India were exempt from the branch licensing requirement while private banks had to follow it in a more limited manner (as compared to public sector banks). Therefore, one can concur with the Narasimham Committee's assessment that this policy may have been an important contributing factor in the poor profitability performance of public sector banks which had to shoulder most of the responsibility in providing banking access to the rural population. Here, a recent study by Subrahmanyam (1993) provides a useful insight. The study estimates the total factor productivity growth (TFPG) for public sector banks over the period 1970–89. It finds a TFPG of around 2–3 per cent per annum for these banks during this period. As the study argues, one reason why the positive TFPG was not realized into accounting profits was the 'preference' by banks for branch expansion at this time.

While considering the costs of policy-induced branch expansion on bank profitability, one should keep in mind also the significant positive impact of the branch licensing policy on financial deepening and resource mobilization in India. Therefore, a relaxation of the branch licensing policy that allows large-scale withdrawal of banks from rural areas may not be appropriate to follow if the current positive trend in financial deepening has to be maintained.[4] An important change in the branch licensing policy since 1991 has been the freedom given to banks to convert non-viable rural branches to satellite offices on certain conditions. Also, banks are allowed to close down loss-making branches in urban/metro centres and rural centres only if these centres are being served by two other commercial banks (except RRBs). Other changes in the policy include the freedom given to banks to open

[4] Within an endogenous growth perspective, since financial deepening leads to a higher rate of economic growth, it can be argued that the social return to providing banking facilities in remote areas may exceed the private return to the individual bank. In this case, there is a market failure which the branch licensing policy addresses.

specialized branches per centre (in the categories of industrial finance, non-resident accounts and treasury management) without the prior approval of the RBI. Further, banks have been permitted to shift their existing branches within the same locality. These changes imply that while banks have been given considerable freedom in rationalizing the structure of their branches, the broad thrust of the pre-reform licensing policy in ensuring that the rural populace has access to banking facilities has been maintained.

The Narasimham Committee also indicates that a further reason for the 'declining profitability' of banks has been the problem of 'over-manning' in public sector banks. As is well known, this problem is of course not only confined to public sector banks, but also afflicts the non-financial units of the public sector. A specific feature of 'over-manning' in the banking sector has been the resistance by unions in the public sector banks to the introduction of computerization and mechanization of banking services leading to a sub-optimal capital–labour ratio in the banking industry. While the unions have agreed (in October 1993) to permit the introduction of computerization in a phased manner in the public sector banks, it should be pointed out that a more comprehensive solution to the problem of 'over-manning' (whether in banks or elsewhere) can only come about with reforms in the existing labour market policies that do not allow flexibility in the use of labour to firms.

In Tables 3.17 and 3.18 we provide some indicators of efficiency and profitability for commercial banks in India. Using deposits per employee as an indicator of bank efficiency, we find that foreign banks out-perform the public sector banks (due in great part to the absence of a requirement for foreign banks to open branches in rural areas). However, public sector banks out-perform Indian-owned private commercial banks both with respect to deposits per office and deposits per employee. Profitability indicators reveal that both foreign and Indian-owned private banks have performed better than public sector banks. One interesting feature of the performance of public sector banks is the steady improvement of the net profit to working funds ratio of the State Bank of India (SBI) group of banks since 1990–1. This has not been the case with the other nationalized banks which witnessed negative profits in the years 1992–3 and 1993–4 after positive profits in the previous two years. The sharp downturn in the profitability of other nationalized banks in the post-1992 period could be in great part due to the adoption of a system of asset classification by commercial banks in

1992–3 (see Chapter 4) that laid greater emphasis on the quantification and provisioning for non-performing loans. The difference in the performance of the SBI group as compared to other nationalized banks with regard to profitability after the adoption of a uniform accountancy standard in 1992–3 indicates that the financial sector reforms have had a differing impact on public sector banks. This could be due to a superior quality of managerial and supervisory staff in the SBI group of banks (possibly due to better recruiting procedures) as compared to the other nationalized banks.

Table 3.17

Efficiency Indicators, Scheduled Commercial Banks

Indicators	June 1969	June 1981	March 1990	March 1993
Deposits Per Office (Rs Crores)				
State Bank of India	0.49	1.36	3.78	5.85
Nationalized Banks	0.64	1.29	3.57	5.15
Foreign Banks	n/a	n/a	58.58	137.42
Regional Rural Banks	...	0.07	0.28	0.47
Other Scheduled Commercial Banks	0.51	0.82	1.80	3.36
Deposits per Employee (Rs Crores)				
State Bank of India	n/a	n/a	0.16	0.26
Nationalized Banks	n/a	n/a	0.19	0.28
Regional Rural Banks	n/a	n/a	0.07	0.10
Other Scheduled Commercial Banks	n/a	n/a	0.12	0.21

Source: Banking Statistics, RBI, various issues.

Table 3.18

Profitability Indicators,[a] Scheduled Commercial Banks

Bank Groups	1990–1	1991–2	1992–3	1993–4
State Bank of India and Associates	0.16	0.21	0.22	0.25
Nationalized Banks	0.20	0.30	−1.72	− 2.25
Indian-owned Private Sector Banks	0.39	0.65	0.34	0.69
Foreign Banks	1.45	1.27	− 2.65	1.72
All Scheduled Commercial Banks	0.26	0.35	−1.08	− 0.92

Note: [a] Net Profit as a percentage of working funds.

Source: Report on Trend and Progress in Banking, RBI, various issues.

OTHER FINANCIAL INSTITUTIONS

We saw (Figure 2.1) that the Indian financial system can be broadly categorized on the basis of organizational form into banks and other financial institutions. The other financial institutions can be further classified into three groups:

A) All India Development Banks (or Development Finance Institutions) consisting of:

i) Industrial Development Bank of India (IDBI): This is the largest development bank with diversified areas of activity. We shall discuss the working and performance of this institution in detail later.

ii)Industrial Credit and Investment Corporation of India (ICICI): This is the second largest development bank also with diversified areas of activity. Once again, the working and performance of this institution will be discussed further on in this chapter.

iii) Shipping Credit and Investment Company of India (SCICI): This is a wholly owned subsidiary of ICICI, and as its name suggests it specializes in providing assistance to shipping companies. Recently it has diversified its scope of activities to include other areas of the industrial sector with an emphasis on exports and infrastructure such as energy, telecommunications and tourism.

iv) Industrial Finance Corporation of India (IFCI): This is the oldest development bank. It was established in 1948. It accounted for over 8 per cent of the total financial assistance to the industrial sector in 1994–5.

v) Industrial Reconstruction Bank of India (IRBI): This institution was established jointly by IDBI, Life Insurance Corporation of India and commercial banks in 1971, with the main objective of creating a specialized institution which concerned itself solely with rehabilitation of sick units. It is a much smaller institution compared to the major development banks. The total disbursement of assistance was Rs 397.6 crores in 1994–5 which accounted for less than 1 per cent of total disbursements to the industrial sector. Given the nature of its lending activities, this institution receives large amounts of subsidized credits and grants.

vi) Small Industries Development Bank of India (SIDBI): This is a specialized institution catering to the needs of the small scale sector, the details of which shall be discussed later.

vii) Risk Capital and Technology Finance Corporation (RCTC): In 1975 the IFCI sponsored the Risk Capital Foundation which aimed at encouraging new entrepreneurs. The Risk Capital Foundation was converted into RCTC on 12 January 1988. It provides both risk capital and technology finance to innovative entrepreneurs and technocrats for their technology oriented ventures. By its very nature and specialization it is a small development bank accounting for a negligible part of total assistance to the industrial sector.

viii) Technology Development Corporation of India (TDCI): This institution began operations in 1989 and provides assistance to firms either directly or through venture funds which it manages. It also provides technology information services.

ix) Tourism Finance Corporation of India (TFCI): The TFCI was incorporated in January 1989. As the name suggests it specializes in providing assistance to tourism projects and tourism related activities.

It is important to note that though many of these institutions are called 'banks' they differ from commercial banks in two important aspects. Firstly, they do not seek deposits from the public, and secondly they specialize in the provision of long-term loans.

B) Investment Institutions, consisting of Insurance companies and Mutual Funds:

i) Life Insurance Corporation of India (LIC).

ii) General Insurance Corporation of India (GIC).

iii) Unit Trust of India (UTI): This is a government owned mutual fund.

C) State Level Institutions: These cater to the needs of the small-scale industries, consisting of:

i) State Financial Corporations (SFC).

ii) State Industrial Development Corporations (SIDC).

Almost all the major institutions in all three categories are government owned (except ICICI and SCICI). All these institutions provide assistance to firms either by providing loans or subscribing to shares and debentures issued by them. They also underwrite new issues and provide guarantees for term loans and deferred payments to enable firms to tap other sources of credit. We present in Table 3.19 the percentage distribution of financial assistance disbursed by all these institutions to the industrial sector. Some of the All India Development Banks do not figure in the table because their share is negligible.

The table indicates that the all India development banks have all along contributed over 60 per cent of financial assistance to the industrial sector. Another important feature is that the UTI has grown in importance over the years and the importance of the state level institutions has been on the decline.

Table 3.19
Institution-wise Details of Financial Assistance to the Industrial Sector[a]

Institution	1980–1	1985–6	1989–90	1990–1	1991–2	1992–3	1993–4	1994–5
IDBI	47.3	42.8	28.1	28.2	29.6	28.4	28.8	30.5
IFCI	6.8	8.2	11.2	12.7	9.9	8.1	8.1	8.5
ICICI	11.5	9.8	13.5	15.9	14.4	15.6	16.5	20.5
SIDBI	...	...	8.9	8.8	7.2	6.1	6.7	7.4
SCICI	...	...	2.2	1.3	1.1	2.3	3.7	4.3
IRBI	1.1	1.4	1.4	1.2	neg.	neg.	neg.	neg.
Sub-total	66.7	62.2	65.3	68.1	62.2	60.5	63.8	71.2
UTI	3.2	10.7	10.7	12.4	17.9	20.1	22.2	13.5
LIC	4.1	5.3	4.5	3.4	6.3	4.4	2.2	3.4
GIC	2.7	2.2	1.7	1.2	1.5	2.1	1.8	1.1
SFCs	15.5	12.3	11.8	10.1	9.5	7.6	5.8	5.9
SIDCs	7.8	7.3	5.4	4.1	4.2	3.2	2.7	2.9
Total	1603.9	4933.7	10033.9	12369.1	16229.3	21304.9	26599.3	33560.3

Note: [a] All the figures in the above are in percentages except the figures in the last row which are in Rs Crores.

Source: Report on Currency and Finance, RBI, various issues.

In the following pages we shall discuss the working of some of these institutions and the changes therein that financial liberalization has wrought.

Let us first consider the all India development banks, restricting ourselves to a discussion of three institutions: IDBI, SIDBI and ICICI.

Industrial Development Bank of India

IDBI was started as a wholly owned subsidiary of RBI in July 1964. It was separated from the RBI (i.e. its ownership was transferred from the RBI to the Government of India) in February 1975. Since then it has been operating as the apex financial institution which is responsible for the coordination of all financial institutions engaged in financing the industrial sector, in accordance with national priorities. As the apex financial institution IDBI has over the years also financed other institutions by (i) refinancing loans granted by SFCs, SIDCs and commercial banks, and (ii) by subscription to the share capital and bond issues of other all India development banks. Till 1990 the IDBI refinanced loans provided to the small scale industries by the SFCs, SIDCs, and commercial banks. In April 1990, IDBI set up a subsidiary company called SIDBI to which it handed over all operations pertaining to the financing of small-scale industries.

Financial liberalization has brought about two important changes: (i) Interest rate deregulation, and (ii) The contraction of subsidized and captive sources of funds.

The interest rates at which the IDBI (and other all India development banks) lent (before 1990–1) either directly for project loans to firms, or as refinance to other financial institutions were fixed by the government. The basic lending rate for direct loans was fixed at 14 per cent and the interest rate on refinance of loans was fixed at 10 per cent with a ceiling on the primary lending rate at 14 per cent. Both these rates had remained constant over a long period. Term loans were rationed among various firms/sectors depending on the priorities set out by the Government of India and the inherent soundness of the projects. The all India financial institutions lent funds on a consortium basis till 1991–2 when they moved to a system of syndicated loans.

In August 1990 as a part of the liberalization programme IDBI and other development banks (except SIDBI) introduced a two-tier interest rate structure. The first tier covered the initial two years of the loan period or the implementation period (whichever was shorter) of the project, over which the interest rate was retained at 14 per cent. The second tier applied to the remaining period of the loan over which the interest rate was raised to 15 per cent. The interest rate charged by the IDBI on refinanced loans was raised to 12 per cent, with the two-tier interest rate system applying to the primary lender. It should be noted that the changes in the interest rate applied to new loans only and not to outstanding loans. In August 1991, the government permitted all term-lending institutions to charge interest rates in accordance with the perceived risks inherent in the projects, subject to a minimum lending rate of 15 per cent. This was clearly an extremely significant policy initiative which basically freed the interest rate on term loans. During 1991–2 the interest rates charged by IDBI ranged between 18 per cent and 20 per cent. The freeing of interest rates was followed by a significant rise in interest rates. During 1992–3 IDBI reduced the interest rates charged on term loans and the interest charged ranged between 17 per cent to 19 per cent. The year 1993–4 saw a further decline in the interest rate which now ranged between 14.5 and 17.5 per cent. In 1995–6 the interest charged ranged between 14.5 and 18.5 per cent.

In December 1993, IDBI introduced a variable interest rate system as an option for borrowers. The interest rate charged under this system is related to the IDBI's long-term prime lending rate (LTPR). The LTPR is determined with reference to the anchor rate derived from the weighted average cut-off yield obtained from auctions of 364-day

Treasury Bills conducted by RBI every fortnight. A mark up factor is added to this anchor rate to account for the term spread, administrative cost and the credit risk. The LTPR is reviewed at half yearly intervals and the changes are applicable on the outstanding loan. Thus, substantial changes have taken place since 1990–1 on the interest rate front.

Another significant change since 1990–1 has been the reduced dependence of IDBI on the Government of India and RBI for funds. Moreover, with the reduction in the SLR for banks, an important captive source of funds for the IDBI, ICICI, IFCI, SIDBI, SFCs, and SIDCs has shrunk. The bonds, shares and debentures issued by all the above mentioned organizations are eligible to be counted under the SLR. This basically implies that with the reduction of subsidized and captive sources of funds the IDBI has had to depend more on the market to raise resources. Nevertheless, the SLR requirements remain an extremely important source of funds for IDBI. In the years 1991–2 and 1992–3 all scheduled commercial banks held various instruments issued by IDBI which accounted for about 25 per cent of total liabilities. It should be noted that the element of subsidy on this source of funds is almost negligible in recent years, as all the instruments held as a part of the SLR carry a rate of interest which is close to the market rate.

The examination of the structure of liabilities of the IDBI (see Table 3.20) in the pre- and post-financial liberalization period reveals the following stylized facts:

i) The total liabilities/ assets have grown over ten times between 1980–1 and 1994–5.

ii) Borrowings from RBI and the Government of India (this source of funds carries a large amount of subsidy as these borrowings are at a rate of interest far below the market rate) have fallen substantially over the years while the importance of borrowings from others and bonds and debentures has grown over the years.

The bank has been increasingly forced to borrow at market rates of interest. In recent years the bank has introduced many new debt instruments in the market, like certificates of deposits and secured and unsecured bonds, all of which have interest rates which are market-related. In October 1992 a fixed deposit scheme was introduced. During 1993–4 floating rate bonds with a maturity period of three years were issued. The interest rate on these bonds was to be 2 percentage points over the weighted average cut-off yield on 364-day treasury bills. Clearly the IDBI has diversified its sources of credit over

Table 3.20

Liabilities of IDBI[a]

Year	Share Capital	Reserves	Bonds and Debentures	Borrowings from RBI	Borrowings from GOI	Borrowings from others	Other Liabilities	Total
1980–1	4.3	3.8	35.4	39.3	5.1	1.7	10.3	3,363
1989–90	3.1	5.3	46.0	20.7	3.8	12.4	8.7	20,419
1990–1	3.1	6.1	49.7	16.2	3.7	14.0	7.1	22,768
1991–2	2.6	6.2	50.8	12.7	3.3	17.1	7.1	28,041
1992–3	2.4	6.8	49.8	11.8	3.4	18.6	6.9	31,083
1993–4	2.2	7.5	45.3	10.4	3.8	20.8	9.8	34,588
1994–5	2.0	8.5	48.2	8.6	3.7	20.1	8.7	38,162

Note: [a] All figures are in percentages except the figures in the last column which are in Rs Crores.
Source: Report on Currency and Finance, RBI, various issues.

the years by introducing debt instruments of varying types. This without doubt has been the outcome of financial liberalization and the IDBI is in the process of transforming itself into a institution capable of raising resources directly from the market with reduced support from the government. How successful it will be in this attempt will be clear only when the SLR requirements are further reduced in accordance with the recommendations of the Narasimham Committee report.

Let us now turn to the ways in which IDBI has provided resources to the industrial sector and the changes therein (see Table 3.21). IDBI provides finance to the industrial sector in two ways, namely direct finance (Rupee and foreign currency loans to firms, underwriting and direct subscription to shares and debentures of firms, and equipment leasing) and indirect finance (refinance of loans, Bills finance, and loans and subscription to shares and bonds of financial institutions). Two stylized facts emerge from Table 3.21:

i) Over the years the importance of direct assistance has increased substantially and,

ii) Refinancing of loans has reduced dramatically.

There could be two possible reasons for this. First, given the contraction of subsidized sources of funds, IDBI has had little incentive to lend to other financial institutions (i.e. refinance the loans they made) at an interest rate far lower than what it could earn if the bank made the loan directly to firms. Second, with the establishment of SIDBI, IDBI stopped functioning as a refinancing institution for the small scale sector.

As a part of the financial liberalization effort the Government of India stipulated in 1990–1 that all India financial institutions should achieve a minimum capital adequacy ratio of 4 per cent by March 1993, and 8 per cent by March 1996. As of March 1995, IDBI had a capital adequacy ratio of 13.4 per cent. Following the new guidelines set out by the RBI for classification of assets, IDBI reported that at the end of March 1993, 92.5 per cent of the loan and other assistance portfolio was classified as standard (i.e. bearing normal risk), 3.1 per cent were substandard and 4.4 per cent were doubtful debts and loss assets. The comparable percentages for 1994–5 were 92.2 per cent, 4.1 per cent and 3.7 per cent respectively.

Another important development in the post 1990–1 period has been an attempt by the IDBI to diversify its activities. In 1991–2 a merchant banking division was established. In August 1993, IDBI decided to sponsor a mutual fund (called the IDBI Mutual fund) and this fund has since been launched. IDBI has also established a commercial bank.

Table 3.21

Scheme-wise Details of Financial Assistance Disbursed by IDBI[a]

Scheme	1980–1	1989–90	1990–1	1991–2	1992–3	1993–4	1994–5
1. Direct Assistance	31.3	49.3	54.7	63.4	73.2	78.8	87.0
a) Rupee Loans	n/a	n/a	52.4	55.6	63.0	61.4	65.5
b) Foreign Currency Loans	n/a	n/a	n/a	7.2	7.2	8.62	10.0
c) Underwriting and Direct Subscriptions	neg.	neg.	neg.	neg.	neg.	7.3	10.0
d) Equipment Leasing	...	...	neg.	neg.	neg.	1.5	1.5
2. Refinance of Loans	43.2	13.5	11.9	9.1	6.4	5.1	3.6
3. Bills finance	15.7	23.2	19.2	16.2	15.4	12.3	8.13
4. Loans to and shares and bonds of Financial Institutions	9.2	13.9	13.9	11.2	4.9	3.8	1.2
Total	1,117.7	3,513.8	4,459.4	5,762.8	6,668.5	8,070.6	10,621.3

Note: [a] All figures are in percentages except the figures in the last column which are in Rs Crores.
Source: Report on Currency and Finance, RBI, various issues.

Table 3.22

Liabilities of SIDBI[a]

Year	Share Capital	Reserves	Bonds and Debentures	Borrowings from RBI	Borrowings from GOI	Borrowings from others[b]	Other Liabilities	Total
1990–1	8.5	0.8	...	7.5	8.1	72.0	3.1	5,309
1991–2	6.7	1.6	...	12.6	12.2	62.2	4.7	6,680
1992–3	6.0	2.6	6.7	11.2	10.8	55.8	6.9	7,484
1993–4	4.8	3.2	9.1	12.4	14.3	41.7	14.5	9,453
1994–5	4.3	4.8	13.5	13.3	16.4	33.8	13.7	10,358

Note: [a] All figures are in percentages except the figures in the last column which are in Rs Crores.

[b] Borrowings from others include (i) consideration payable to IDBI against transfer of outstanding portfolio relating to small scale sector and (ii) foreign borrowings.

Borrowings from others in 1993–4 and 1994–5 include amounts placed with SIDBI by foreign banks in lieu of shortfall in their advances to the priority sector.

Source: Report on Currency and Finance, RBI, various issues.

In the post-liberalization period IDBI has attempted to transform itself into a financial institution with a reduced dependence on the government for subsidized and captive sources of funds and having a diversified field of activity.

Let us now turn to an analysis of the working of SIDBI.

SMALL INDUSTRIES DEVELOPMENT BANK OF INDIA

SIDBI was set up as an wholly owned subsidiary of IDBI by an Act of Parliament in 1989 and commenced operations in April 1990. SIDBI took over the outstanding portfolio of loans to the small scale sector from IDBI. SIDBI has been assigned the role of the principal financial institution for promotion and financing of the small scale industries and to coordinate the functioning of institutions engaged in similar activities.

From an examination of the structure of liabilities of SIDBI (see Table 3.22), the following important conclusions emerge:
i) SIDBI is still substantially dependent on the Government of India, RBI and IDBI for funds.
ii) There is a gradual increase in the share of bonds and debentures.
SIDBI still depends to a great extent on subsidized sources of credit.

As regards the lending activities of SIDBI a study of the scheme-wise details of financial assistance disbursed by SIDBI (see Table 3.23), result in the following observations:
i) The share of direct loans has risen to 55.5 per cent in 1994–5.
ii) Indirect assistance, especially in terms of refinance has declined significantly.

Table 3.23

Scheme-wise Details of Financial Assistance Disbursed by SIDBI[a]

Scheme	1990–1	1991–2	1992–3	1993–4	1994–5
1. Direct Assistance	...	6.3	17.0	31.0	55.5
2. Indirect Assistance	95.6	92.7	81.4	65.9	41.2
a) Refinance	69.3	63.2	52.0	41.8	36.5
b) Bills Rediscounting	7.9	7.8	6.4	4.4	4.7
c) Short term Bills	18.4	21.7	23.0	19.8	...
3. Others	4.6	1.0	1.5	3.1	3.2
Total	2263.2	2588.11	2787.28	3331.32	3385.30

Note: [a] All the figures in the above are in percentages except the figures in the last row which are in Rs crore.

Source: Report on Currency and Finance, RBI, various issues.

A major reason for the decline in the importance of refinance has been that the performance of the financial institutions eligible for refinance (i.e. mainly the SFCs and SIDCs) has not been satisfactory over the years. We saw in Table 3.19 that the importance of the SFCs and SIDCs has fallen over time. They contributed well over 20 per cent of financial assistance to the industrial sector which dropped to below 10 per cent in 1994–5. Though the data needed to evaluate the performance of SFCs and SIDCs are not available, these institutions seem to be saddled with a large amount of bad debts and thus face a severe resource crunch. Given this situation, SIDBI has preferred to increase the extent of its direct lending.

In the process of financial liberalization, the rates of interest SIDBI could charge to its direct borrowers have risen substantially but the interest rates charged are lower as compared to those charged by IDBI and ICICI. In 1990–1 the interest charged ranged between 6.5 per cent and 11.5 per cent, while rising to between 7 per cent and 15.5 per cent in 1991–2. This was a sharp increase but was not comparable to the increase in interest rates of IDBI and ICICI. During 1992–3 and 1993–4 the interest rates charged ranged between 8.5 per cent to 17 per cent. During 1994–5 the interest rates charged ranged between 9 and 14.5 per cent. The generally large range of the interest rates charged are due to the presence of a large number of financing schemes introduced by SIDBI each of which carries a different extent of interest rate subsidy. SIDBI has been lending to the small scale sector at rates of interest much below the market rates. This is a conscious policy decision of the government aimed at reducing the adverse impact that an extraordinarily sharp rise in interest rates would have on the small scale sector.

Given that SIDBI is the financial institution which refinances loans (to SFCs and SIDCs who are in serious financial difficulties) and lends directly only to the small scale sector at subsidized rates of interest it was important to ensure that it was not forced to borrow at market rates of interest. It was through continued support to SIDBI that the government made certain that the flow of long-term loans to the small scale sector was not disrupted. Given the current structure of SIDBI's liabilities and lending operations, this support would have to continue for some years to come.

We now turn to an analysis of the working of ICICI.

INDUSTRIAL CREDIT AND INVESTMENT CORPORATION OF INDIA

ICICI was set up as a private sector development bank in 1955. Its share capital was subscribed to by foreign institutions (including the

World Bank), banks, and insurance companies. Presently, a large part of its share capital is held by government-owned institutions such as banks and insurance companies. This is largely because of the nationalization of banks and insurance companies. ICICI caters to the credit needs of large firms and it also underwrites and directly subscribes to issues of shares and debentures.

Interest rate deregulation has been discussed earlier. As regards the sources of funds, after 1990–1, the SLR funds available to ICICI have declined and in 1991–2 and 1992–3 these have accounted for less than 7 per cent of total liabilities. We present in Table 3.24 the structure of liabilities.

The following characteristics emerge:

i) Overall the structure of liabilities has been rather stable with bonds and debentures and foreign borrowings being the major source of funds.

ii) In recent years borrowings from the IDBI are on the decline and other liabilities are gaining in importance indicating a diversification of source of funds in the post 1990–1 period.

Turning to lending operations, Table 3.25 shows the structure of financial assistance provided. ICICI does not refinance loans so all its assistance is direct assistance in the form of direct loans or direct subscriptions to shares and debentures. Deregulation has not therefore brought about a major reorientation of its lending activities except that in 1993–4 and 1994–5 direct subscriptions to shares and debentures increased sharply. Financial services have also grown in importance.

As of March 1994 the capital adequacy ratio was 11.9 per cent which was above the norm of 8 per cent set for all India development banks. The annual reports of ICICI for the years 1992–3 and 1993–4 reveal that the percentage of non-performing assets to total assets was 8.8 per cent and 8 per cent respectively.

Like the IDBI, the ICICI has since 1990–1 attempted to diversify its operations into various fields of industrial finance. In 1991–2 an investment company was set up as a subsidiary of the ICICI in collaboration with J.P. Morgan & Co. ICICI entered the commercial banking sector in January 1994, with the launch of 'The ICICI Banking Corporation Ltd.' In the same year another subsidiary called ICICI Asset Management Co. Ltd. was set up to operate the schemes of the ICICI Mutual Fund.

Financial liberalization has not forced the ICICI to reorient its lending operations substantially because it has always given only direct loans to firms and does not engage in refinance operations.

Table 3.24

Liabilities of ICICI[a]

Year	Share Capital	Reserves	Bonds and Debentures	Borrowings from GOI	Borrowings from IDBI	Foreign Borrowings	Other Liabilities	Total
1980–1	3.3	4.0	44.8	neg.	13.1	28.3	6.5	745.3
1989–90	1.5	6.5	38.0	1.9	5.7	35.3	11.1	5,901.7
1990–1	1.5	6.6	33.3	2.4	6.4	33.3	16.5	7,721.7
1991–2	1.5	6.7	27.3	2.7	3.4	39.9	18.5	10,821.1
1992–3	1.8	7.3	24.5	3.7	2.1	34.8	25.8	13,112.6
1993–4	1.5	7.7	24.2	4.2	1.1	32.3	19.1	16,026.2
1994–5	1.5	9.2	28.6	4.4	0.5	24.7	29.1	19,605.1

Note: [a] All figures are in percentages except the figures in the last column which are in Rs Crores.
Source: Report on Currency and Finance, RBI, various issues.

Table 3.25

Scheme-wise Details of Financial Assistance Disbursed by ICICI[a]

Scheme	1980–1	1989–90	1990–1	1991–2	1992–3	1993–4	1994–5
1. Direct Assistance	86.3	59.9	65.6	76.1	78.7	70.0	71.2
a) Rupee Loans	53.1	43.6	47.5	45.4	56.2	57.5	56.1
b) Foreign Currency Loans	33.2	16.3	18.1	30.7	21.9	10.6	15.1
c) Underwriting of shares and debentures	neg.	neg.	3.9	neg.	neg.	1.9	neg.
2. Direct subscriptions to shares and debentures	neg.	6.4	5.4	3.0	3.7	10.7	18.5
3. Financial services[b]	11.7	32.7	28.5	20.5	17.5	19.1	9.71
Total	183.56	1,357.1	1,967.53	2,351.27	3,315.2	4,413.3	6,879.3

Note: [a] All figures are in percentages except the figures in the last row which are in Rs Crores.
[b] Financial Services include deferred credits and leasing.
Source: Report on Currency and Finance, RBI, various issues.

Liberalization has nevertheless forced ICICI to diversify its sources of funds to a large extent.

Let us now turn to a discussion of the operations of the investment institutions among which the UTI is easily the most important institution.

Unit Trust of India

UTI was set up in 1964. It is a 50 per cent subsidiary of IDBI, the rest of the share capital being held by LIC, commercial banks, ICICI and IFCI. We noted in Table 3.19 that the UTI's share in the total financial assistance to the industrial sector grew from a mere 3.2 per cent in 1980–1 to 22.2 per cent in 1993–4 but then dropped to 13.5 per cent in 1994–5. We also noted earlier that the share of UTI and other mutual funds in the savings of the household sector in financial assets rose from 4.9 per cent over the period 1986–7 to 1990–1 to 6.7 per cent over the period 1991–2 to 1994–5. Thus the importance of the UTI as a financial intermediary has increased a great deal in the post 1990–1 period.

UTI was never constrained in any way either by regulation or by policy decisions of the Government of India in the manner in which it invested its resources, and it has invested in both equity and fixed income securities. Financial liberalization of this sector, thus has involved a removal of legal barriers to entry in the mutual funds business in a phased manner, and a strengthening of regulations aimed at ensuring transparency, the provision of reliable information to investors and ensuring the prevention of mutual funds being used by private business groups to raise cheap resources to finance their own investments. Till 1987–8 the UTI held a monopoly position in the mutual funds business. In 1987–8 commercial banks and publicly owned financial institutions were allowed to set up mutual funds and in 1993–4 the private sector was permitted to enter too.

In an important policy initiative on mutual funds during 1993–4, the Securities and Exchange Board of India (SEBI) announced a set of regulations. Mutual funds were required to be formed as Trusts and be managed by a separate asset management company (AMC) and supervised by a board of trustees. This regulation was aimed at providing for an 'arms-length relationship' between the various constituents of the mutual fund. The regulations stipulate that the AMC must have a minimum net worth of Rs 6 crores of which the sponsors must contribute at least 40 per cent. Offer documents of schemes announced by mutual funds need the approval of SEBI before they can be offered to the public and an advertisement code has also been prescribed in order to enforce fair and truthful disclosure by mutual funds. SEBI has specified a procedure for calculating and declaring the Net Asset Values of the various mutual fund schemes. The regulations also include a detailed set of rules regarding investments. For example, it is stipulated that no individual scheme of the mutual fund should invest more than 5 per cent of its corpus in any one company's shares.

Table 3.26 presents the resource mobilization by Mutual Funds over the period 1987–8 to 1994–5.

Table 3.26

Resource Mobilization by Mutual Funds in India[a]

Year	Subsidiaries of Banks	Subsidiaries of Public Sector FIs	Unit Trust of India	Private Sector Mutual Funds	Total
1987–8	12.4	...	87.6	...	2,017.9
1988–9	8.4	...	91.6	...	3,783.7
1989–90	13.4	4.7	81.9	...	6,694.2
1990–1	36.4	10.1	53.5	...	6,154.3
1991–2	20.2	3.7	76.1	...	11,252.9
1992–3	9.3	5.8	84.9	...	13,021.0
1993–4	1.3	2.2	82.9	13.6	11,243.3
1994–5	6.7	5.1	76.5	11.7	11,343.9

Note: [a] All the figures in the above are in percentages except the figures in the last column which are in Rs Crores.

Source: Report on Currency and Finance, RBI, various issues.

Though the shares of other mutual funds is increasing, UTI is by far the largest yet.

Let us now turn to an analysis of the structure of liabilities and assets of the UTI. Table 3.27 shows the structure of liabilities of UTI.

Table 3.27

Liabilities of UTI[a]

Year	Unit Capital	Reserves	Development Reserve Fund	Dividend Equalization Reserve Fund	Current Liabilities and Provisions	Total
1989–90	72.4	15.5	0.2	0.5	11.4	18,504
1990–1	70.3	14.2	0.2	0.4	14.8	23,367
1991–2	69.5	12.5	0.3	0.3	17.4	35,737
1992–3	72.9	14.3	0.3	0.2	12.3	42,026

Note: [a] All the figures in the above are in percentages except the figures in the last column which are in Rs Crores.

Source: Report on Currency and Finance, RBI, various issues.

Unit Capital is by far the largest source of funds. UTI has about 39 different schemes which are both open-ended and closed-ended. The most important among these is the Unit Scheme 1964 which is an open-ended scheme.

The investments of the UTI have undergone significant changes over the period. We present in Table 3.28 the structure of UTI's assets.

Table 3.28

Structure of Assets of UTI[a]

Assets	1989–90	1990–1	1991–2	1992–3
Govt securities/deposits	13.2	21.8	16.1	9.4
Debentures and Bonds	20.3	18.9	17.2	20.7
Equity Shares	18.9	18.1	24.4	35.3
Preference Shares	neg.	neg.	neg.	neg.
Bridge Finance and Deposits with Companies	11.5	10.0	10.0	10.5
Deposits with Banks	24.7	15.0	13.1	7.8
Term Loans	6.7	7.5	7.5	8.5
Rights Entitlements and application money	...	...	0.6	0.4
Current Assets	4.2	8.2	10.7	7.0
Fixed Assets	0.4	0.4	0.3	0.3
Total	18,504	23,367	35,737	42,026

Note: [a] All the figures in the above are in percentages except the figures in the last column which are in Rs Crores.

Source: Report on Currency and Finance, RBI, various issues.

After 1990–1 the share of investments in government securities and deposits with banks has declined, while the share of investments in equity shares has dramatically increased.

Given that a satisfactory regulatory framework is now in place, both the UTI and other mutual funds can be expected to operate in an environment with transparent rules and increased public confidence. Their role in the mobilization of savings would in the future depend on the return they provide to investors.

We consider next two insurance firms (wholly government owned), namely Life Insurance Corporation of India (LIC), which holds a monopoly on the life insurance business, and General Insurance Corporation (GIC), which controls the general insurance business. We concentrate on the LIC, firstly, because it is the larger of the two and secondly because life insurance has had an important share of the financial savings of households (during 1991–2 to 1994–5 it was 9.3 per cent of financial savings of households).

LIFE INSURANCE CORPORATION OF INDIA

LIC was established in September 1956 by nationalizing all life insurance companies operating in India at that time. LIC was set up by an Act of Parliament viz. LIC Act with a contribution of Rs 5 crores by the Government of India. Since nationalization LIC has successfully built up a huge 'Life Fund' (life fund is the total of premiums received till date and interest earnings less expenses of management and claims) of Rs 49,655.82 crores as of 31 March 1994. LIC has 2,008 branch offices and 100 divisional offices. It employs about 1,23,785 people directly and has 5,24,427 active agents. Since its inception, LIC has had to operate under severe constraints regarding the way it could allocate its investible resources among various instruments. Under section 27A of the LIC Act the corporation is required at all times to keep invested 75 per cent of the accretion to the controlled fund (defined as all funds appertaining to life insurance business of an insurer) according to the following directives:

i) In Central Government marketable securities being not less than 20 per cent.

ii) In loans to National Housing Bank including (a) above being not less than 25 per cent.

iii) In State Government securities including government guaranteed marketable securities inclusive of (b) above being not less than 50 per cent.

iv) In socially oriented sectors including public sector, co-operative sector, house building by policy holders, own-your-home schemes, inclusive of (c) above being not less than 75 per cent. LIC is allowed to use the remaining 25 per cent of the controlled fund to invest in the private sector, loans to policy holders and construction and acquisition of immovable property. As of March 1992, the LIC owned about 13.3 per cent of all outstanding central and state government securities. These restrictions have significantly reduced the yields on investments. The situation has improved in recent years with the yields of government securities increasing significantly.

In April 1993, the Government of India appointed a committee under Chairmanship of Shri R.N. Malhotra, former Governor of RBI, to look into the possibilities of reforms of the insurance sector. The committee submitted its report in January 1994 with a reform package containing wide ranging suggestions on both organizational and functional aspects of the insurance sector. Some of the important recommendations are :

i) The private sector should be allowed to enter the insurance business.

ii) The proportion of LIC and GIC investments in Government securities should be reduced.

iii) Government stake in the LIC and GIC should be reduced through disinvestment.

The recommendations of the committee notwithstanding little has been done to reform the insurance sector. This is one sector of the financial market which has yet to be touched by the reform process.

Our brief overview of the other financial institutions and the effects of financial liberalization on their workings suggests the following broad conclusions.

i) Captive and subsidized sources of funds to almost all the all India development banks have been reduced and consequently they have been forced to turn to the market for funds.

ii) There has been a phased deregulation of interest rates.

iii) SIDBI which lends and refinances loans that are exclusively made to the small scale sector continues to receive support from the Government of India and RBI in terms of subsidized credit.

iv) The refinancing operations of both SIDBI and IDBI have reduced substantially after 1990–1.

v) The mutual funds business has been opened up for entry to private firms thus ending the monopoly position that UTI enjoyed. A comprehensive set of regulations regarding the organization and operations of mutual funds is now in place.

vi) The insurance sector has yet to be touched by the reform process.

III. The Evolution of Financial Markets in India

There are three major sets of financial markets by function—money, credit, and capital (Figure 3.4). In this section we describe the changes in these markets brought about by financial liberalization. The money market comprises call money, certificates of deposit, commercial paper and commercial bills.[5] The credit market consists of short-term loans by commercial banks and long-term loans by term-lending institutions. As the market for long-term credit has been analysed in the previous section as part of the discussion on term-lending institutions, we restrict

[5] One component of the money market that we do not examine is the inter-corporate market for short-term funds. The inter-corporate market is unregulated with little precise information on its size. Since the focus of this study is organized financial markets, the inter-corporate market necessarily falls outside its scope.

our review of credit markets to that for commercial bank credit. Finally, the capital market consists of the government securities market and the market for corporate stocks and debentures.

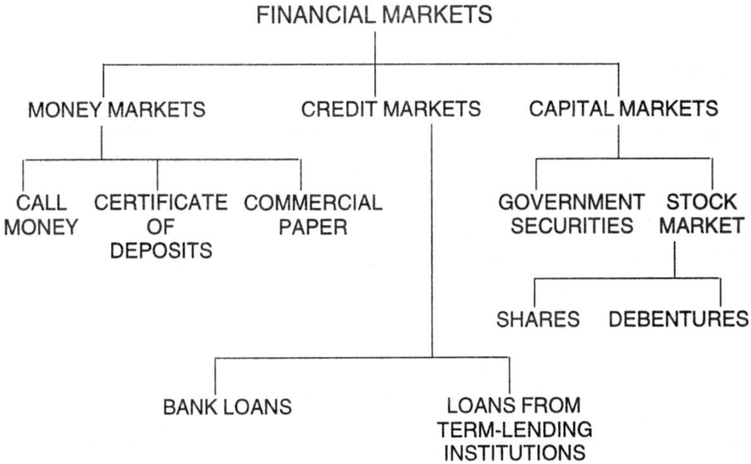

Figure 3.4 Functional Classification of Financial Markets

Money Markets

Money markets are markets for short-term financial assets that are close substitutes for money usually with maturities of less than a year. The deregulation of money markets and their development are an essential component of financial reform. Firstly, well-functioning money markets provide a relatively safe income-yielding outlet for the short-term investment of funds both for banks and firms. The money market can also be an important source of short-term funds to banks in need of quick liquidity. Therefore, a well-developed money market allows banks to economize on their holdings of excess funds and to deploy these funds more profitably elsewhere, decreasing the cost of bank intermediation. Moreover, a deep money market allows firms direct access to short-term funds and thus, avoid bank intermediation costs.

Indian money markets were fairly underdeveloped till the mid-eighties. The most prominent of the money markets during this time was the inter-bank call money market which was a restricted one with a narrow base and a limited number of participants. Key money market instruments which are common in the developed markets of the advanced market economies such as certificates of deposit and commercial paper did not exist. Since then, however, money markets in

India have undergone a great deal of change. Instrumental in this change have been the recommendations of the Vaghul Committee (RBI, 1987) whose objective was to examine the entire spectrum of money markets in India and to recommend specific measures for their development.

Since 1991, with the initiation of the stabilization-cum-structural adjustment programme, there has been an acceleration in the pace of change in the Indian money markets. This was a consequence of RBI's move towards greater use of indirect tools for monetary policy with the money market 'increasingly becoming the fulcrum for central bank intervention in the economy' (*EPW* Money Market Review, 15 October, 1994, p. 2711). Also, with the gradual phasing out of automatic monetization of the budget deficit, monetary policy has become less subservient to fiscal policy and begun to take on an independent shape of its own.

THE CALL MONEY MARKET

The call money market consists of overnight money and money at short notice for periods of up to 14 days and essentially serves to balance the short-term liquidity needs of banks. Prior to December 1973, the call money rate was market-determined. However, as part of an overall move towards administered interest rates, the Indian Banks Association (IBA) fixed a ceiling of 10 per cent for the call money rate in December 1973. In various phases this ceiling was reduced to 8.5 per cent by March 1978. With the onset of high inflation in the economy due to the oil shocks and the consequent upward revision in administered interest rates, the ceiling was raised to 10 per cent in April 1980. The 10 per cent ceiling stayed in place for much of the eighties with the average call money rate being quoted at the ceiling rate during this period.

A characteristic of the call money market till the late eighties was the existence of a few large lenders and a large number of borrowers. As the Vaghul Committee noted in its report, the absence of participants, who alternated as both borrowers and lenders served to inhibit the active development of the market during this time. The large lenders were the LIC and UTI who in any case were only allowed to lend. It was felt that since both the LIC and UTI had a sizeable short-term float, the latter could be profitably deployed in the call money market. The borrowers on the other hand were commercial banks whose individual needs for short-term funds often coincided (for example, to meet CRR requirements during a particular day of the week). Given the limit set on the call money rate and the absence of a large number of lenders, banks in need of liquidity were often unable to obtain the requisite short-term funds.

In April 1988, in light of the Vaghul Committee's recommendation that a discount house be established that 'could facilitate the smoothening of short-term liquidity imbalances and ... lead to the integration of the short-term money market', (RBI, 1987, p. 26), the RBI instituted the Discount and Finance House of India (DFHI). In July 1988, the DFHI was allowed to participate as both lender and borrower in the call money market. Then in October 1988, the operations of DFHI were exempted from the provisions of the ceiling rate set by IBA. These two steps provided a strong impetus to the development of the call money market as it meant that the imbalances in the supply and demand for funds that had plagued the market to date could be greatly remedied by the active participation of DFHI on both sides of the market. Since the DFHI's involvement in the call money market, there has been a significant increase in its annual turnover, with the latter close to tripling in the period 1990–1 to 1994–5 (Table 3.29). DFHI's daily average lending in the call money market increased from Rs 546 crores in 1990–1 to Rs 1,600 crores in 1994–5.

In May 1989, as a further step towards the liberalization of the money markets, the ceiling on the call money rate was withdrawn. In May 1990, in order to widen the call money market, RBI allowed the GIC, IDBI, and National Bank for Agriculture and Rural Development (NABARD) to participate as lenders. This was followed, in October 1990, by the grant of entry to all participants in the bills rediscounting market to the call money market as lenders. In October 1993, RBI permitted the financial institutions to borrow in the call money market up to an aggregate limit of Rs 1,000 crores with individual limits for borrowing being fixed from time to time.

Since the withdrawal of the ceiling on the call money rate, the fortnightly call money rate has shown a tendency to fluctuate significantly. This has been true in particular from July 1990 to August 1992, and then again from September 1994 to August 1995 (Figure 3.5). The sharp imbalances in the demand and supply of bank reserves that have led to the volatile behaviour of the call money rate have been due to a combination of several factors. The most important of these has been a bunching up of the banks' needs for short-term funds in order to meet CRR requirements. RBI monitors the holding of reserves by commercial banks as these are necessary to meet CRR requirements on a fortnightly basis—the days on which banks have to report their reserves to the RBI being the first, third and (when applicable) the fifth Friday of the month. Therefore, banks with an expected shortfall in the required reserve on a reporting Friday, tend to enter the call money market heavily on the preceding days, thereby leading to a liquidity crunch.

Another contributing factor has been the occasional withdrawal of liquidity from the banking system by the government. This occured in September and December 1994, on account of the half-yearly advance tax payments and the flotation of six State Government loans. It should also be noted that since non-bank financial institutions like LIC and IDBI are major lenders in the call money market, a sale of shares of public sector enterprises, by the government in the capital market can also lead to a decline in the amount of funds in the call money market (as in December 1994). Finally, the volatility of call money rates has in addition resulted from the asset–liability mismatch of some large banks which had invested in medium- and long-term assets by borrowing from the call money market with the intention of 'rolling over their requirements in the future' (Economic Survey, 1994–5, p. 57).

With the deregulation of the interest rate and the widening of the market through the participation of more non-bank financial institutions as both lenders and borrowers, the call money market has been playing an increasingly important role in equilibrating the banking system's demand and supply of short-term funds. Clearly, with the growth in the size of the call money market (as evident by the increase in DFHI's annual turnover), the need for commercial banks to hold on to excess reserves to meet any unanticipated deposit withdrawals by bank customers has been greatly reduced, thereby lowering bank intermediation costs. The setting up of DFHI in 1988 and its emergence as 'a major force in the call money market' (*EPW* Money Market Review, 15 October 1994) have also contributed to the development of the market.

However, in spite of the widening of the call money market and DFHI's attempts to smooth out liquidity needs, there has been a relatively high degree of instability in the call money rates in the post-1990 period. This has not yet shown signs of abatement as evident in the recent episode of instability during the period September to December 1994 (see Figure 3.5). As a consequence of the volatility in the call money market in the second half of 1994, several firms and financial institutions held back their proposals to issue floating rate bonds in the Indian capital market (*EPW* Money Market Review, 15

October 1994). Another fall-out of the high levels of the call money rate in late 1994 has been the arbitrage opportunities that it presented to players in the foreign exchange market. Banks borrowed dollars from their overseas branches to sell in the swap market in India and hedged by booking dollars forward (*EPW*, 1994). As a result, there was a sharp increase in the forward premia for the US dollar in the inter-bank market which jumped from 1.5 paise to 14 paise (or roughly 5.7 per cent on an annualized basis) in September 1994. With an existing large inflow of foreign portfolio investment, the increase in the demand for rupees in the foreign exchange market created a further upward pressure on the exchange rate.

In order to reduce the instability in the call money market, RBI has implemented several measures in the past few years. Firstly, since December 1992, the RBI began to enter into repurchase agreements (repos) with commercial banks using dated government securities as collateral. The period of the repo has varied between overnight to fourteen days, the latter being the length of the reserves make-up period (for the CRR). The objective of the repo was to even out liquidity in the banking system within the reserves make-up fortnight. However, as Rangarajan (1994) notes, the RBI has only used repos to drain reserves from banks and not to replenish them. Given this policy stance, the usefulness of the repo as a means of preventing sharp increases in the call money rate is clearly limited. Secondly, since 7 January 1995, the RBI asked banks to maintain 85 per cent of their CRR requirements on a daily basis. While this may prevent surges in the call money rate in the days immediately preceding the reporting Friday, it might actually increase the possibility of greater day to day volatility in the call money rate. Moreover, since banks would prefer to 'play safe' and hold on to excess reserves (in case they are short of the requisite balances on any particular day), this policy decision runs counter to the logic of the reform process in the money markets, an important objective of which is the minimization of the excess reserves that banks need to hold. Since December 1994, RBI has shown a willingness to play a more active role in the money markets and to provide liquidity to the call money market in order to stabilize the call money rate. In December 1994–January 1995, as the call money rate touched 50 per cent, RBI injected Rs 3,000 crores into the market via the DFHI and the Securities and Trading Corporation of India (STCI) (*EPW* Money Market Review, 11 March 1995, p. 476). Then again in September 1995, as the call money rate shot up to 70-80 per cent, RBI provided support to the market to the extent of Rs 2,500–3,000 crores (*EPW* Money Market Review, 11 November 1995, p. 2841).

Table 3.29
Cumulative Turnover of DFHI in Money Market Instruments[a]

Instruments	1990–1	1991–2	1992–3	1993–4	1994–5
Call Money	202,790	294,460	457,010	589,434	529,183
Commercial Paper	107	42	...	212	...
Certificates of Deposit	8	22	33	7	184
Commercial Bills	12,675	6,995	786	32	334

Note: [a] In Rs Crores.
Source: DFHI and RBI, *Annual Report,* various issues.

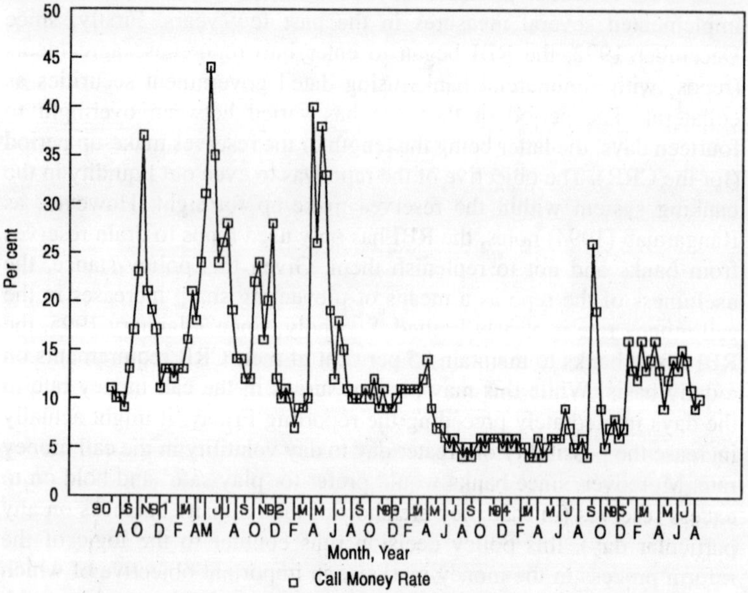

Figure 3.5 Call Money Rate, July 1990 to August 1995 Fortnightly Weighted Average

Source: RBI, *Annual Report,* DFHI, *Annual Report,* and *EPW* Money Market Reviews.

COMMERCIAL PAPER

Commercial paper (CP) consists of unsecured promissory notes sold directly by the issuers to investors or via agents like merchant bankers and security houses. Since the issuance of commercial paper is not related to any underlying self-liquidating trade, the maturity of this instrument is flexible and can be adapted to the needs of both borrower and lender. The CP market is particularly attractive to highly rated corporate borrowers who can obtain funds at a cost lower than the cost of borrowing from banks. On the other hand, CPs provide institutional investors with an attractive outlet for their short-term funds as they can obtain higher returns from investing in CPs than they could by investing in the banking system. As the Vaghul Committee notes,

> the issue of commercial paper imparts a degree of financial stability to the system as the issuing company has an incentive to remain financially strong. The possibility of raising short-term finance at relatively cheaper cost would provide an adequate incentive for the corporate clients to improve their financial position and in the process the financial health of the corporate sector should show visible improvement (RBI 1987, p. 20).

The Vaghul Committee, therefore, strongly advocated the introduction of commercial paper in the Indian money markets. Following the Committee's recommendation, in 1988–9 the RBI allowed the issuance of CPs while providing stringent restrictions on the type of company that could issue CPs. RBI initially stipulated that the companies issuing CPs should have a tangible net worth of Rs 10 crores, that the working capital limits of the company be not less than Rs 25 crores, that the company must have a minimum credit rating of P1+ from the Credit Rating Information Services of India Ltd. (CRISIL), and that the maximum amount of CP the company would be allowed to raise be limited to 20 per cent of the maximum permissible bank finance. Also, the maturity period of the CP was restricted to between 3 and 6 months and the maximum denomination of the CP being issued had to be Rs 25 lakhs or multiples thereof, subject to a minimum size of Rs 1 crore. The above restrictions were gradually relaxed in the next few years. The RBI permitted from the beginning, however, the free determination of the interest rate on CPs and free transferability of the CP.

There has been a sizeable growth in the primary market for CPs with the quantum of outstanding CPs increasing from Rs 64.7 crores in end-June 1991 to Rs 3264 crores in end-March 1993. The total amount of CPs outstanding decreased to Rs 604 in end-March 1995 due to the stringent money market conditions prevailing in 1994–5. Most of the CPs outstanding have been held by commercial banks. To a great extent, CPs are fulfilling their role as envisaged by the Vaghul Committee in that they are being increasingly used by highly rated corporate borrowers to obtain short-term funds from banks at interest rates that are lesser than the bank lending rate—for example, the effective interest rate range on CPs in November–December 1993 was 9.35 to 9.5 per cent as compared to the bank prime lending rate of 14 per cent. The widening gap between the interest rate on CPs and the bank lending rate motivated the IBA to advise banks not to subscribe to CPs with an interest rate below 12.5 per cent in 1993–4. Consequently, the typical interest rates offered on CPs rose to 14 –15 per cent by March 1995.

Notwithstanding the activity in the primary market, the secondary market for CPs has remained inactive till the end of 1995. This is evident in the low and fluctuating annual turnover figures (as compared to total outstandings) of DFHI (Table 3.29). Since an important and attractive feature of the CP is its potential marketability, the lack of an active secondary market for the CP has greatly limited its usefulness as a money market instrument. An inhibiting factor in the development of the secondary market in the early stages, has been the large minimum denomination of the issue thereby putting the CP effectively out of the reach of smaller investors. With the lifting of the restriction on the denomination of issue by the RBI and the emergence of screen-based trading in the National Stock Exchange (NSE) for CPs (along with other short-term debt instruments), there is reason to believe that the secondary market for CPs will pick up perceptibly in the future.

CERTIFICATES OF DEPOSITS

A Certificate of Deposit (CD) is a certificate issued by a bank to depositors of funds that remain on deposit at the bank for a specified period of time. Unlike a bank deposit, a certificate of deposit can be purchased and sold in the short-term money markets. In the mid-eighties, the short-term bank deposit rates were significantly lower than other comparable interest rates in the system. In its report, the Vaghul Committee felt it was premature to develop the CD as a money market instrument at that time as long as the short-term bank deposit rates were not aligned with the other interest rates. In 1988–9, in an effort to correct this, the RBI revised upwards the rate on term deposits of 46 to 90 days. In the same year, the RBI introduced the CD as a new instrument in the money market.

While the interest rate on CDs was allowed to be market-determined, the period of maturity of the CD was restricted to being from within three months to one year. Also, the total outstanding CDs issued by any bank at a point in time, could not be more than one per cent of its fortnightly average deposits in the current financial year. The restrictions on the denomination and size of issue for CDs were the same as for CPs—multiples of Rs 25 lakhs with a minimum size of issue of Rs 1 crore. This was reduced to Rs 10 lakhs and Rs 50 lakhs respectively in 1989–90. The bank-wise limit on the issue of CDs was progressively raised till October 1993 when the limit was finally withdrawn. Also, since 1992 the RBI has permitted several non-bank public sector financial institutions to issue CDs, including IDBI, ICICI, IFCI, IRBI, SIDBI, Exim Bank, SCICI and TFCI.

While the primary market for CDs is larger than that for CPs, the former has had its share of ups and downs in the past few years. The amount of CDs outstanding issued by scheduled commercial banks increased from Rs 5,373 crores in end-December 1991, to a peak of Rs 12,557 crores in July 1993, before declining to Rs 8,017 crores in end-March 1995. Moreover, DFHI's involvement in the CD market was initially minimal though increasing significantly in 1994 (Table 3.29). Effective interest rates for CDs have tended to vary a great deal in the past four years, ranging from 9 to 17 per cent (on CDs with one year of maturity) in July 1991, increasing to 12 to 25 per cent in June 1992 then declining to 12 to 14 per cent in March 1995. Similar to the CP market, there has been little secondary activity to date in the CD market with most holders of CDs willing to hold the instrument to maturity because of the high return on the latter.

Commercial Bills

In the early stages of the money market development in India, rediscounting of commercial bills of exchange was an important segment of the markets. Given that till the late eighties, the call money market was relatively underdeveloped and alternate instruments such as CPs and CDs did not exist, the bill rediscounting market provided an important source of short-term liquidity for banks in need of funds. However, over the past few years bill rediscounting has fallen in importance as a money market instrument with the total bills outstanding declining from Rs 4,612 crores in April 1992 to Rs 1,048 crores in March 1995. DFHI's annual turnover in the bill market has also shown a steady decline till 1993 (Table 3.29).

IV. The Credit Market

In the Mckinnon–Shaw paradigm, the credit market has a crucial role to play in the success of the financial liberalization programme. In the context of relatively underdeveloped capital markets and with little internal resources, private firms depend largely on banks for investment funds. A greater availability of bank credit can have a significantly positive effect on the economy-wide investment rate. Also, with a more appropriate pricing of bank credit, scarce investible funds will go only to the most efficient firms in the economy. Yet, as Mckinnon (1973) notes, credit markets are typically the most repressed of financial markets in a less developed economy. This was certainly the case in India till the onset of the reforms in 1991. There were severe restrictions placed on commercial banks by the government regarding both the pricing and allocation of credit. As we have discussed in Chapter 2, the most important of these were the mandatory lending requirements to the 'priority sectors'. As Table 3.30 indicates, the share of bank credit going to the priority sectors increased from 24.5 per cent in 1972 to 40.7 per cent in 1984. This share stayed fairly stable over the eighties.[6] Since the onset of the reforms, there has been a decline in the share of bank credit going to the priority sector, with most of the

Table 3.30

Sectoral Deployment of Gross Bank Credit (per cent)

Sector	June 1972	March 1984	March 1990	March 1995
Priority Sectors	24.5	40.7	40.1	34.6
Agriculture	8.9	16.8	16.2	12.9
Small Scale Industries	12.1	14.9	15.4	14.9
Other priority sectors	3.5	9.0	8.3	6.8
Industry (medium and large)	75.5	41.1	38.0	40.7
Wholesale Trade	n/a	6.4	5.4	5.3
Other Sectors	n/a	11.8	16.5	19.4

Note: Gross Bank Credit excludes public food procurement credit.
Source: RBI (1985) and RBI *Annual Report,* various years.

decline occurring in the share of bank credit going to the agricultural sector. Interestingly, disaggregation of bank credit by type of organization reveals (Table 3.31) that the share of bank credit going to the public sector has increased in the period 1990–3 while the share going to the private sector has decreased in the same period. In the context of the reforms, this counter-intuitive finding can be possibly due to the substitution by private sector firms from bank loans to other sources of funds (see Chapter 5 for an elaboration of this point). Table 3.31 also reveals that since 1990, there has been a reversal of the trend towards greater term lending by commercial banks, a trend that has been observed over the seventies and eighties. The decline in the share of long-term loans in total bank credit could be due to a decline in the average maturity of bank deposits. Similar to the decline in the maturity pattern of bank loans, there has been a reversal of a tendency by

[6] Foreign banks in India had to adhere to a lower priority sector target of 15 per cent as compared to private (domestically owned) and public sector banks. This was raised to 32 per cent in July 1993 (but the definition of priority sector for foreign banks was modified to include export credit).

households to hold term deposits of longer maturity, a tendency that was observed earlier in the seventies (Table 3.32). In part, this could be related to the use of bank deposits as a means of cash management by private and public sector firms. In part, it could also be related to the increasing uncertainty regarding the expected inflation rate in the late eighties. Clearly, the shortening of maturities on the liability side has acted as a disincentive to banks to be locked into assets of longer term maturity.

Table 3.31

Distribution of Outstanding Credit according to Type of Organization and Account (per cent)

Organization and Account	June 1973	June 1981	March 1990	March 1993
Organization:				
Public Sector	18.3	24.0	12.8	15.5
Co-operative Sector	1.7	1.9	1.4	2.1
Private Sector	74.2	62.5	69.3	66.4
Individuals	5.5	11.6	15.8	15.8
Others	0.3	0.0	0.7	0.3
Account:				
Cash Credit	50.0	40.9	36.2	39.5
Overdrafts	8.0	6.6	7.3	7.3
Demand Loans	6.1	5.2	3.6	5.1
Term Loans	12.2	23.6	30.7	28.6
Packing Credit	5.1	4.1	5.0	5.1
Export Bills	3.9	3.5	3.8	4.6
Inland Bills	13.9	12.6	10.4	8.3
Advances against Import Bills	0.8	3.5	1.6	0.8
Miscellaneous	...	...	1.4	0.7

Source: RBI (1985) and *Banking Statistics*, RBI, various issues.

Over the years, the directed credit programme became increasingly complex and bureaucratic with sub-targets for different sectors (for example, there were specific targets for agriculture and exports) and classes of borrowers (namely, 'weaker sections'/scheduled castes etc.). By the late eighties, there was evidence of growing political and administrative intervention in the credit decision-making process (MOF 1991, p.10). Also, with the stipulation of concessional lending rates to be charged on priority sector credit, there was a significant element of cross-subsidy in the structure of bank lending rates. Thus, the rate at which credit was made available to medium and large industry was much higher than that to the priority sectors. This has been particularly true in the late eighties with the lifting of a ceiling on lending rates to medium and large industry. The combination of fixed targets for bank lending to particular sets of borrowers (irrespective of the risk-return characteristics of these borrowers), and below-market returns on such lending, may have been an important contributing factor responsible for the deteriorating loan quality and the declining profitability of commercial banks in India in the seventies and eighties.

Table 3.32

Maturity Classification of Term Deposits with Scheduled Commercial Banks[a] (per cent)

Period of Maturity	1969	1980	1990	1993
6 months or less	20.2	4.7	8.4	18.4
More than 6 months and not exceeding 1 year	39.1	n/a[b]	4.4	8.2
More than 1 year and not exceeding 2 years	8.8	2.8	15.6	21.4
More than 2 years and not exceeding 3 years	5.3	17.9	31.6	14.3
More than 3 years and not exceeding 5 years	20.4	12.8	16.9	22.3
Above 5 years	6.2	61.8	23.1	15.4

Note: [a] Data refers to end-March.
[b] Break-up not available.

The reforms in the financial sector have not so far encompassed a reduction in the priority sector lending requirements.[7] Partly this is due to the possible repercussions such a move may have, particularly among the well-organized and politically influential large and medium farmers. To some extent, it could also be due to an awareness among policy-makers of the need to put in place an effective system for the financing of agriculture (and small-scale industry) *before* priority lending requirements are reduced. As we will argue in Chapter 5, agriculture is particularly prone to market failures of the Stiglitz–Weiss type. Hence, there is little reason to expect that banks will *voluntarily* lend to agriculturists once the lending requirements are withdrawn.

With little change in the restrictions on the use of credit by banks, most of the reforms in the credit market have occurred with respect to regulations on the pricing of credit. There has been a gradual rationalization of bank lending rates from six different rates in October 1991, to four in April 1992 to finally, three in April 1993 (Table 3.33).

[7] Since October 1993, however, banks have been permitted some flexibility in their priority sector advances; small-scale industry being redefined to include units with investment in plant and machinery of up to Rs 60 lakhs (previously it was Rs 35 lakhs).

Interest rates have been deregulated in a phased manner, with the central bank maintaining a system of administered interest rates for advances below Rs 2 lakhs. However, in October 1994 the minimum lending rate on bank advances over Rs 2 lakhs was discontinued and banks were allowed total freedom to set their own lending rates.

The tendency in the credit market has been for commercial banks to use the SBI Advance Rate as the prime lending rate. In Figure 3.6, we plot the real lending rate and the spread between the lending and deposit rate. Except for the oil price shocks, the real lending rate has remained positive at around 8 to 10 per cent. Both the extremely high level of the real interest rate and the spread between the lending and deposit rate can be seen as an outcome of the distortion in bank use of funds with a significant proportion of the latter 'locked' into low return priority sector loans and government securities (and non-interest bearing reserves). In the Indian context, it is difficult to argue that the high real interest rate on loans to private corporate firms may have led to a more productive use of investible funds. Since bank loans are mostly for working capital purposes, a more plausible argument would be that the high interest costs faced by private firms may have been passed on to the firms' customers via higher product prices (Taylor 1983; van Wijnbergen 1983; Sen and Vaidya 1995).

Table 3.33

Structure of Bank Lending Rates

Category of Account	October 1991	April 1992	April 1993	September 1993	October 1994
Upto and inclusive of Rs 7,500	11.5	11.5	12.0[a]	12.0	12.0
Over Rs 7,500 and upto Rs 15,000	13.0	13.5[b]			
Over Rs 15,000 and upto Rs 25,000	13.5				
Over Rs 25,000 and upto Rs 50,000	15.5	16.5[c]	16.5	15.0	13.5
Over Rs 50,000 and upto Rs 2 lakhs	16.5				
Over Rs 2 lakhs (minimum rate)	20.0	19.0	17.0	15.0	Free

Note: [a] upto and inclusive of Rs 25,000.
[b] over Rs 7,500 and upto Rs 25,000.
[c] over Rs 25,000 and upto Rs 2 lakhs.

Source: Report on Trend and Progress in Banking, RBI, various issues.

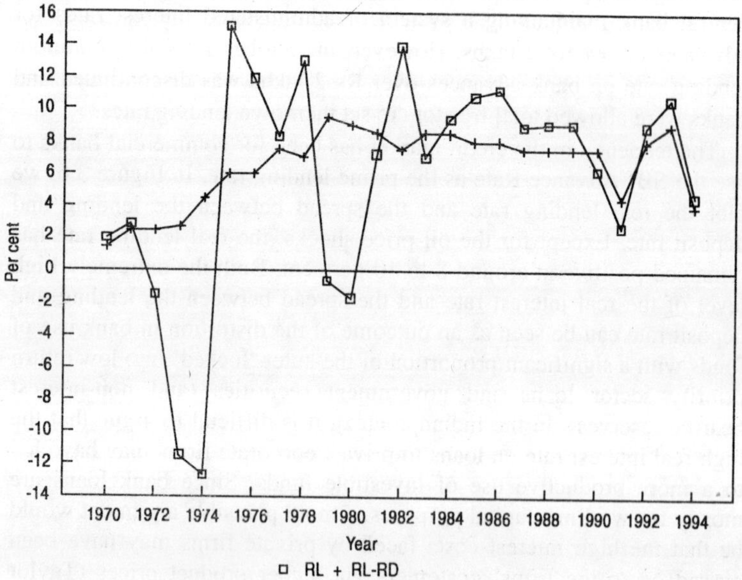

Figure 3.6 Commercial Bank Real Lending Rate[a] (RL) and Spread between Lending and Deposit Rates (RL–RD)[b]

Note: [a] SBI Advance Rate.
[b] Data refers to financial year.

Source: Reports on Currency and Finance, RBI, various issues.

V. The Capital Market

Government Securities

The government securities market consists of the markets for Treasury bills (T bills) and dated securities. In a strict sense, T bills are money market instruments since they have a maturity period of less than one year.[8] However, we include T bills in our discussion in this section on government securities because of the strong overlap in the reforms regarding the T bills and dated securities markets. Till the mid-eighties, the T bills and dated securities markets in India were fairly under-developed. The returns on these instruments were kept artificially low with the intention of depressing the cost of borrowing of the government. For example the interest rate on a thirty-year security was

[8] Dated securities, on the other hand, are of maturities of more than one year up to a maximum of thirty-one years.

less than the interest rate on a five-year term deposit. The demand for government paper was, therefore, restricted to the captive market among banks and to certain financial institutions (such as insurance and provident funds) created by means of the SLR. In the case of treasury bills, the bulk of the T bill issue consisted of *ad hoc* 91-day T bills. This was essentially a mechanism of monetizing the budget deficit. The marketable 91-day T bills were sold on tap at a low fixed discount and consequently, not very attractive to invest in. As a result, approximately 90 per cent of the total T bills outstanding ended up with RBI (RBI, 1985).

Since 1986, there has been a phased deregulation of the government securities markets in India. The reforms in these markets were based on the Chakravarty Committee report whose main recommendations have already been discussed in Chapter 2. The principal recommendation of the Committee with regard to the government securities markets, was to suggest an upward revision of interest rates in these markets. While the increase in rates of return on T bills and dated securities would be implemented in the context of administered interest rates, the Committee was of the view that such a step could initiate the transition from direct tools of monetary policy (such as credit controls and the use of the CRR) to the use of indirect instruments such as open market operations as the dominant tool of monetary policy. The Committee also felt that higher rates of return on government securities could 'facilitate a better cost–benefit analysis of government expenditure programmes' (RBI, 1985, p. 183). In what follows, we review developments in the T bills and dated securities markets in turn.

TREASURY BILLS

In order to develop the T bill market as a prelude to the use of open market operations as a tool of monetary policy, the Chakravarty Committee recommended that the discount rate on T bills be such that the yield on them be marginally positive in real terms. Following this recommendation, a scheme for 182-day T bills was introduced in November 1986, initially on a monthly auction basis and without any rediscounting facilities with RBI. The 182-day T bill was phased out on 16 April 1992, and the 364-day T bill, on an auction basis, was introduced on 28 April 1992. In January 1993, the government also introduced a scheme of auctions for 91-day T bills. There has been a significant growth in the primary market for T bills, with the total amount outstanding of auction-based 91-day T bills increasing from Rs 250 crores in January 1993 to Rs 3,450 crores by mid-August 1994. Significantly, in August 1994 only 16 per cent of auction-based 91-day

Table 3.34

DFHI's Annual Turnover in Treasury Bills

Year	Total Turnover (Rs Crores)
1990–1	32,330
1991–2	23,410
1992–3	16,020
1993–4	19,970
1994–5	30,921

Source: RBI and DFHI, *Annual Reports.*

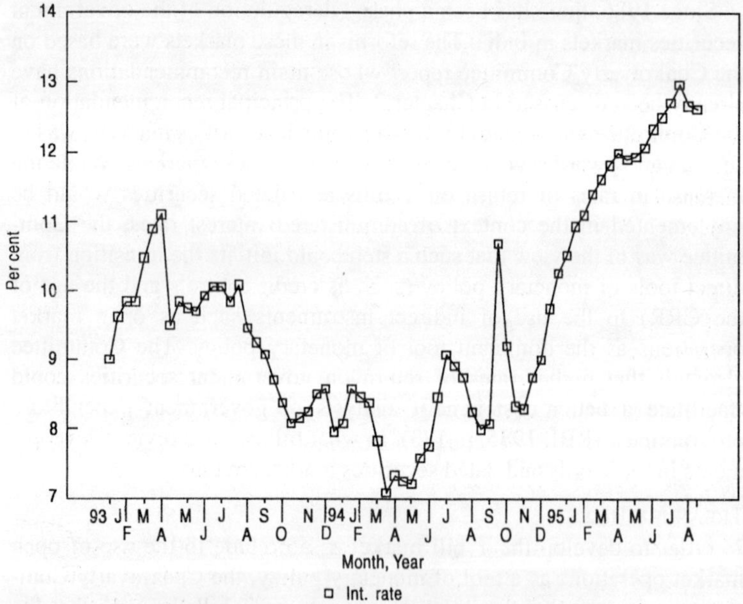

Figure 3.7 The 91-Day T Bills Interest Rate, January 1993 to August 1995[a]

Note: [a] Fortnightly Implicit Yield at Cut-Off Price.
Source: RBI, *Annual Reports.*

T bills outstanding was held by RBI. The total amount outstanding of 364-day T bills increased from Rs 666 crores in April 1992 to Rs 7,160 crores in mid-August 1994. An important reason for the growth in the primary market for T bills has been the use of open market operations by RBI to absorb a part of the excess liquidity in the banking system caused by the surge in foreign capital inflows. However, as with other segments of the money markets, secondary activity in T bills has not yet shown signs of picking up, with DFHI's annual turnover in this category actually declining in the period 1990–1 to 1994–5 (Table 3.34).

The interest rate on the 91-day T bill has tended to fluctuate a great deal in the period 1993–4 to 1994–5, with the range being 7 to 11 per cent (Figure 3.7). The interest rate on the 364-day T bill has been more stable (Figure 3.8), and there are indications that the 364-day T bill rate is emerging as the benchmark for the other interest rates in the financial sector. One sign of the growing integration of short-term financial markets is similarity of behaviour between T bill rates and the call money rate. As is evident from Figures 3.5, 3.7 and 3.8, all three interest rates have tended to decline over the period 1993–4 in a period of easy liquidity, and then increase in September 1994–August 1995 due to the liquidity crunch in money markets at that time.

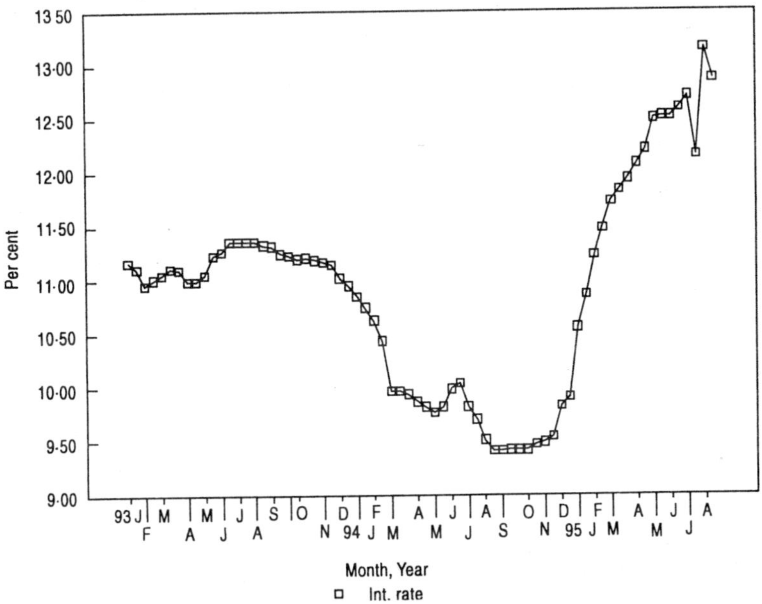

Figure 3.8 The 364-Day T Bills Interest Rate, January 1993 to August 1995

Source: RBI, *Annual Reports.*

DATED SECURITIES

Following the recommendation of the Chakravarty Committee, there has been a gradual alignment of the interest rate on dated securities with other interest rates in the financial sector, along with a reduction in maximum maturity from twenty to ten years. For example, in 1994 the ceiling on the government securities interest rate was 13.5 per cent while the minimum lending rate of banks was 15 per cent. Also, from April 1992 the entire central government borrowing programme has been conducted through auctions. Tables 3.35 and 3.36 give the maturity structure and ownership pattern of central and state government securities. These tables indicate that prior to the reforms, there had been a considerable lengthening of maturities in both central and state government securities, as most of the securities outstanding were of maturities of above fifteen years. At the same time, with the SLR inching upwards over the eighties, commercial (and co-operative) banks held an increasing proportion of total securities outstanding between 1982 and 1990. Unfortunately, with the post-1991 data not available, it is not possible to determine whether there have been significant changes in the maturity structure of central and state government

Table 3.35

Maturity Structure of Central and State Government Securities (per cent)

Maturity Period (as at end-March)	Central Govt. Securities	State Govt. Securities
Upto 5 years:		
1978	15	27
1982	13	47
1990	11	8
Above 5 years and upto 10 years:		
1978	17	69
1982	17	26
1990	10	26
Above 10 years and upto 15 years:		
1978	8	...
1982	11	25
1990	13	26
Above 15 years and upto 31 years:		
1978	57	4
1982	58	2
1990	70	38

Source: RBI Bulletin, December 1994.

securities in the nineties. However, data for 1993 indicate a significant increase in the proportion of central government securities held by commercial banks (as compared to 1990). Since this occurred at a time when the SLR was being progressively reduced, the increase is clearly related to the upward movement in the coupon rates of central government securities and reflects a *voluntary* decision by commercial banks to invest in government securities in the post-reform period.

Table 3.36

Ownership Pattern of Central and State Government Securities[a] (per cent)

Category of Holder	Central Govt Securities	State Govt Securities
Central and State Governments:		
1978	2.2	0.9
1982	1.2	0.2
1990	0.5	neg.
1993	neg.	neg.
RBI (own account):		
1978	25.4	...
1982	29.5	...
1990	19.6	...
1993	10.6	...
Commercial and co-operative banks:		
1978	42.4	68.4
1982	45.4	72.2
1990	55.5	85.2
1993	64.6	72.7
Insurance:		
1978	16.2	23.3
1982	14.5	17.5
1990	17.2	7.2
1993	16.3	9.0
Provident Funds:		
1978	11.3	3.5
1982	6.6	7.6
1990	2.4	5.0
1993	1.1	1.1

Note: [a] As at end-March.
Source: *RBI Bulletin*, December 1994.

An important development in the institutional infrastructure in the government securities market has been the creation of the Securities and Trading Corporation of India (STCI) in 1993, which has been entrusted with the task of developing an efficient secondary market in government securities and public sector bonds.[9] Also, in 1995, RBI

[9] Mention should be made of a new financial innovation in the government securities market in the form of zero coupon bonds introduced in 1994. The main characteristic of these bonds is that interest is not paid on a periodic basis (as is the case with other types of bonds); instead, these bonds are sold at a discount and redeemed at par on maturity.

issued guidelines and procedures for the enlistment of primary dealers in the government securities market. Primary dealers are particularly important in providing breadth and depth to securities (and money) markets since they have an incentive to build a customer base to 'manage interest rate risk in bad times in order to survive and prosper in good times' (Meek 1991, p. 24).

THE STOCK MARKET

Many commentators on the process of financial liberalization have been sceptical of the role of stock markets in developing countries. In an extremely influential paper, Singh (1992) argues that even a well-developed stock market may 'do more harm than good'. The reason cited is that the possible negative aspects of stock markets like short-termism, speculation and the tendency of large firms to expand via take-overs rather than new investments, would, in all probability, outweigh possible positive aspects like encouragement of savings, more efficient allocation of investment resources and the discipline of corporate managements through competitive selection in the market for corporate control. Singh favours a bank-based financial system. He, of course, is well aware of the dangers of such a system and warns against the following possible fall-outs of a bank-based financial system:

(a) Crony capitalism, which finances schemes for particular individuals and families with political connections rather than promoting long-term industrial development.

(b) industry-finance links of the bank-based type can in principle, and sometimes in practice lead to monopolistic positions in product markets and thwart entry by new firms thereby hindering efficient industrial development.

(c) imprudent or inadequate regulation of banks has sometimes jeopardised the integrity of the financial system as a whole (for example Chile, following financial liberalization in the early 1980s) Singh (1992 p 44).

We have noted earlier in detail the problems plaguing the banking sector in India and the reforms relating to banks and term-lending institutions. Singh suggests that while encouraging stock markets, four important precautions are necessary for developing countries. Firstly, an attempt must be made to insulate the real economy from the influence of the stock market. Secondly, the effects of a prospective market for corporate control must be given serious consideration. Thirdly, Singh suggests that publicly owned financial institutions must be used to maintain orderly markets. Lastly, Singh prefers the encouragement of competition in the product markets to discipline managements as opposed to the take-over mechanism of the stock market. On this last aspect (i.e. encouragement of competition in product markets), major changes have taken place in the Indian economy, as we will see in Chapter 5.

India has had fairly well-developed stock markets (compared to other developing countries) and their role in the overall financial system has dramatically increased since the eighties. We have had occasion to point out earlier (Table 3.5) that the savings of the household sector in corporate securities as a percentage of total financial savings rose from a mere 3.2 per cent during 1981–2 to 1985–6 to an impressive 8.7 per cent during 1991–2 to 1994–5. In Table 3.37, we present the distribution of India's shareholding population across major cities. The share of the five largest cities dropped from 66.2 per cent in 1983, to 55.3 per cent in 1992. Comparable figures for the twelve largest cities are 78.6 per cent and 67.5 per cent respectively. Clearly, over years the people residing in smaller cities, towns, and rural areas are increasingly holding their savings in corporate securities.

Table 3.37

Distribution of India's Shareholding Population across Major Cities (Percentage of Shareholding Population Accounted for by the City)

City	1983	1992
Bombay	35.3	27.3
Calcutta	10.0	8.6
Delhi	9.5	8.3
Ahmedabad	7.4	7.6
Madras	3.9	3.5
Total of 12 Largest Cities	78.6	67.5
Rest of India	21.4	32.5
Total	100	100

Source: The Stock Exchange Official Directory, BSE, vol. 2, 1995.

In 1993, India ranked twenty-second in the world in terms of market capitalization, twenty-fourth in terms of value traded and second in listed domestic securities. Currently there are 22 stock exchanges of which 20 are associated with particular cities. The largest stock exchange in the country is the Bombay Stock Exchange (BSE) which accounts for more than 80 per cent of transactions. Recently two new exchanges were set up, namely, the Over the Counter Exchange of India (OTCEI) which was established in August 1989, and became operational on 29 September 1992 and the National Stock Exchange of India (NSE) which was set up in November 1992 and started operations on 30 June 1994.

Market capitalization in the BSE at the end of March 1995 was Rs 468,837 crores as compared to Rs 10,219 crores in December 1984.

Market capitalization as a ratio of GDP rose from 4.7 per cent in March 1983 to 51.4 per cent in March 1995. The ratio of market capitalization as a ratio of GDP for all the stock exchanges put together rose from 7 per cent in March 1983 to 68.8 per cent in March 1994. This, by any standards, is a phenomenal increase.

An important feature of the pattern of stock holding in India is that a large proportion of shares belong to government-owned financial institutions, the most important being UTI. The 30 firms whose shares form the basis of the BSE sensitive index have a government-owned institutional share holding which ranges between 13 per cent to over 50 per cent. The government is thus capable of indirectly influencing the market and has done so on occasions of a major downswing by asking the financial institutions to prop up the market by increasing their buying activity.

The financial institutions also exercise their voting rights in co-ordination with each other. This has enabled many managements to retain control of companies without needing to own a significant share of the paid up capital. Moreover, this pattern of share ownership has automatically restricted the threat of corporate takeovers to existing managements as no takeover bid, in most cases, is possible without the support of financial institutions and they have in general always been supportive of incumbent managements. In recent years there have been some takeovers but none of them involved firms with a substantial equity holding by financial institutions. Thus, at least two of Singh's concerns noted earlier have to a large extent been taken care of via the publicly owned financial institutions.

The financial liberalization process has brought about fundamental changes in the operations of the stock markets in the case of both new issues and the secondary market.

The New Issues Market

The important function of the new issues market is to act as a conduit for funds to the corporate sector by attracting new investible funds and allocating them among various firms. In the process of financial reforms, the most important step regarding stock exchanges was taken in 1992 with the passing of the Securities and Exchange Board of India (SEBI) Act (for details regarding the SEBI Act and guidelines issued by SEBI see Gopalsamy 1994; Gokarn 1995), which substantially changed the rules regarding new issues. Prior to the passing of this Act all capital issues were governed by the Capital Issues (Controls) Act (1947) whose main objectives were as follows:

i) to ensure that investment does not take place contrary to the objectives of the Five Year plans, or flow into unproductive or wasteful channels,
ii) to encourage the growth of joint stock companies with a sound capital structure,
iii) to direct and distribute appeals for public subscriptions to new issues of capital so as to avoid any concentration or overcrowding in a particular period of the year,
iv) the Act also served as a checkpost to ensure that a company before entering the capital market was in the possession of all other clearances from the government (e.g. the industrial license).

According to the Act all companies (either incorporated in India or abroad) which made an issue of capital in India, and Indian companies which made an issue of capital abroad, required the consent of the Controller of Capital Issues.

The principal criteria adopted by the Controller of Capital Issues (CCI) were the adequacy of capital and the soundness of capital structure. In all normal cases a debt to equity ratio of 2:1 was favoured. Higher debt to equity ratios were allowed for some capital intensive industries. The interest rates payable on debentures were fixed at 14 per cent for non-MRTP and FERA companies and 12.5 per cent for FERA and MRTP companies.[10] If the new issue was being made at par it did not require the consent of the CCI but the consent was mandatory if the issue was being made at a discount or a premium. No company was allowed to approach the market more than once in twelve months. Prior to 1992, the primary issues market was very closely regulated by the government in almost every aspect. The various regulations especially in respect of pricing of new issues discouraged corporations from using new issues to raise funds.

In 1992, with the passing of the SEBI Act the Capital Issues (Controls) Act was repealed and with it the abolition of the office of CCI, was effected. SEBI was hereafter made the regulatory authority for new issues of companies and was given the necessary legal powers to regulate and reform the capital markets. The most important fall-out of this was the freeing of pricing and the setting up of new guidelines concerning new issues. Companies are now free to approach the capital market after a clearance is obtained from SEBI. According to the SEBI guidelines regarding pricing of new issues, three categories of new issues were allowed complete freedom in pricing:

[10] MRTP companies refer to all firms with a capital base of over Rs 20 crores. FERA companies refer to foreign companies in India and Indian joint-stock companies with a foreign equity holding of over 40 per cent (see Chapter 5 for details).

i) Issue by new companies set up by existing companies with a five-year track record of profitability.
ii) Issue by existing private/closely held companies with a three-year track record of profitability, and
iii) Issue by existing listed company.
A new company coming up with a first issue of equity and other companies not falling in any of the above three categories are required to make the public issue at par value.

SEBI set out detailed rules aimed at improving disclosure standards, introduction of prudential norms and simplification of issue procedures. Companies were required to disclose all material facts and specific risk factors associated with their projects while making public issues and a code of advertisement of public issues was introduced. According to the new guidelines, the 'due diligence certificate' by the lead managers regarding disclosures made in the offer document, has been made a part of the offer document itself for better accountability and transparency on the part of the lead managers. Rules regarding private placement of securities and preferential allotment to Foreign Institutional Investors (FII) and other financial institutions have been framed.

SEBI has also issued guidelines regarding the underwriting of new issues. Underwriting is optional for all new issues, subject to the condition that if an issue is not underwritten and is unable to collect 90 per cent of the amount offered to the public, the entire amount collected is to be returned to investors. If the issue is underwritten then the underwriting agreements have to be filed with the stock exchanges where the security is listed. The lead managers to the issue are required to ensure that the underwriters have the ability to discharge their underwriting obligation if the need so arises. Rates of commission for underwriting have also been fixed by SEBI. Strict rules have been framed to regulate the activities of merchant bankers.

The SEBI initiated a host of measures intended to improve disclosure standards and safeguard the investor's interests with regard to debentures of all kinds. Some important regulations were as follows:
i) Fully Convertible Debentures (FCD) having a conversion period of more than 36 months were disallowed unless accompanied by an optional 'put and call' option.
ii) Premium amount on conversion and time of conversion for FCDs was to be predetermined and stated in the prospectus and interest on FCDs was freed.
iii) All debentures (Fully, Partly or Nonconvertible) required credit rating if the conversion/maturity exceeded 18 months.

In September 1992, the Government of India allowed unrestricted entry, in terms of volumes of investments, in both primary and secondary markets to reputed FIIs such as pension funds, mutual funds, investment trusts and asset management companies. FIIs were required to obtain an initial registration with SEBI before making investments. As of March 1995, there were 308 FIIs registered with SEBI, and as on end-March 1995 their cumulative net investments in both primary and secondary markets were estimated to be Rs 4,720 crores. Investment norms for Non-Resident Indians (NRI) in both primary and secondary markets were liberalized. Under the new rules both overseas corporate bodies and NRIs were allowed to buy corporate securities without prior permission from the RBI.

Clearly, with the setting up of SEBI the accent was more on truthful disclosure of information by companies going in for new issues, safeguarding of investor's interests and the opening up of the stock market

Table 3.38

New Capital Issues by Non-Government Public Limited Companies[a, b]

Year	Equity Shares Amount (Rs Cr.)	Preference Shares Amount (Rs Cr.)	Debentures Amount (Rs Cr.)	Total Amount (Rs Cr.)
1985–6	898	1.2	843.3	1742.5
	(758)	(9)	(83)	(850)
1986–7	1007.5	0.7	1555.7	2563.9
	(424)	(3)	(94)	(521)
1987–8	1103	6.8	667.3	1777.1
	(174)	(38)	(46)	(225)
1988–9	1033.6	3.3	2187.9	3224.8
	(269)	(6)	(79)	(341)
1989–90	1220.2	7.9	5281.8	6509.9
	(269)	(4)	(134)	(407)
1990–1	1284.3	13.1	3014.8	4312.2
	(246)	(3)	(115)	(364)
1991–2	1916.1	1.5	4275.5	6193.1
	(366)	(3)	(145)	(514)
1992–3	9981.1	0.5	9844.0	19825.6
	(867)	(1)	(169)	(1037)
1993–4	10113.0	63.4	9324.9	19501.3
	(987)	(4)	(145)	(1136)
1994–5	17441.4	131.3	8871.0	26443.7
	(1554)	(9)	(121)	(1684)

Note: [a] The data exclude bonus shares and issues privately placed with financial insitutions.

[b] Figures in parenthesis indicate number.

Source: Report on Currency and Finance, RBI, various issues.

to foreign investors, rather than on the consistency of the investments with the objectives of Five Year plans. The new guidelines issued by SEBI have had a tremendous impact on the new issues market. We present in Table 3.38 details of new capital issues by non-government public limited companies over the period 1985–6 to 1994–5 and the following important points emerge:

i) The number of new issues and the amount of capital raised has increased dramatically after 1991–2. In 1992–3 the amount of capital raised via new issues was over three times the amount raised in 1991–2 and the number of new issues doubled. This increase has been sustained in 1993–4 and 1994–5. The new issues market has been extremely buoyant after reforms were introduced.

ii) The rise has been more dramatic for equity shares than for debentures both in terms of number and the amount of capital raised. The number of new issues of equity more than doubled between 1991–2 and 1992–3 while the amount raised increased over five times. The predominance of debentures in the new issues market has given way to primacy of equity shares. A possible reason could be the stringent rules regarding new issue of debentures and the freeing of pricing of new equity issues.

As we will observe later, sources of funds statements show, that in 1992–3 equity shares constituted over 20 per cent of the total sources of funds, while this figure stood at a paltry 7.8 per cent in 1991–2. This is consistent with the significant increase in the number and amount of new issues between 1991–2 and 1992–3. With the establishment of SEBI and the reform of laws governing new issues, the relationship between the real economy and the stock market has clearly deepened. Recent experience suggests that firms have been able to access the stock market for funds when bank funds became relatively more expensive in the process of reforms of the banking sector and term-lending institutions. It should be noted that even when the stock markets were sluggish during 1994–5 new capital issues were not affected. If the process of financial liberalization creates an environment in which firms are able to substitute one source of funds for another depending on the relative costs of funds, then this can surely be considered as a major achievement. It is of course too early to comment on whether this has actually happened.

In 1992, the Government of India allowed Indian corporations with good track records to issue convertible debentures—Foreign Currency Convertible Bonds (FCCB)—or equity—Global Depository Receipts (GDR)—on foreign stock markets. In Table 3.39 details of the amounts raised and actual inflows are presented.

Table 3.39

Euro Issues and Amount of Inflow (US $ Million)

Year	Capital Raised			Amount of Inflow		
	GDRs	FCCBs	Total	GDRs	FCCBs	Total
1992–3	240.5	...	240.5	85.8	...	85.8
1993–4	1522.4	995.5	2517.9	1462.9	913.9	2376.9
1994–5[a]	1852.8	102.5	1955.3	1742.0	92.6	1843.6
Total	3615.7	1098.0	4713.8	3290.8	1006.5	4297.3

Note: [a] end-January 1995.
Source: Government of India, Economic Survey, 1993–4.

Though the amounts raised on foreign markets are modest and the number of firms allowed to tap foreign markets are not large, an important beginning has been made by Indian firms seeking funds on foreign stock markets. This is another major step towards encouraging Indian firms to diversify their sources of funds. The advantage of this diversification would be that any unforeseen disruption in one source of funds would not dramatically affect the resource position of firms.

Apart from equity shares (ordinary and preference) and debentures (fully convertible, partly convertible and non-convertible), a large number of innovative financial instruments have been introduced on the stock market. All new instruments introduced require the approval of SEBI. We describe a few of them below:

i) Secured Premium Notes (SPN) with Detachable Warrants: The SPN is redeemable after a predetermined period of four to seven years. The detachable warrant ensures the holder of the right to apply for and be allotted equity shares of any new issue by the company.

ii) Non-Convertible Debentures with Detachable Warrants: This instrument allows of an option to buy a specific number of shares at the time of a new issue, at a predetermined price within a definite timeframe.

iii) Zero Interest Fully Convertible Debentures: This is a zero interest debenture which is automatically converted into shares after a predetermined period.

iv) Equity Shares with Detachable Warrants: This new instrument is essentially an equity share with a right to apply for a predetermined number of shares at a specific price. The detachable warrants are separately registered and traded on the stock market.

v) Fully Convertible Cumulative Preference Share: This instrument consists of two part—A and B. Part A is fully convertible into equity shares on the date of allotment of a new issue, and part B can be redeemed at par or converted into equity shares, after a specified lock-in period.

vi) Preference Shares with Warrants Attached: Each preference share carries a warrant which entitles the holder to apply for equity shares at any time between the third and fifth year from date of allotment.

vii) Secured Zero Interest Partly Convertible Debentures with Detachable Warrants: This instrument also has two parts—A and B. Part A is convertible into equity shares at a fixed price on the date of allotment. Part B is non-convertible and is redeemed at par at the end of a specified period and it carries a separately tradeable warrant which enables the holder to receive an equity share for every warrant held at a predetermined price.

viii) Fully Convertible Debentures with Interest (Optional): This instrument does not yield any interest for a specified period, after which the holders are given the option to apply for equity shares.

All the above mentioned new instruments variously entitle the holder to get a firm allotment of shares at the time of a new issue. They have significantly enlarged the menu of instruments available to investors in the primary issues market. Genuine derivative instruments are yet to be introduced.

There is no doubt that reforms have been extremely successful in transforming the primary market in two years.

THE SECONDARY MARKET

The number of companies listed on all the stock exchanges was 7,811 as on 31 March 1994, out of which 3,585 were listed on the Bombay Stock Exchange (BSE). In the discussion that follows we restrict our observations mainly to the BSE both because it is the largest stock exchange and data pertaining to it are readily available.

The BSE was constituted in 1875. Historically it was managed by approximately 540 members who were all brokers. Till recently all brokerage houses have been relatively small family-run firms. In the post-reform period this has changed substantially with corporate membership being introduced. The most important legislation which controls the working of all stock markets is the Securities Contracts (Regulation) Act (SCRA) 1956. The Act stipulates various guidelines for recognition of stock exchanges, trading methods and practices etc. With the passing of the SEBI Act in 1992, certain changes have also been made in the SCRA which allow SEBI to exercise powers under the Act which were previously the prerogative of the Government of India. SEBI has introduced certain changes in the rules regarding the broker-client relationship, the most important being the segregation of client and broker accounts. Capital adequacy norms for brokers have also been stipulated. Insider trading has been banned and strict fines have been imposed. A major development on the Bombay Stock exchange since liberalization has been the introduction of a computerized trading system in March 1995. In addition, the two new stock exchanges, i.e. the OTCEI and NSE have computer-based trading systems.

Only members of the stock exchange and their authorized clerks are allowed to transact business. Dealings on the secondary market are broadly of two types namely, ready delivery contracts and forward contracts. Ready delivery contracts are settled on the same day or within a period of seven days. Forward delivery contracts are settled on fixed settlement days when sometimes the delivery is executed or the transaction is reversed and the difference is claimed. Forward delivery contracts can also be 'carried over' to a future settlement day by paying a brokerage charge. This practice is popularly referred to as *badla.* The trading of options is currently not allowed.

One drawback of the way the *badla* system operates is that of speculative dominance which has on occasion affected the entire system causing a suspension of operations. A classic example of this is the stock market scam which came to light in June 1992 and led to suspension of trading for several weeks on the stock exchanges. Between October 1991 and May 1992, the BSE experienced a speculative bubble engineered by an illegal diversion of funds from the banking system. In August 1992, a Joint Parliamentary Committee was appointed to probe this scandal. A full discussion of the stock market scam is beyond the scope of this study and one can only note that the trading system on the major stock exchanges left a lot to be desired. As a consequence of the scam, SEBI introduced new guidelines to govern the operations of the *badla* system which were not accepted by the BSE. The latter subsequently suspended *badla* deals in March 1994, thus affecting liquidity on the stock exchanges. SEBI announced guidelines for the introduction of 'carry forward' trading in a revised form in October 1995.

Thin trading in a majority of the listed companies has been a persistent problem in the stock exchanges. On the Bombay stock exchange according to the latest data available only 69 per cent of the listed securities are traded on any given day. Prior to computerization this figure stood at 56 per cent. In 1991, only 8.5 per cent of the listed companies were traded on all trading days and this figure has dramatically risen to 38.2 per cent in 1995. Computerization has made a significant difference on this front.

The average monthly turnover on the BSE has been rising steadily over the years. Between 1987–8 and 1994–5 the average monthly turnover has increased over ten-fold (see Table 3.40). The turnover dropped sharply in 1992–3 mainly because of the 'stock market scam', which lead both to a disruption of trading and a sharp drop in prices.

Table 3.40
Monthly Market Turnover on Bombay Stock Exchange

Year	Turnover (Rs Crores)
1987–8	659
1988–9	1714
1989–90	2449
1990–1	3001
1991–2	5981
1992–3	3808
1993–4	7045
1994–5	5646

Source: The Stock Exchange Official Directory, BSE, vol. 2, 1995.

We have mentioned earlier that foreign institutional investors have been allowed to invest on the stock markets in India. Though their investments on the stock markets have been relatively small, they are relatively active traders accounting for about 13 per cent of the total transactions between April 1994 and March 1995. The large increase in volumes on the BSE are partly on account of very active trading by FIIs. This might be a cause for some concern because the FIIs as a whole, are likely to be in a position to influence price movements. Nevertheless, there exists a countervailing force in terms of the publicly owned financial institutions which can if the need so arises prevent the market from declining on account of the trading strategies of FIIs. Though apprehensions regarding the possible destabilizing effects of FII activity have often been voiced in the media and in other forums, a situation where this actually happens is yet to materialize.

To summarize the movements of prices on the Bombay Stock market we present in Figure 3.9 the monthly figures of the Bombay Stock Exchange sensitive index (Sensex) which is an index consisting of thirty shares listed on the BSE.

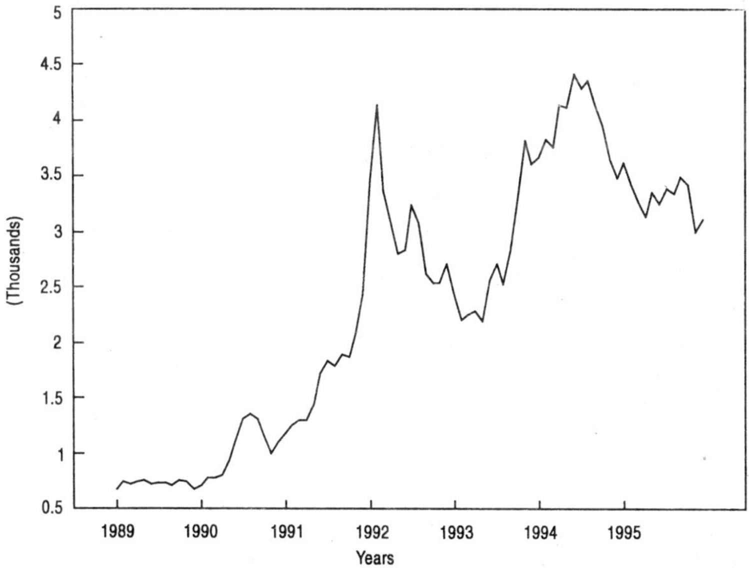

Figure 3.9 The Bombay Stock Exchange Sensitive Index
Source: Report on Currency and Finance, RBI, various issues.

The sensex has generally been on the rise over the period 1988 to 1994. The sharp increase between October 1991 and May 1992 and subsequent dramatic drop in the index during 1992–3 is due to the stock market scam. In 1994–5 too the sensex dropped.

The functioning of the secondary markets leaves a lot to be desired. The relative infrequency in the trading of a large number of scrips has adversely affected liquidity, as has the banning of *badla* or forward trading. Though no hard evidence is available, there have been frequent instances of price rigging. As derivatives and options are yet to be introduced, the menu of alternative instruments is also limited. SEBI has attempted to streamline rules and regulations but this process is far from over. The recent surge of activity on the primary markets has been sustained for three years but it is doubtful whether this can continue without major improvements in the working of the secondary markets.

REVIEW OF EMPIRICAL WORK RELATING TO THE STOCK MARKET

Empirical work relating to the stock markets is recently beginning to pick up. Over the past years research in this area has been rather sparse. A brief review of the relatively recent studies is presented below.

We have pointed out earlier that there has been a significant relaxation of rules regarding the pricing of new issues. In a recent study on the pricing of Initial Public Issues (IPO), Shah (1995) uses data on all new listings on the BSE between 1 January 1991 and 15 May 1995, to arrive at the following important conclusions:

i) The IPO market in India is prone to large degrees of underpricing. The data set used indicates that price at first listing was on an average 105 per cent above the issue price.

ii) The average time between the date of issue and the date of listing is 11 weeks, which by any standards is very large.

iii) The frequency of trading of the new issues is rather low after the first day of listing.

iv) During the first calendar year (approximately first 200 days of trading) on an average, IPOs earn 40 per cent in excess of market returns.

The phenomenal underpricing and consequent abnormal returns are possibly indicative of price rigging by promoters. The mispricing of IPOs suggests that many non-exploited arbitrage possibilities exist and calls into question the efficiency of the stock market. There is every likelihood that the situation is aggravated by the very limited liquidity of the IPOs after the first day of listing. As SEBI guidelines evolve over time and the market matures this anomaly is likely to reduce.

Weak form efficiency (i.e. current prices reflect all information contained in past prices) has been extensively tested with data pertaining to the BSE. The majority of the studies (see Barua, Raghunathan and Varma 1994 for an extensive survey) conclude that BSE is efficient.

Tests of the semi-strong form efficiency (i.e. current prices reflect all publicly available information) are few. Ramchandran (1985) and Srinivasan (1993) find in their event studies, that the market is efficient in responding to information content of bonus issues (stock splits) and rights issues. There is a great deal of ambiguity regarding the ability of the market to respond to political events (see Subramanian 1989).

Ignatius (1992) compares returns on the BSE Sensex with those on the New York stock exchange (S & P 500 Index). He finds a mildly significant week-end effect on the returns on BSE and also a seasonality of returns with December providing significantly higher monthly returns. In the case of weekly returns, the fourth week has the highest return. The study also suggests that the BSE and New York Stock Exchange are segmented (i.e. not integrated).

Thomas (1995) in an interesting paper studies the conditional heterosedasticity in the BSE Sensex between the period April 1979 and March 1995. Some of the important conclusions arrived at are as follows:

i) Daily and weekly returns on BSE have strong ARCH effects. This finding is consistent with studies relating to other stock markets.
ii) There exists much higher volatility of returns after March 1985.
iii) The BSE Sensex shows excess volatility in the month after the Central Government budget is presented while the stock market scam of 1992 is also associated with excess volatility.
iv) The BSE Sensex and the S&P 500 are unrelated in terms of both returns and volatility.

Goyal (1995) studies the nature and trends in volatility of stock returns. He estimates volatility of stock returns on a daily basis for the period May 1993 to December 1994 and on a monthly basis for the period 1986 to 1994, for two indices, i.e. the BSE Sensex and the BSE National Index. He arrives at the following important conclusions:
i) The daily volatility of returns peaks at the beginning and at the end of the settlement period.
ii) Volatility of monthly returns peaks every year in the months of March and July.
iii) The banning of the *badla* has contributed to decrease in the volatility, and
iv) Globalization of the Indian capital market has not added to volatility.

It is obvious from our brief review that research in this field is extremely inadequate in India compared to the rich empirical literature that has developed in the advanced nations. This is a serious handicap for policy makers while dealing with issues relating to stock exchanges. The years to come will clearly need a quantum jump in research activities in this field.

VI. The Non-Banking Corporate Sector

The Non-Banking Corporate Sector (NBCS) consists of two analytically distinct sets of institutions—non-financial firms who use the deposits that they mobilize to finance their own operations, and non-banking financial companies who intermediate funds from lenders to borrowers. The term non-banking financial companies covers investment companies, finance corporations, chit funds[11], *nidhis* and

[11] Under the chit fund scheme, the promoter of the 'chitty' collects subscriptions at specified periods from each enrolled member of the chit fund. The amount so collected called the capital of the chitty is given out as the prize amount to one of the members selected either by lot or auction. Chit funds in India are governed by the Chit Funds Act of 1982. Most of the chit funds are located in the southern states (for further details, see RBI 1985, pp. 338–9.

mutual benefit funds,[12] hire-purchase finance companies, loan companies and leasing companies. As Table 3.41 makes clear, there has been a significant increase in the total deposits mobilized by the NBCS, which went up from 1.1 per cent of the GDP in 1980–1 to 10.4 per cent of GDP in 1992–3. While deposits of non-financial firms constitute the bulk, there is a clear indication of the growing import- ance of the non-banking financial companies in the intermediation of funds over the eighties. Deposits of the non-banking financial companies as a percentage of total deposits of the non-banking financial companies and scheduled commercial banks combined increased from 0.5 per cent in 1980–1 to 9.4 per cent in 1992–3. As the Chakravarty Committee notes, 'the growth and emergence of the non-banking financial intermediaries could be traced to the need for provision of finance to activities which were not served by the organised banking system, as also to a class of customers whose demands were not fully satisfied' (RBI 1985, p. 91).

Table 3.41

Deposits with Non-Banking Corporate Sector (NBCS)
(Rs Crores)

Year	1980–1	1989–90	1990–1	1991–2	1992–3
Aggregate Deposits[a]	1357 (n/a)	33531 (20.2)	44063 (18.2)	52928 (17.4)	65213 (17.6)
Non Financial Companies[b]	84.2	62.0	59.6	52.8	57.4
Financial Companies[b]	15.8	32.7	35.5	41.5	36.5
Miscellaneous[b]	n/a	5.3	4.9	5.7	6.1
NBCS Deposits as % of Total Deposits of Banks + NBCS[c]	3.2	16.5	18.3	18.6	21.9

Note: [a] Figures in parenthesis indicate percentage of regulated deposits.
[b] As percentage of total NBCS deposits.
[c] Deposits of scheduled commercial banks (excluding RRBs).

Source: RBI (1985) and *Report on Currency and Finance,* RBI, various issues.

[12] These funds represent a group of persons who have agreed to help one another by contributing specified sums to a common fund and extending financial assistance to the needy members. The common fund called the *nidhi* must be supplemented by deposits from its members. Profits derived from the operations of the *nidhi* are shared among its members. *Nidhis* are registered under the Companies Act of 1956.

In the light of the increasing importance of the NBCS in the functioning of the Indian financial system, RBI constituted a committee under the chairmanship of Dr A.C. Shah in May 1992 which submitted its report in September 1992 (RBI, 1992). The following steps have been initiated since 1992:

i) All companies having net owned funds of over Rs 50 lakhs and above were required to register with RBI. By the end of March 1994, 891 applications for registration were received.

ii) RBI has issued guidelines on prudential norms for income recognition, accounting standards, provision for bad debts, capital adequacy and concentration of credit and investments. These guidelines are generally similar to those prescribed for commercial banks.

iii) Interest rates on deposits offered by non-banking non-financial companies has been fixed at 14 per cent.

iv) Non-banking financial companies and residuary non-banking companies are required to get themselves rated at least once every year.

VII. The Credit Rating Agencies

In a deregulated environment where private sector firms (both old and new) have the freedom to set interest rates on their debt instruments, credit rating agencies have an important role to play in mitigating some of the informational problems that plague debt markets. In the Indian context, one important development in recent times has been the creation of three independent credit rating agencies.

Credit Rating Information Services of India Limited (CRISIL)

CRISIL was jointly set up by ICICI, UTI, LIC, GIC, Asian Development Bank and some other financial institutions as the first credit rating agency in the country. It started operations in January 1988. Its primary objective is to rate debt obligations of Indian companies thereby providing a guide for investors as to the risk of timely payment of interest and principal in a particular debt instrument.

In Table 3.42 we provide the details of credit rating by CRISIL since its inception. There is a phenomenal rise in the number of instruments (and the amounts involved therein) since 1991–2. This rise is because of SEBI's new guidelines which make credit rating compulsory for all private sector debt instruments.

Investment Information and Credit Rating Agency of India Limited (ICRA)

ICRA was incorporated in January 1991 as an independent and professional credit rating agency promoted by the IFCI jointly with

Table 3.42

Details of Credit Rating by CRISIL (Rs Crores)[a]

	1987–8	1988–9	1989–90	1990–1	1991–2	1992–3	1993–4	1994–5
1. Debentures	65.0	143.0	681.1	24.0	3,989.0	13,653.0	6,227.0	7641
	(1)	(9)	(15)	(7)	(114)	(160)	(77)	(103)
2. Fixed Deposit Schemes	...	763.0	1,189.5	1,471.0	1,252.0	5,350.0	5,116.0	9,130
		(17)	(37)	(46)	(26)	(33)	(69)	(97)
3. Commercial Paper	...	...	227.8	196.0	524.0	782.0	4,801.0	1,629.0
			(20)	(24)	(12)	(34)	(211)	(137)
4. Others	...	...	...	...	100	26.0	527.0	6,144.0
					(3)	(2)	(9)	(47)
Total	65	906.0	2,098.4	1,691.0	5,865.0	20,011.0	16,671.0	24,544.0
	(1)	(26)	(72)	(77)	(155)	(229)	(366)	(384)

Note: [a] Figures in parentheses indicate the number of debt instruments which were given a credit rating.

Source: Report on Currency and Finance, RBI 1993–4 and 1994–5.

other leading investment institutions, commercial banks and financial service companies. The agency commenced its commercial activities from September 1991. In Table 3.43 we present the details of credit rating operations of ICRA. One interesting contrast between ICRA and CRISIL is that the former has rated a much greater number of commercial paper than the latter.

Table 3.43

Details of Credit Rating by ICRA (Rs Crores)

	1991–2	1992–3	1993–4	1994–5
1. Debentures	2,038.9	4,558.0	1,998.9	1,779.8
	(33)	(51)	(28)	(45)
2. Fixed Deposit Schemes	104.5	246.0	1,082.7	540.3
	(12)	(27)	(42)	(87)
3. Commercial Paper	72.0	524.0	1,668.9	3,023.2
	(3)	(8)	(69)	(80)
Total	2,215.4	5,328.0	4,750.5	5,343.3
	(48)	(86)	(139)	(212)

Note: [a] Figures in parenthesis indicate the number of debt instruments which were given a credit rating.

Source: Report on Currency and Finance, RBI 1993–4 and 1994–5.

CREDIT ANALYSIS AND RESEARCH LIMITED (CARE)

CARE was incorporated in April 1993 and was promoted by IDBI, Canara Bank, UTI, private sector banks and financial services companies.

VIII. Concluding Remarks

There is little doubt that all important sets of financial institutions and financial markets have undergone a significant change since the onset of the reforms. Yet it is clear from our analysis that the pace and extent of the reform has not been uniform across all sectors. This differential pace is the outcome of a conscious attempt by the government to shield certain important sectors from the adjustments that would have ensued, had the reforms been more comprehensive and rapid. In general, the strategy followed seems to have been one of a fairly gradual reform with an initial focus on those institutions and markets where reforms would have a less disruptive impact.

For example, in the banking sector, an important omission in the reform process has been the non-withdrawal of priority sector lending requirements in order to protect agriculturalists and the small-scale sector who would clearly not have been in a position to bear the consequences of a sudden and complete movement towards a market-oriented credit allocation process. On similar lines, access to subsidized sources of credit has been maintained for SIDBI but not for IDBI and ICICI. On the stock market front, the reform of the new issues market has been much more comprehensive than the secondary market. It was easy to reform the new issues market because the existing system had obvious weaknesses and the reform was unlikely to cause any major disruptions. On the other hand, reform of secondary markets has been slower (and has been accompanied by major disruptions, e.g. the banning of *badla* transactions) clearly because it is difficult to formulate a new system which has all the favourable characteristics of the old system and none of its disadvantages.

4

The Regulatory Framework

In a classic article, Diaz Alejandro (1983) argued that a *laissez-faire* system should not be the ultimate goal of policy makers in the reform of the financial sector. According to Diaz Alejandro, the failure of the highly publicized financial liberalization programme of Chile in the late 1970s was in a large measure due to the introduction of a free-enterprise financial system in the economy, without having the requisite regulatory safeguards in place. However, while it is now widely agreed that it is essential to have a strong regulatory framework in place before liberalizing the financial sector, relatively little attention has been paid in the literature to the actual design of the regulations themselves. Here, the policy maker faces a difficult choice. On the one hand, stringent and pervasive regulations can lead to an inefficient and uncompetitive financial sector and negate the very purpose of the reform process. On the other hand, weak and minimal regulations can contribute to an unstable financial sector that is susceptible to panics and frauds. If these panics and frauds cause a major financial crisis or a loss of faith in financial transactions by economic agents, then this could not only abort the financial liberalization process itself but in certain cases (such as a disruption in the payments system), also have a significantly negative consequence for real sector activities. It could well be argued then that the design of an 'optimal' regulatory framework—that is, a framework that encourages competition and efficiency in financial services and at the same time ensures a safe and sound financial sector—is perhaps the most difficult and complex component of the financial liberalization process.

In the design of a regulatory framework for the financial sector, it is important to make a distinction between banks and other financial intermediaries. All financial intermediaries finance entities in financial deficit (typically, the government, non-financial firms and some households) using the funds of entities in financial surplus (typically, households). What then makes banks special? Firstly, banks screen potential borrowers and monitor actual borrowers on behalf of the depositors. Secondly, a bank transforms the illiquid primary securities issued by firms (bank loans) into secondary liquid assets (bank deposits) held primarily by households. Thirdly, banks are central to the payments system and provide liquidity services to many financial and non-financial firms. An implication of the first function of banks—the screening and monitoring role—is that banks have superior information about the true value of the loans of their borrowers and cannot communicate this information to the market. The non-marketability of bank assets may therefore be said to constitute the essential difference between banks and other financial intermediaries (van Damme 1994). As a consequence of the absence of a market for bank loans, depositors often have little precise information about the value of the bank loan portfolios. This could lead to a situation where rational depositors choose to reallocate their resources by withdrawing from certain banks based on macroeconomic information or rumours. Banks which would otherwise be solvent can face withdrawals because of the possibility that there exist banks which are not solvent. Given that loans are not marketable in the short run, there is a strong possibility that banks which were healthy to start with may become insolvent in the presence of a large-scale withdrawal of deposits. The possible presence of insolvent banks creates an externality for other banks, since risk-taking by a single bank can have consequences for the banking system (Gorton 1994). Also, an implication of the participation of banks in the payments system would be that with a major banking panic that leads to the insolvency of several banks, the payments system will be severely disrupted and real activity depressed.[1]

The points noted above highlight the special role of banks in the financial intermediation process and underscore the need for a regulatory framework for banks that would be substantially beyond the regulatory mechanisms necessary for other financial intermediaries. The regulatory framework for banks—termed 'prudential regulation' in the literature—consists broadly of capital adequacy norms, restrictions on the line of activities that banks can participate in, restrictions on entry, and deposit insurance. In the case of other financial intermediaries, it can be argued that what would be necessary is to have certain minimal regulations in place such as disclosure requirements and prevention of fraudulent practices. In this sense, the regulation of

[1] As Bernanke (1983) has shown, the financial crisis preceding the Great Depression of 1929–33 in the United States was a major contributing factor to the recession that followed.

other financial intermediaries would be no different from that of the capital markets. However, in the Indian context, there is one peculiar feature of certain financial intermediaries that needs to be addressed. This is to do with development banks which unlike banks do not issue deposit liabilities that are a component of the means of payment, but like banks hold illiquid primary assets (term-loans). Given the peculiar nature of the term-lending institutions, certain features of the regulatory framework of banks such as capital adequacy norms may be applicable to them.

Since the onset of the financial sector reforms in 1991, an important task of policy makers has been to set up an appropriate regulatory framework for the Indian banking sector. Here again, as with other aspects of the reform process, the Narasimham Committee report has provided guidance on the actual design of the regulatory mechanism. In this chapter, we discuss the recommendations of the Narasimham Committee on the regulatory framework and the progress in implementing these recommendations to date. We concentrate on banks and developmental financial institutions; as we have argued, prudential regulation is only relevant to these two sets of institutions (and much more so to banks). The issues relevant to regulations of other financial intermediaries and the capital market it should be noted have already been discussed in the previous chapter.

I. The Prudential Regulation of Banks

In principle, the regulatory framework for banks should be designed so as to address six issues: i) deposit insurance; ii) policies regarding entry of banks, including issues of market structure; iii) policies that place restrictions on certain types of lending activities, iv) accountancy norms including income recognition and provision for non-performing assets; v) the supervision system and vi) capital adequacy norms. We discuss each of these in turn.

Deposit Insurance

There is a common misconception in the literature that deposit insurance can be viewed as a motivation for bank regulation rather than as part of the optimal regulatory package. There is no doubt that deposit insurance contributes greatly to the moral hazard in banking—with either fully or partially insured liabilities, banks may have the incentive to take on far too many high-risk investments or may simply neglect their task of monitoring the performance of their borrowers. On the other hand, without deposit insurance, runs on banks are a distinct possibility. Diamond and Dybig (1983) provide a theoretical rationale on why this may be the case. One important function of banks as we have noted earlier is term transformation. Firms like to finance their projects with long-term credits while households prefer to hold short-term deposits for liquidity reasons. A bank, therefore, transforms the credit portfolio demanded by its borrowers into a deposit portfolio demanded by lenders. In the Diamond-Dybig model, depositors do not know in advance when and whether they will require to withdraw their deposits. For the bank, the problem is of a different nature: it cannot differentiate between bank customers who really need cash and other customers who 'pretend' that they are also liquidity-constrained.[2] Here, with the term transformation of its liabilities, the bank may have to liquidate its assets at a discounted value if there are too many withdrawals at one time. Apprehending that the bank may not be able to repay its depositors in the future, customers who would otherwise have converted their deposits into cash in the future do so now, thus precipitating a run on the bank. Therefore, in this model, deposit insurance provides a means of preventing bank runs and thereby saving illiquid but solvent banks from failing.

The above argument has been the most persuasive motivation for deposit insurance and explains why this safeguard is a standard feature of modern banking systems. Deposit insurance in India is provided by the Deposit Insurance and Credit Guarantee Corporation (DICGC) which also provides guarantee cover to eligible financial institutions for their priority sector advances to small borrowers and small scale industries. DICGC was established in 1961 and is a wholly-owned subsidiary of RBI, its paid-up capital of Rs 15 crores being contributed entirely by the central bank. DICGC has three funds, namely the General Fund, the Deposit Insurance Fund and the Credit Guarantee Fund. The share capital of the corporation is held in the General Fund. Establishment and other expenses are met entirely from the interest on investments out of this fund. The Deposit Insurance Fund has been built up by premiums received from insured banks and augmented by interest on investments out of this fund. It is utilized exclusively to meet deposit insurance claims. The Credit Guarantee Fund has been accrued from the guarantee fees received for the guarantees given by the corporation and interest on investments out of this fund and is used solely to meet guarantee claims.

[2] As in all asymmetric information models, the individual's need for liquidity in the future is *private* information—i.e. the bank cannot verify who is the genuinely liquidity-constrained customer and who is not.

All commercial banks (including RRBs) are registered as insured banks, affording uniform protection to depositors. Every depositor of an insured bank which goes into liquidation is entitled to receive from the DICGC, through the liquidator, repayment of his or her deposits in all the branches of the bank, held by him or her in the same capacity and right, up to a maximum amount prescribed from time to time (RBI 1983, p. 154). In May 1993, the limit of insurance cover was enhanced from Rs 50,000 to Rs 100,000 per depositor per bank. In July 1993, the insurance premium was increased from 4 paise to 5 paise per Rs 100 per annum (i.e. from 0.04 to 0.05 per cent per annum). In end-March 1993, the number of insured banks under the Deposit Insurance Scheme was 1,931 comprising 276 commercial banks (including 196 RRBs) and 1,655 co-operative banks in 16 states and three union territories. With the growth in the banking system in the seventies and eighties, there has been a large increase in the number of fully protected bank accounts, which at 3,497 lakhs in 1993 comprised 99 per cent of total bank accounts. Interestingly, insured deposits as a proportion of total assessable deposits declined from 74 per cent in 1981 to 68 per cent in 1993 (indicating the growth in large corporate deposits in recent times). There has also been a significant increase in the total assets of the DICGC in the eighties, rising from Rs 159 crores in 1981 to Rs 1,693 crores in 1993. By law, the DICGC has to invest its surplus funds in central government securities and around 60 per cent of its assets are in that form of investment. Since its inception till end-March 1992, the total amount of deposit insurance claimed and provided in respect of 24 commercial banks and 24 co-operative banks aggregated to Rs 135.9 crores and Rs 13.2 crores, respectively.

One omission in the Narasimham Committee report was any reference to a policy perspective on the deposit insurance scheme currently in operation in India (in fact, issues relating to deposit insurance have not been mentioned anywhere in the 146-page document). This omission is indeed striking given that with the increasing importance of private banks, bank runs are a distinct possibility. There is little doubt that a well-designed deposit insurance scheme will contribute to the prevention of bank runs and at the same time reduce the moral hazard in banking operations. Two features of the Indian scheme deserve mention as they have certain weaknesses well-known in the literature on deposit insurance in other countries. The first pertains to the flat fee payable by banks to the DICGC for their insured deposits. This is indeed a common characteristic of most deposit insurance schemes in existence currently. The insurance premium paid by banks to the regulatory authorities is independent of the riskiness of the loan portfolio. As is well recognized, such a deposit insurance scheme subsidizes risk-taking since it allows banks to borrow at the risk-free rate. One solution that has been proposed to this problem in the literature is to have bank-specific premiums that are linked to the riskiness of the bank's portfolio. However, as Gorton (1994) points out, if it were possible to price the risk of the loan portfolio, then banking panics would indeed not be an issue to begin with, because banks could sell their loans. Given the non-marketability of bank loans, and that the true riskiness of the portfolio can only be known to the bank management, it would never be possible to adequately price the riskiness of a bank's loan portfolio. Therefore, there will always be an element of risk-taking in deposit insurance. Hence, a system of deposit insurance has to be complemented with other prudential regulations such as capital adequacy norms and a strict supervisory system that restricts the risk-taking activities of banks.

Another solution that has been proposed in the literature is to partition a bank's assets and liabilities such that insured deposits can only be invested in assets of readily ascertainable market value and to make the deposits translatable into a *pro rata* share of the value of these assets (Black 1970; Fama 1980). This would clearly rule out bank insolvency which as we have noted primarily arises from the uncertain and varying value of some classes of bank assets. This would also rule out undue risk-taking behaviour on the part of banks, as the value of their liabilities would now reflect the risk-return characteristics of their assets. However, as Goodhart (1993) argues, such a solution would negate the very special role that banks play in the intermediation process. Banks are particularly important in financing small and medium-sized firms. Such firms cannot tap the capital market directly (by issuing equity or through public debt) as these firms lack reputation or a healthy equity position either of which factors discourage investors from directly holding claims on these firms. Small- and medium-sized firms, often with limited equity, no reimbursement history, or a reputation for solvency, must be closely monitored (Diamond 1991). Given the natural monopoly aspect of the information provision (discussed in Chapter 1), it is logical for such firms to apply for bank debt.[3] Therefore, if banks are restricted to using insured deposits only to invest in marketable assets (such as government securities), they will

[3] As firm-level studies of the financing of investment indicate, small and medium-sized firms obtain a larger proportion of their external funds from banks as compared to large firms who rely relatively more on capital markets (e.g., see Fazzari *et al.* 1988).

either have to reduce their lending activities (which as we have noted are non-marketable), or fund these activities by offering higher interest rates on non-insured deposits (to encourage depositors to shift to non-insured deposits). This will either lead to a drying up of external finance to small and medium firms or make the cost of external finance prohibitive to such firms. In either case, the outcome would not be desirable from a policy perspective.

A second feature of the deposit insurance scheme in India that deserves attention is the public ownership of the DICGC. One obvious reason for the public ownership of the deposit insurance fund is the absence of private insurance funds in India even among other insurance claims (such as life, property, and casualty insurance). However, there is no intrinsic reason why deposit insurance has to be provided by a publicly-owned institution; for example, Gorton and Mullineaux (1987) have shown that private insurance was effective in the United States during the nineteenth century. A private insurance company would have better incentives to measure a bank's risk precisely and to monitor the latter's loan portfolio more closely, than the officers of a public deposit insurance corporation who need not face the financial consequences of poor monitoring and risk assessment. There are, however, problems that can be anticipated with the private provision of deposit insurance. For example, in the face of systemic risk (i.e., non-diversifiable risk), a severe macroeconomic shock could render well-capitalized private insurance companies insolvent. Here again, the government would have to step in as a lender of last resort. In any case, given the lack of private corporations in any sphere of insurance claims, clearly there is a long way to go before we can contemplate the provision of deposit insurance by private companies in India.

We can propose two reforms to the current system of deposit insurance in India. Firstly, given the moral hazard problems that are occasioned by wholly insured deposits, it would be desirable to only partially insure each customer's deposits (say 75 to 90 per cent of each customer's deposits could be insured). This would lead to a greater monitoring of banks by depositors and, more importantly, act as a strong disincentive to banks to indulge in risky activities (given that now they would have to repay a part of their deposit liabilities if they became insolvent). Such a proposal has merit in that it balances the need to provide deposit insurance to prevent bank runs, with the necessity to make banks somewhat responsible for their actions. A second reform we propose is to invest in the DICGC a capability to monitor and penalize errant banks. In the present system, the power to monitor and penalize banks is vested exclusively with the Board of Financial Supervision (which we shall discuss later in the section). The present system is clearly inadequate in that it does not provide the DICGC with either a supervisory or monitoring role; all that the DICGC does is to collect insurance premiums from banks and pay out insurance claims to depositors. In other words, it simply exists to 'foot the bill'. One advantage of giving the DICGC a role in monitoring banks independent of the Board of Financial Supervision is that it allows multiple regulators for the same task. This may guard against the possibility of collusive behaviour between a single regulator and the regulated bank. Also, giving the DICGC an independent role in monitoring banks may permit a gradual transition to risk-based insurance premiums as the DICGC gets to learn more about bank loan portfolios. The disadvantage of having more than one regulator is that it gives rise to the problem of 'moral hazard in teams' as each regulator will shift the responsibility for a bad outcome on to other regulators (Dewatripont and Tirole 1994). On balance, we feel that it may be desirable to have more than one agency supervising and monitoring the Indian banking sector given the strong possibility of regulatory collusion or oversight in a situation where regulatory mechanisms are relatively weak.

Issues Pertaining to Entry and Market Structure

There is now a widely-shared view among regulators that unlike most other industries, the banking industry should not be characterized by free entry (Caprio and Summers 1993). As Gorton (1994) persuasively argues,

> Entry into banking must change the way banks are regulated because bank regulation depends on restricting entry into the banking industry. Entry by competitors reduces charter value since banks no longer have a monopoly on an important source of firm finance. Entrants underprice loans or debt in order to capture market share in financing corporations. Incumbent banks must then lower the interest rates they charge on loans, resulting in reduced profitability. But, there are two side effects. First, in attempts to maintain profitability banks enter new activity which are not necessarily a source of public concern *per se,* but become entwined with traditional banking activities and, hence, a source of concern. Second, and most important, with a less valuable charter, banks will engage in riskier activities. Without the incentive effect of a valuable charter, the level of bank risk-taking will increase (p. 107).

By promoting a high charter value in the banking industry, regulators create incentives for banks to limit risk on their own, and therefore make it less necessary for the former to intervene directly. This is particularly important in an environment where off-balance-sheet products (such as options and derivatives) become important activities for banks and so make it difficult for the regulator to monitor the riskiness of a bank's portfolio.[4] However, restricting entry into the banking industry has a clear disadvantage in that it may undermine the goal of bringing about greater competition and efficiency in the banking sector. While there is no doubt that the restriction of entry into the banking sector will lead to some degree of inefficiency in banking services, this has to be weighed against the benefits of having a safe and sound banking sector. Here, the regulator must use the high charter value created as a result of restrictions on entry, as both a carrot and a stick to individual banks. With the creation of a high charter value, banks have an incentive to limit risk-taking on their own. However, high charter value also leads to excess demand for bank licences. Therefore, the regulator can always allow new banks to enter if it feels that the desired level of efficiency is not being observed in the banking industry.

With respect to the freedom of entry, following the Narasimham Committee's recommendations, RBI announced in 1992–3 guidelines for the entry of new private sector banks. These guidelines attempted to ensure that the new entrants were professionally managed, financially viable and would be able to bring about technological upgradation of the banking sector. Some of the important guidelines are as follows:

i) New private sector banks have to be registered as public limited companies under the Companies Act, 1956.

ii) The RBI may, on merits, grant a licence under the Banking Regulation Act, 1949 for new private banks.

iii) The shares of new banks should be listed on stock exchanges.

iv) In order to avoid a concentration of headquarters of new banks in metropolitan cities and other over-banked areas, while granting a license, preference will be given to those banks whose headquarters are located in areas which do not have the headquarters of any other bank.

[4] There is another important reason why the charter value of banks needs to be maintained at a high level. Measures of prudential regulation such as capital requirements and restrictions on trading activities are in effect taxes on bank profits. If there are no good substitutes to bank loans, then banks can pass on these taxes to their borrowers. With the increasing importance of non-bank financial companies in the intermediation process, that may no longer be the case. If these regulations become too onerous for a banking firm to bear, it may exit from the banking industry and choose to be a non-bank finance company instead. As we noted earlier, banks have a special role to play in the intermediation process and their 'disappearance' may lead to certain kinds of borrowers being 'squeezed out' of the credit market and therefore, have potentially significant negative effects on real sector activity.

v) New banks will not be allowed to have as a director any person who is a director of any other banking company, or of companies which among themselves are entitled to exercise voting rights in excess of 20 per cent of the voting rights of all the shareholders of the banking company.

vi) New banks will be subject to a minimum paid-up capital of Rs 100 crores. They will also be subject to prudential norms in respect of banking operations, accounting practices and other policies as are laid down by RBI.

vii) They will also have to observe the priority sector lending requirements as applicable to other domestic banks.

viii) The existing branch licensing policy shall apply to new banks.

The Narasimham Committee envisaged the following market structure in the Indian banking sector in the post-reform period: i) three or four large banks (including SBI) which could become international in character; ii) eight to ten national banks with a network of branches throughout the country engaged in general or universal banking; iii) local banks whose activities would be confined to a particular region;[5] and iv) rural banks whose operations would be limited to the rural areas and whose predominant business would be the financing of agriculture and allied activities (MOF 1991, p. 69). The Committee viewed the above scenario, particularly those relating to i) and ii), to follow from mergers between existing public sector banks. These mergers would be market-driven and based on profitability considerations rather than imposed by regulatory authorities.

The Committee also believed that the government could begin a programme of phased privatization of the public sector banks by allowing the profitable and highly reputed ones to issue fresh capital to the public. This has already begun with the State Bank of India Act of 1955 being amended in 1993 to allow for private share-holding. Consequently, SBI was the first public sector bank to tap the capital market with an equity-cum-bond issue of Rs 2,532 crores in 1993–4. The Banking Companies Acts were amended in 1994 to allow public sector banks to tap the capital market for public contribution to their capital up to 49 per cent. The Oriental Bank of Commerce was the second public sector bank to issue equity and raised a sum of Rs 387 crores in

[5] Again, this suggestion is problematic; in fact, the US experience with restrictions on intrastate branching shows that geographical specialization of banks is *not* a good idea. As Calomiris and Gorton (1991) argue, the US with a larger number of local banks than Canada has witnessed a higher frequency of banking panics and bank failures due in great part to location-specific real shocks.

October 1994, diluting the government's equity holding in the bank from 100 to 66 per cent.

One feature of the Indian banking sector that needs to be noted is the dominance of SBI and its associate banks among the Indian banks. This is clearly evident from an examination of Table 4.1, which provides the salient features of the current market structure in the Indian banking sector. Moreover, among the eighteen nationalized banks, three banks —Bank of India, Bank of Baroda and Canara Bank—held 35 per cent of total deposits outstanding in 1994.[6] This figure is not surprising given the fact that there exist considerable economies of scale and scope in banking services. If this is the case, it remains to be seen as to what extent the entry of several private sector banks will cause competitive pressures in the industry.[7]

Table 4.1

Structure of Commercial Banking, March 1994[a]

Market Structure Indicators	SBI Group	Nationalized Banks	RRB	Foreign Banks	Private Sector Banks
Number of Banks	8	19	196	24	28
Branch Network	20.6	49.2	23.5	0.2	6.5
Deposits	27.0	57.1	2.6	7.7	5.6
Advances	33.6	51.8	2.8	6.7	5.1

Note: [a] Figures in percentages except number of banks.

Source: IBA (1994).

Restrictions on Trading Activities

Since the initiation of the reforms, restrictions on uses of funds by banks have been considerably relaxed. For example, the ceiling on bank investment in bonds of Public Sector Enterprises (PSEs) has been withdrawn. Also, banks have been permitted to subscribe to shares/debentures of non-financial firms up to a limit of 5 per cent of incremental deposits (with a limit of 1.5 per cent of incremental deposits on the acquisition of corporate shares). Lending norms have also been considerably liberalized with banks being given operational autonomy in respect of fixation of inventory and receivable levels; term financing of a project and the financing of infrastructure facilities.

[6] Due to non-availability of data on deposits, the Punjab National Bank was excluded from the calculations on deposit concentration.

[7] See Bhaumik and Sarkar (1996) for a recent attempt to empirically determine whether new entry in the banking sector has fostered competition.

ACCOUNTANCY NORMS

Since 1992–3, there has been a phased introduction of a system of income recognition, asset classification, and provisioning for public sector banks. This was done on the recommendation of the Narasimham Committee, which believed that 'a proper system of income recognition and provision (was) fundamental to the strength and stability of the banking system' (MOF 1991, p. 54). With increasing freedom being given to banks in their use of funds, a uniform and transparent accountancy standard is critical to the effective monitoring of bank solvency. Assets have been classified into four categories: i) standard; ii) sub-standard; iii) doubtful; and iv) loss. A non-performing asset (NPA) is defined as a credit facility in respect of which interest remained 'past due' (i.e. thirty days beyond due date) for four quarters up to March 1993, three quarters up to March 1994, and two quarters from the year ending March 1995 onwards. An asset is considered sub-standard if it is an NPA for a period not exceeding two years, doubtful if it is an NPA for a period exceeding two but less than three years, and loss if it is an NPA for over three years. While the provisioning requirement for a loss asset was 100 per cent, provisioning norms in the case of sub-standard and doubtful assets were gradually tightened and stood at 30 per cent in March 1993. Given the large number of NPAs where the outstanding balance was under Rs 25,000, aggregate provisioning was decided on (standing at 7.5 per cent in 1995) for the total outstandings on such NPAs rather than a case-by-case evaluation. Table 4.2 gives the break-up of assets under

Table 4.2

Classification of Loan Assets of Public Sector Banks, 1993–4

(per cent)

Category of Assets	SBI Group	Nationalized	Total
Standard	77.7	75.7	76.4
Sub-standard	5.7	8.1	7.3
Doubtful	13.8	14.0	13.9
Loss	2.9	2.2	2.4

Source: Report on Trend and Progress in Banking, 1993–4, RBI.

each of the four categories for the SBI Group and the nationalized banks. Approximately 23 per cent of total advances of the public sector banks could be considered to be non-performing, with about 15 per cent in the doubtful or loss category. There has been some attempt by the government to expedite the recovery of banks' dues with the setting up of appellate tribunals (called debt recovery tribunals) in several metropolitan cities.

THE SUPERVISION SYSTEM

Prior to the reforms, the supervision of banks was done by a department of RBI. The Narasimham Committee felt that while the RBI would normally be the appropriate agency for regulation, 'the present system (had) over-burdened the Reserve Bank of India ... and (had) not allowed undivided attention being paid to the (supervisory) aspect and to develop the necessary skills and expertise' (MOF 1991, p. 131). It, therefore, proposed a separation of the function of supervision of banks from the traditional central banking functions of the Reserve Bank of India and suggested that a quasi-autonomous Banking Supervisory Board be set up to take over the job. The Committee also proposed that the Board should have supervisory jurisdiction not merely over banks but also over developmental finance institutions and non-bank financial intermediaries as it felt that having an integrated system of supervision would be more advantageous. Following this recommendation, the Board of Financial Supervision (BFS) was constituted under the aegis of RBI in November 1994, with the Governor of RBI appointed as the Chairman of the Board. An advisory council to BFS was also constituted to tender advice on matters relating to supervision and inspection. It comprises five members who are 'eminent personalities in the areas of economics, banking, law, agricultural credit and accountancy' (RBI Annual Report 1994–5, p. 13). The BFS has been authorized to exercise powers of supervision and inspection in relation to banks, financial institutions and non-banking financial companies.

There is a lack of consensus in the literature on whether supervision and the monetary policy functions should be combined within the same agency. One argument given for the separation of the two functions is that combining these functions within the same agency may lead to a conflict of interest. For example, in its role as the agency in charge of monetary policy, the central bank may wish to increase interest rates (to control the inflation rate). At the same time by wearing the hat that ensures the stability of the financial sector, it may worry about the adverse effects of interest rates on the profitability and solvency of the banking system. Goodhart and Schoenmaker (1995) argue that,

> the potential for conflict between regulatory and monetary objectives depends to some large extent on the structure of the banking and financial systems. The more such a system involves intermediaries financing maturity mismatch positions through wholesale markets in a competitive milieu, the greater such dangers of conflict will be (p. 547).

In their survey of 24 countries in the 1980s, Goodhart and Schoenmaker also found that 11 of these countries had combined agencies while the rest had separated ones. While there is no compelling theoretical argument or empirical evidence for one regime over the other, it can be argued that in the Indian context it would be desirable to have a supervisory agency which is more or less independent of the RBI and the government. In a context where it is unlikely that the government will divest its controlling stake in the twenty-seven banks that comprise the nationalized banking sector, there is a strong possibility of a conflict of interest between the government's two positions—one as an owner of a bank and the other as the regulator of banks. A clear example would be that of an ailing public sector bank which is in danger of becoming insolvent. There is a strong incentive for the bank management here to 'gamble for resurrection'—i.e., to invest in some high return but high risk assets in the hope that they will make good. This would be particularly true in a deregulated environment where the career prospects of bank managers are tied up with the performance of the bank. As part-owner of the bank, the government too has an incentive to 'turn a blind eye' to the management's actions since it benefits if the investments prosper but does not lose unduly if the bank fails (thanks to deposit insurance). On the other hand, as a regulator, the desirable action for the government in this case would be to ask for a recapitalization along with a possible change in the bank's management. Clearly the conflict of interest that is evident here can lead to deliberate regulatory oversight and have a potentially dangerous consequence on the solvency of banks. It can be argued then that the granting of 'quasi-autonomous status' to the BFS does not go far enough; it may in fact be necessary to give the BFS *complete autonomy* so that it carries out its responsibility without falling prey to possibly hazardous conflicts of interest.[8]

Capital Adequacy Norms

The requirement that banks maintain minimum capital adequacy ratios is an essential component of the prudential regulation of banks. There has been an international harmonization of capital adequacy norms with the adoption of a common capital adequacy standard known as the Cooke Ratio, prescribed by the Basle Committee on Banking Regulations and Supervisory Practices (the so-called Basle Accord of 1988) appointed by the Bank of International Settlements (BIS). The

[8] This issue is also tied up with the question of central bank independence. The greater the independence of the central bank from the government, the lower is the possibility that the central bank will succumb to such conflicts of interest. We discuss issues relating to central bank independence in Chapter 7.

underlying principle behind the Cooke Ratio is a risk-weighted approach to capital adequacy so that institutions with a higher risk profile maintain higher levels of capital. For the purpose of calculation of capital, BIS classifies capital into two broad categories—Tier 1 capital consisting of share capital and disclosed reserves, and Tier 2 capital consisting of undisclosed and latent reserves, general provision, hybrid capital and subordinated debt. BIS recommends that Tier 2 capital should not exceed Tier 1 capital. The BIS norm for capital adequacy is 8 per cent of the risk-weighted assets, i.e. Tier 1 and Tier 2 capital must be equal to at least 8 per cent of total assets of the bank after applying risk-weighting coefficients to the assets. The Narasimham Committee has recommended that all banks in India reach this figure in a phased manner, with the smaller banks given more time than the larger ones to achieve this norm, latest by March 1996. Reasonably satisfactory progress has been made by public sector banks to reach the target. As at end-March 1995, thirteen of the twenty-seven public sector banks had attained a minimum capital to risk-weighted asset ratio of 8 per cent, eleven had reached 4 per cent, and the remaining three less than 4 per cent. The move to reach minimum capital adequacy ratios has been greatly facilitated by the infusion of fresh capital in several public sector banks by the government in its 1993–4 and 1994–5 budgets. Sums of Rs 5,700 crores and Rs 5,600 crores were kept aside in the 1993–4 and 1994–5 budgets respectively by the government to recapitalize public sector banks.

BIS also recommends that the stipulation of a minimum capital to risk-weighted asset ratio (CRAR) must be complemented by a policy of intervention if the ratio persistently falls below the minimum for a particular bank (the policy of intervention could be either to sell or liquidate the concerned bank). As Dewatripont and Tirole (1994) argue, such a policy is essential if the capital adequacy norms are to have the right incentive effects on the bank's managers and shareholders. The reason for this is simple: as the bank's net worth declines possibly due to some 'bad investments', there is an inducement for managers and shareholders to gamble for resurrection and engage in highly risky activities (the perverse incentive effect of deposit insurance). In the absence of capital adequacy norms, this will lead to a perverse evolution of the bank's balance sheet as it takes on more and more risky activities. However, in the presence of capital adequacy norms, a fall in the CRAR for the bank will lead the regulator to ask for a recapitalization from the bank's shareholders. Such a requirement acts as a disincentive to the bank's shareholders to take on more risk and counters the tendency of the management to 'go for broke' (since shareholders will now interfere in the management if the CRAR falls below the minimum). If, in fact, shareholders refuse to recapitalize, then regulators must be prepared to interfere with the bank management and possibly sell or liquidate the bank. Dewatripont and Tirole note that the threat of a shift in control to the regulator in the event of bad performance by a bank, acts as a disciplining device to managers of banks and deters unnecessary risk-taking.

We have reason to believe that the positive incentive effects of capital adequacy requirements on bank risk-taking and managerial performance will not be adequately internalized by managers of public sector banks. This could be for two reasons. Firstly, as cited earlier, recapitalization of a bank by the shareholders in the face of a falling CRAR must be accompanied by a greater interference in the bank's management. Since the government has a soft budget constraint with respect to the recapitalization requirement (it could always put the amount aside from the budget), it will not have as much motivation to interfere in bank management as private shareholders. Secondly, in the case of large public sector banks, the government has an incentive (for obvious political and economic reasons) through the regulatory authorities to bail out a failing bank (i.e. a bank where the CRAR is persistently below the minimum) rather than sell or liquidate. Here again, the disciplining role of the capital adequacy norm may not be fulfilled—bank managers will realize that in the event of the bank failing, they will in all probability retain their jobs.[9] We, therefore, feel that with the pervasive state ownership of banks, capital adequacy norms have limited value in assuring the solvency of the Indian banking sector.

II. Regulation of Development Banks

The Narasimham Committee report devotes an entire chapter to issues related to the regulation of development banks. We have already dealt with some of them, like interest rate deregulation and reduction of subsidized and captive sources of credit. Without doubt, financial liberalization has substantially altered the milieu in which the development banks function. In such an environment, regulations are needed to keep a watch on the asset quality of these institutions.

Before financial and real sector liberalization measures were introduced, the grant of an industrial license to a firm was followed,

[9] Unless of course the bank failed as a result of deliberate fraudulent practice by the bank management, as happened during the financial scam of 1992–3.

almost automatically, by the sanction of assistance by the development banks. The Narasimham Committee report argues that liberal lending norms (to firms possessing a license), particularly the high leverage (debt equity ratios of 2:1 were the norm) allowed and preferred (because the fiscal system favoured debt over equity), led to weak financial structures of firms and thus made them susceptible to sickness when faced with increased market uncertainties in the liberalized environment. We have noted earlier, that in September 1992 sick units in the private sector had bad and doubtful debts outstanding to the tune of Rs 12,586 crores. Thus, prior to the reforms, the quality of the portfolios of the development banks left a lot to be desired. We have also noted that over the past few years the two largest development banks (IDBI and ICICI) have to some extent been successful in improving the quality of their portfolios according to the reported classification of assets. Clearly, with licensing requirements being dramatically reduced, those development banks with better abilities of techno-economic evaluation of projects would over the years improve their asset quality. Due to lack of information, the same cannot be said of the SFCs, SIDCs and SIBDI, and in all probability the quality of their assets has not improved substantially. A lot thus remains to be done on this front. Most of the required regulations are in place. Strict implementation of the regulations has yet to be achieved.

An important issue highlighted by the Committee is the possible blurring of the distinction between commercial banks and development finance institutions in a deregulated financial environment. This view of the Committe seems to be inappropriate, at least in the medium term, for two important reasons. Firstly, given the obvious difference in the nature of liabilities of the two institutions, it is difficult to visualize a situation where their structure of assets would tend to converge, even if such a situation is in principle allowed to materialize in a deregulated environment. Secondly, as pointed out by Mayer (1988), long-term debt and short-term debt that can be rolled over are not equivalent. The former (long-term loans) involves a commitment from the financial intermediary and the borrower, which is absent from a working capital (short-term) loan. Therefore, it can be argued that the development finance institutions, given their long experience in the provision of term loans, have a competitive advantage in this area. It is unlikely that commercial banks would be able to acquire the requisite skills which could erode this advantage in the short to medium term.

Another aspect to which the Committee report devotes a lot of space is the lack of competition among the various term-lending institutions. We have seen earlier (Table 3.19) that the six largest term-lending institutions account for well over 60 per cent of total assistance to the industrial sector and that IDBI is by far the largest among them. As the apex bank, the IDBI is the co-ordinating agency of operations of all the development banks, and the development banks taken together have been operating as a consortium. Apart from regular meetings of institutional heads, almost all development banks are represented on each others' boards of directors which facilitates in co-ordinating the consortium agreements. With areas of activities being neatly divided between banks, development banks and state level institutions, borrowers have little choice in selecting the institution to approach for loans. Even within the development banks, some like SIDBI, IRBI, SCICI and TFCI have specialized areas of activity. The report argued that this situation is incompatible with the deregulation of interest rates in particular and a more competitive financial sector in general and recommended a move towards a system of syndicated lending. Though consortium lending had its advantages (for example, firms did not have to approach several institutions for funds), the greatest drawback was that if a particular loan application was rejected the borrower had no other option to turn to. This created serious barriers to entry for firms. Moreover, this kind of co-ordinated lending did not pressurize each institution to scrutinize each project independently.

Before the financial sector reforms were initiated the consortium financing agreements included assistance to projects costing above Rs 10 crores. Leasing finance, equipment finance, and bills discounting were outside the consortium financing agreements. In 1990–1 the financial institutions were allowed to sanction assistance to projects costing Rs 20 crores or less without reference to the inter-institutional fora. By 1991–2 the formalized system of consortium financing had given way to an informal system of loan syndication as recommended by the Narasimham committee. There, nevertheless, still exists some co-ordination between the various institutions and they do not compete in the true sense of the term.

Though more competition is likely to improve the allocation of funds, the costs of competition to the financial institutions may outweigh its benefits. Competition may lead to lower profits and the erosion of net worth and thus adversely affect the financial strength of the development banks. Not all development banks (especially SFCs, SIDCs, SIDBI, i.e. institutions specializing in lending to the small scale sector) are currently in a good financial position. Moreover, their specialization in the past may put them at a disadvantage if they are suddenly forced to operate in areas which require skills they do not possess. Another impediment to promoting competition between institutions hitherto protected is that some institutions, especially those lending to the small-scale sector, still receive subsidized credit from either the RBI or the central government. For these subsidies to be passed to the targeted sector a clear demarcation of areas of activities is inevitable. If such subsidies are progressively done away with, then the scope and feasibility of promoting competition may improve. Thus, financial institutions catering to the needs of the small scale sector need to be protected from competition, at least in the short and medium term. Exposing them to competition at this stage may prove disastrous. A phased move in this direction is likely to be the optimal strategy.

As mentioned earlier all the development banks except ICICI and SCICI are owned by the government, thus ensuring that they are directly under the control of the government. In the current and future liberalized environment, the autonomy (freedom from direct government control) of these institutions is important. The interest rate deregulation has in effect given a great deal of autonomy to these institutions. In addition, the drastic reduction in subsidized and captive sources of credit has further diluted the need for strict control over these institutions (except those assisting sick firms and small scale industries) because the targeting of subsidies is no longer an important issue. Dilution of ownership, if not outright privatization, is another option that needs to be given serious thought to in the future. IFCI and IDBI have taken some concrete steps in this regard in 1994–5 by going in for the new issue of shares on the stock markets thus diluting the extent of government ownership.

III. Concluding Remarks

During the era of financial repression, when banks and developmental financial institutions were entrusted with well-defined 'social responsibilities', there was little recognition of the need for a sophisticated regulatory framework. It was generally perceived that public ownership *per se* would adequately substitute for a strong regulatory framework. It has been realized by the policy-makers that such a perception is no longer valid in the current regime. Our discussion highlights the fact that a serious search for the 'optimal' regulatory framework for the Indian financial sector is currently underway.

5

Real and Financial Sector Interactions

Two important issues are often neglected in the literature on financial liberalization. The first concerns the need to reform the real sector at the same time as the financial sector; as Caprio and Summers (1993, p.15) argue, '...reforms in the financial sector cannot prudently run too far ahead of those in the real sector'. This is of particular relevance in the Indian context where both the allocation of resources and the current production levels were governed for several decades by a rigid system of industrial licensing and centralized planning, and the market mechanism had a limited role to play. The second issue deals with the consequences of financial sector reform on the financing of real sector activities (i.e. both on current production and investment). It is clear that financial deregulation (for example interest rate decontrol) can lead to a sharp disruption in the financing of industry and agriculture and hence have an adverse impact both on production and investment in the short to medium term.

In this chapter we discuss, in the first section, the reforms that have currently been undertaken in the real sector and are relevant to the success of financial sector reforms. The second and third sections deal with the financing of industry and agriculture and the influences of financial sector reforms therein.

I. Reforms in the Real Sector

The need to synchronize reforms in the real and financial sectors in economies which are attempting to move away from a system of centralized planning towards greater market orientation is obvious. Abrupt changes in financial variables like the interest rate may precipitate a spate of bankruptcies of hitherto viable firms, especially if they operate in a tightly regulated regime which curtails their flexibility and consequently their ability to respond to shocks. Another important consideration is the possibility that dismantling a tightly-structured control regime in the real sector itself, is likely to lead to some amount of financial distress among firms not capable of operating in a relatively free environment. It is important to note that in this case financial distress among firms arises due to developments in the product market. In such a situation financial liberalization can only add to the woes. It is thus important that real sector reforms are given enough time to settle in so that firms can come to terms with these sets of reforms before they are exposed to shocks of financial liberalization. When referring to reforms in the real sector the literature generally stresses three specific areas:

i) Reduction of legal barriers to entry;

ii) Streamlining of exit procedures and bankruptcy laws; and

iii) Privatization of public enterprises.

Reform in these three areas would constitute a major step towards reducing microeconomic rigidities and thereby lead to a resource allocation guided primarily by market forces.

After independence, industrialization was deemed to be the primary instrument in raising the standard of living. In order to achieve this, a strategy of planned development was envisaged and state-owned public enterprises were supposed to play a vital role in industrial development. Three basic sets of legislation provided the legal and operational framework for strict control of the operations and growth of non-financial firms according to priorities set out in the various Five-Year plans. They are:

i) Industries (Development and Regulation) Act, 1951 and the Industrial Policy Resolution, 1956;

ii) The Monopolies and Restrictive Trade Practices Act (MRTP), 1969; and

iii) Foreign Exchange Regulation Act (FERA).

The Industries (Development and Regulation) Act stipulated that no new units could be set up nor substantial expansion be made to existing units without a license from the Central Government. The Act also empowered the government to exempt any class of industrial firms from all or any of the provisions of the Act. Under this provision the government exempted all firms with an investment of less than Rs 10 lakhs (called small scale industries) in land, building, and machinery. This exemption limit has been progressively raised and currently stands at Rs 60 lakhs. The government has over the years also followed a policy of reserving items for exclusive manufacture in the small scale sector, the list for which currently comprises 843 items.

The Industrial Policy Resolution, 1956, classified industries into three categories based on the role that the state was expected to play in each category. The divisions were:

i) Industries in schedule A, mostly public utilities, basic and strategic industries, which were exclusively reserved for the state to develop.

ii) Industries listed in schedule B, mostly heavy industries which were to be progressively owned by the state but private firms were also allowed to enter.

iii) Industries outside the schedules A and B which were open to private firms.

The MRTP Act stipulated that all firms with a capital base of over Rs 20 crores were to be classified as MRTP firms and were permitted to enter only selected industries and that too, on a case by case, basis. In addition to industrial licensing all investment proposals by these firms required separate approvals from the Department of Company Affairs.

The FERA was passed by Parliament in January 1974. It provided the regulatory framework for the commercial and manufacturing activities of branches of foreign companies in India, and Indian joint-stock companies with a foreign equity holding of over 40 per cent. The Act specified a list of industries where such firms would be allowed to operate and all new investments and substantial expansions required a separate approval from the Department of Company Affairs.

As a result of these laws, industry in India was subject to rather formidable legal barriers to entry. The reform process of this sector began in 1975–6 and has concentrated on a reduction of these legal barriers to entry. In November 1975, twenty-four industries were taken out of the purview of the industrial licensing provisions of the Industries (Development and Regulation) Act. This deregulation process received a further impetus in 1985–6 when twenty-five more industries were de-licensed. This de-licensing was extended to even MRTP and FERA companies. Moreover, the threshold of bringing a unit under MRTP was increased from Rs 20 crores to Rs 100 crores, and a list of thirty industries was drawn up in which MRTP and FERA companies could directly seek a licence, without seeking prior permission from the Department of Company Affairs. On 24 July 1991, a path-breaking Industrial Policy Statement was tabled in Parliament. There were a few more announcements made in subsequent years. As a result, the current position with respect to the above-mentioned acts is :

i) Industrial Licensing stands abolished irrespective of the level of investment except for sixteen industries.

ii) The number of industries reserved for the public sector presently is six.

iii) The MRTP Act was amended to remove the threshold limit of assets. This Act now only seeks to curb Monopolistic and Restrictive Trade Practices.

iv) Under the new policy guidelines on foreign investment, automatic permission is granted for foreign equity participation upto 51 per cent in a specified list of high technology and high investment priority industries. Separate clearances are still required for foreign firms to be able to operate in other areas.

Thus it can be asserted that legal barriers to entry had been substantially reduced by the time financial sector liberalization began.

THE BANKRUPTCY PROCEDURE

Let us now turn to reform of exit procedures and bankruptcy laws. Bankruptcy is a screening mechanism designed to eliminate those firms which are economically inefficient and whose resources can be better used in some other activity (White 1989). A bankruptcy filing initiates a collective legal procedure by which all claims against the firm are settled. In the event of bankruptcy, the control of the firm's assets shifts from the debtor to the creditor. In the event of there being only one creditor, a formal bankruptcy procedure is not necessary since all that must be ensured is that a transfer of ownership and control does take place in the default state, i.e. the terms of the debt contract are upheld. However, in the case of multiple creditors, a formal bankruptcy procedure is necessary. Without it individual creditors would engage in a costly and unproductive race to be the first to sue the firm for repayment of their own claims. Since creditors who sued first would receive a payment in full with other creditors receiving nothing, this would lead to a significant increase in bankruptcy costs (due to the duplicative monitoring expenses of the creditors and the costs of the lawsuits). While in principle there is no reason why creditors and debtors may not be able to work out their own bankruptcy procedure, in practice the large transaction costs involved in the design of such a procedure may preclude such a possibility. This is perhaps the reason why most countries have a 'standard-form' state-sponsored bankruptcy procedure.

A good bankruptcy procedure should provide an incentive to inefficient firms to shut down and at the same time provide an incentive to efficient firms to continue operations. In particular, as argued by Hart (1995), a good bankruptcy procedure should have the following goals:

1. It should achieve an *ex post* efficient outcome (that is, an outcome that maximizes the total value of the proceeds—measured in money terms—received by the existing claimants).
2. It should preserve the bonding role of debt by penalizing managers adequately in bankruptcy states. However, bankruptcy should not be so harsh that managers try and avoid it at all costs, e.g. by gambling with the company's assets.
3. It should preserve the absolute priority rule (APR), that is, the most senior creditors should be paid off before proceeding down the line to others of less seniority. Equity holders should come last in the APR.

While goal 1 is self-explanatory, goal 2 follows from the disciplinary role that debt plays in the case of a public limited company where there are too many small investors who cannot individually exercise control over the management. One important difference between a public limited company (run by an independent group of managers appointed by the board of directors of the company) and an owner-managed firm is that in the case of a public limited company, the goals of the managers may differ from those of the shareholders; in particular, as argued by Baumol (1959) and Marris (1964), managers may choose to overpay themselves and give themselves extravagant perks, or carry out unprofitable but power-enhancing investments. In such a case, the shareholders have an incentive to place debt in the firm's capital structure. The reason for this follows from the specific nature of the debt contract. In a debt contract, the agent borrows money from the investor and promises to make certain repayments. If he makes them, he retains control of the firm's assets. If he does not make them, control shifts to the investor. Therefore, the placement of debt in the firm's capital structure *forces* managers to curb their empire-building tendencies.[1] However, for debt to preserve its 'bonding role', managers must be penalized in bankruptcy (Goal 2).

Goal 3 is desirable for two reasons. Firstly, if the structure of debt priority that was agreed to contractually can always be violated within bankruptcy, then people would be unwilling to lend to the company in the first place, since their claims would be unprotected. Secondly, a discrepancy between entitlements inside and outside of bankruptcy can lead to inefficient rent-seeking in the form of one group of people bribing management to deliberately bring about bankruptcy and another group attempting to prevent it.

One point of contention in the bankruptcy literature has been goal 3. White (1989) has argued that a strict enforcement of this goal may lead

[1] For a more complete discussion of these issues, see Hart (1995, Ch. 6).

to inefficient decision-making outside of bankruptcy as managers have an incentive to gamble with the creditors' assets as they 'try desperately to avoid bankruptcy's draconian treatment of equity under the APR' (p. 149). If managers are given a choice of reorganization/rehabilitation over liquidation, they would prefer the former, given that by reorganizing, they are transferring income from creditors to equity. In addition, 'managers' personal interests strongly favour reorganization because existing management is usually retained in reorganizing, while in liquidation managers' jobs are eliminated' (Ibid, p. 147). This implies that managers of inefficient firms prefer reorganization even when they should be favouring the liquidation option as the logical one.

Clearly, an environment of allowing greater competitive activity would need streamlined legal and administrative procedures for exit. This has been recognized by the government but little has been done on this front. The quest for a suitable exit policy is now being undertaken. The comprehensive label of exit policy covers a set of policies regarding industrial decline, retrenchment, reconstruction of financially weak firms and liquidation of closed units (for a detailed discussion of the issues involved, see Saha, 1995).

There exist several legal barriers to exit. Some of the important ones are :

i) Industrial Disputes Act, 1947: according to Chapter V-B of this Act no large industrial unit is allowed to retrench workers or close down the firm without the permission of the central government.

ii) Urban Land (Ceiling and Regulation) Act, 1976: this legislation prevents firms from selling land without permission of the concerned state government. This permission has nearly always been denied by state governments and thus becomes a barrier to any restructuring or even formal exit of firms.

iii) The Sick Industrial Companies (Special Provisions) Act (SICA), 1985: this act was amended in 1992 and according to it a unit is said to be sick if (a) the unit has been registered under the Factories Act for five years, and (b) it has accumulated losses which are in excess of its net worth. The Act provided for the setting up of the Board for Industrial and Financial Reconstruction (BIFR). Any firm that becomes sick is required to make a reference (within sixty days of its audited accounts being published) to BIFR for determination of the measures to be adopted with reference to the said company. Till December 1991, public sector enterprises were outside the purview of the act. The reform package initiated in 1991 brought the public sector enterprises under the purview of this act too.

Once a reference is made to BIFR, it uses a consensus approach to approve a suggested rehabilitation package (which necessarily involves more loans being sanctioned to the sick unit), which needs to meet with the approval of all the parties concerned (management, trade unions, creditors and shareholders). In very few cases does the BIFR actually suggest the winding up (i.e. liquidation) of a company. All this entails an inordinate amount of time spent between a unit becoming sick and a rehabilitation package being adopted, or the unit being wound up. During this period (which may exceed five years) the unit stays in a state of 'suspended animation', i.e. production is stopped and workers and creditors are not paid.

The problem of industrial sickness is rather large (details are available in the Economic Survey of 1994–5 published by the Government of India). In September 1992, there were 1,599 large and medium sized units in the private sector which were declared sick, with an outstanding debt of Rs 6,805 crores. Sickness in the small-scale sector is also rampant with 233,441 units declared sick with an outstanding debt of Rs 3,346 crores. Thus a total sum of Rs 10,151 crores was outstanding from units in need of financial restructuring or closure. For all practical purposes these can be considered to be bad debts. In addition, 828 large and medium sized units in the private sector were declared weak (i.e. had a high probabilty of being declared sick in the future) with outstanding debts of Rs 2,436 crores. This amount can be considered as of doubtful debts. Thus the total of bad and doubtful debts outstanding to sick and weak units in the private sector was a whopping Rs 12,586 crores. In 1993–4, 120 public sector enterprises were declared sick. Details about oustanding debt are not available though the figure is expected to be rather high.

As indicated earlier BIFR rarely suggests winding up a sick unit. Even if winding up is recommended this is an extremely time-consuming and complicated process which could take as long as ten years. The winding up of a firm is guided by the Companies Act, 1956. Winding up operations are undertaken by the relevant High Courts. The High Court passes a winding up order and appoints an official liquidator, who is required to take physical custody of the firm and collect all financial records and prepare an account of available assets. With regard to the priority of claimants on the firms assets, Section 529A of the Companies Act states that payments of (a) workmen's dues and (b) debts due to secured creditors shall have priority over all other debts. The experience has been that given the phenomenal delays involved in each step of this process, very little can be realized from the sale of the sick unit. This implies that the controlling interests of the firm bear a very low cost of bankruptcy while the major claimants (workers and secured creditors) bear a high cost (Anant *et al.* 1992).

This inefficient functioning of the exit process with its large delays clearly has important implications on bankruptcy costs. The exit process thus is a very complicated and time consuming process in India. The impact on the financial sector is obvious. Loans made to sick units are difficult to recover. This has an adverse impact on the financial health of the institutions making loans to sick units.

Though no real reforms have been initiated in this context yet, an important first step in the reform of bankruptcy laws and exit procedures in India has been the submission of a report by a Committee (Goswami Committee) which was set up by the Government of India to study various aspects of industrial sickness and corporate restructuring (MOI 1993). Among several recommendations of the Committee, two that are relevant to our earlier discussion are:

i) The responsibility of industrial and corporate reorganization must shift from secured creditors and the state to the defaulting debtor firms.

ii) BIFR should make use of the winding up provisions of SICA more frequently so as to facilitate the sale of unviable units.

In the Indian context, one of the problems of the existing bankruptcy procedure has been the preference of the government to reorganize rather than liquidate an ailing firm. This has clearly led to the existence of far too many firms that should have been shut down in the first place. In a limited sense, the second recommendation cited above meets the goals of a good bankruptcy procedure outlined earlier. The first recommendation seems to be problematic in light of our earlier discussion, because it is important to have an independent authority take charge of the firm rather than the existing management, who might have an incentive not to opt for liquidation even when it is warranted. What is required is the streamlining of the process of liquidation so as to get rid of the delays involved in the current procedures.

Not many empirical studies are available which try to investigate the causes of industrial sickness. Anant *et al.* (1992) have attempted to diagnose the causes of sickness in the textile and engineering industries which were industries with the largest number of sick units. The most important conclusion arrived at was that, *citerus paribus,* higher fixed costs and higher debt equity ratios increased the probability of a firm becoming sick. This conclusion comes as no surprise as it is consistent with the received theories of financial distress of firms.

With regard to privatization, no real policy initiatives have been taken. The Government has disinvested a small part of its equity holding in some public sector enterprises but this has been done solely for revenue-raising purposes and the Government has no intention of privatizing these firms (Vaidya 1994). In 1990–1 the share of public sector enterprises in value added in the manufacturing sector stood at 32.76 per cent, the rest being contributed by the joint (7.34 per cent) and private sectors (59.9 per cent). Thus public sector enterprises still play a major role in the industrial sector. Though outright privatization is not on the policy agenda, various steps have been taken to make public sector enterprises more autonomous and to free them from governmental interference in their operations. Most importantly, a policy to introduce a system of signing a 'Memorandum of Understanding' with the respective managements has been initiated, which would provide managements with greater autonomy and also make them more accountable. Nevertheless, decisions on investments are still under the direct control of the government.

II. The Financing of Industry in India

The success or failure of financial liberalization would to a great extent depend on how firms in both the private and public sectors respond to the new financial environment. An extremely important consideration here is the ability of firms to cope with shocks (such as higher interest rates) which would arise in the process of financial liberalization. The sources by which firms raise funds and the ease with which they can substitute one source for another would clearly be an important determinant of the ability of firms to respond to such shocks without having to drastically change their investment plans. If due to financial liberalization, firms are forced to reduce investment, the economy could well slip into a minor or major recession depending on the extent of disruption caused. In Chapter 3 we have looked at the aggregate sources and uses of finance of the private non-financial sector. Here, we provide a more detailed examination of the sources and uses of funds for firms in the industrial sector, particularly in the years preceding and following the onset of reforms. Though not enough time has elapsed to arrive at any firm conclusions on these issues, on the basis of available data we attempt to identify the changes that have occurred between the late eighties and early nineties, in the way Indian firms have financed their investments. In our analysis of the financing of investment, we make a distinction between private and public sector firms since it can be argued that the reform process may have a differential impact on these two sets of firms.

In a comprehensive study of the patterns of corporate sector financing over the period 1970–85 in eight developed countries, using data from the national flow of funds statements and company accounts, Mayer (1990) arrived at three major conclusions:

i) In no country do securities markets contribute a large portion of corporate sector financing.

ii) In these countries retentions or internal finance was the most important source of funds.

iii) Of total external finance, bank loans were the most important.

Singh and Hamid (1992), in a study of nine developing countries over the decade of the eighties, using company accounts of the largest fifty companies quoted on the stock market of each country, report the following two important stylized facts (among others):

i) Firms in developing countries use external finance to a much greater extent than developed countries.

ii) The large corporations in these countries use more equity than debt to finance the growth of their net assets.

According to Singh and Hamid this difference between the developed and developing countries is likely to be due to factors like differences in institutional environments, tax regimes, and the degree of development of the capital market.

Our analysis is based on data from company accounts. The analysis of large private sector companies is based on a data set compiled by the Reserve Bank of India. The data set covers the period 1986–7 to 1992–3. It refers to a sample of private corporate firms with a paid-up capital of over one crore. The size of this sample increases marginally over the period. The firms in the sample account for well over 40 per cent of all non-financial firms in the private corporate sector in terms of paid-up capital. The data set pertaining to public sector enterprises refers to 200 large central government enterprises out of a total of 246. This data set covers the period 1986–7 to 1991–2. In case of both the sectors (i.e. private and public) we shall be referring to the sources and uses of funds statements derived from the consolidated balance sheets of the firms in the respective samples. The focus is thus on the flows of finance instead of stocks.

Let us consider the private corporate sector first. Tables 5.1, 5.2 and 5.3 present the pattern of financing, the uses of funds, and some financial ratios relating to the sample of firms, respectively.

Table 5.1

Sources of Funds of Large Non-Financial Enterprises in the Private Sector[a]

	1986–7	1987–8	1989–90	1990–1	1991–2	1992–3
No. of Firms	621	621	645	648	650	650
1) *Internal Sources/Retentions*	38.8	40.6	33.2	39.2	29.9	26.3
2) *External Sources*	61.2	59.4	66.8	60.8	70.1	73.7
a) Shares	3.3	7.3	7.3	10.4	7.8	22.9
b) Capital Receipts	0.3	0.4	0.2	0.2	0.2	0.1
c) Borrowings from Banks	11.0	4.7	8.8	8.0	9.0	10.8
d) Borrowings from Financial Institutions	9.4	9.4	8.4	12.9	14.6	15.4
e) Borrowings from Govt. and Semi Govt. Bodies	0.5	0.7	1.2	1.3	1.5	1.0
f) Borrowings from others	19.3	16.6	20.9	7.8	15.7	9.5
g) Trade and other Current Liabilities	17.4	20.2	19.9	18.9	21.3	14.0
h) Misc. Non Current Liabilities	neg.	neg.	0.2	neg.	neg.	neg.
Total	4,617	4,741	11,560	13,159	19,139	21,846

Note: [a] All figures in the table are percentages except the total which is in Rs Crores.
Source: RBI Bulletin, various issues.

Table 5.2

Uses of Funds of Large Non-Financial Enterprises in the Private Sector[a]

	1986–7	1987–8	1989–90	1990–1	1991–2	1992–3
No. of Firms	621	621	645	648	650	650
1) Gross Fixed Assets	57.8	54.5	37.9	54.6	49.6	54.0
a) Land and Buildings	7.6	6.5	3.1	5.6	3.7	4.9
b) Plant and Machinery	44.8	33.7	31.2	33.3	28.5	47.9
c) Capital Work in Progress	2.6	10.0	2.0	13.1	14.7	neg.
d) Others	2.8	4.2	1.6	2.6	2.6	2.2
2) Inventories	13.7	14.0	19.1	18.4	14.6	16.4
a) Raw Materials	2.3	5.1	6.5	6.4	2.7	2.2
b) Finished Goods	4.1	2.4	5.1	4.3	6.0	8.1
c) Work in Progress	4.2	4.7	4.4	4.4	4.3	2.7
d) Stores, spares and others	3.2	1.7	3.1	3.3	1.6	3.3
3) Loans, Advances and other Debtors	24.8	23.5	23.7	21.7	28.0	23.6
4) Investments	4.9	4.3	16.1	2.4	3.1	neg.
5) Other Assets	neg.	neg.	neg.	neg.	1.0	1.1
6) Cash and Bank Balances	– 2.0	3.4	3.2	2.4	3.6	4.3
Total	4,617	4,741	11,560	13,159	19,139	21,846

Note: [a] All figures in the table are percentages except the total which is in Rs Crores.
Source: RBI Bulletin, various issues.

Table 5.3

Financial Ratios of Large Non-Financial Enterprises in the Private Sector[a]

	1986–7	1987–8	1989–90	1990–1	1991–2	1992–3
No. of Firms	621	621	645	648	650	650
Current Assets to Current Liabilities	1.3	1.3	1.29	1.35	1.35	1.39
Gross Profit to Total Net Assets (%)	8.9	8.3	10.9	11.1	10.9	9.4
Gross Profit to Sales (%)	9.2	8.6	10.1	12.5	12.8	11.8
Debt to Equity (%)	80.3	83.5	91.8	99.4	101.6	94.3

Note: [a] Debt comprises (1) all borrowings from government and semi-government Financial Institutions other than banks and other institutional agencies, (2) borrowings from banks and other borrowings. Equity comprises paid-up capital and all reserves.

Source: RBI Bulletin, various issues.

The following important observations emerge from Table 5.1:

1) Internal sources have not been the dominant source of finance over the period. In fact, generally speaking, the importance of this source has been decreasing and the decrease has been rather dramatic after 1990–1, the year in which financial sector reforms were initiated.

2) Borrowings from banks, which are predominantly in the nature of short-term credit, have generally accounted for 8 per cent to 11 per cent of the total except for the year 1987–8. After 1990–1 this share has risen marginally.

3) Borrowings from financial institutions (both Indian and foreign) are generally in the nature of term loans. Their share has been rising and stood at 15.4 per cent in 1992–3.

4) The share of borrowings from others (which include debentures, inter-corporate loans and deposits from the public) has varied a great deal over the years. It has ranged between 7.8 per cent and 19.3 per cent.

5) Trade credit and other current liabilities has always been an important source of finance.

6) The importance of shares as a source of finance has increased over the years with a dramatic rise from 7.8 per cent in 1991–2 to 22.9 per cent in 1992–3.

Turning to the uses of funds of the private corporate sector (presented in Table 5.2), the following conclusions emerge:

1) Funds available to this sector have generally been rising.

2) The share of funds used to finance investment in fixed assets fell sharply during 1991–2. The fall in 1991–2 can be attributed to the sharp rise in term-lending rates following the interest rate deregulation initiated in August 1990. The turnaround was rather quick because in 1992–3 this share rose sharply from 49.6 per cent in 1990–1 to 54.0 per cent.

3) The most important component of gross fixed assets is investment in plant and machinery. The share of funds used to finance investments in plant and machinery also fell sharply in 1990–1 to 28.5 per cent and rose significantly in 1992–3 to 47.9 per cent, a level far above that witnessed in this period.

4) Investment in inventories ranged between 13 per cent and 19.1 per cent over the period. Financial investments have declined sharply after a peak of 16.1 per cent in 1989–90.

5) The share of cash and bank balances has been in the range of 2 per cent to 4.3 per cent over the period.

The profitability ratios (as they are gross of interest payments they would essentially be influenced by developments in the product markets) presented in Table 5.3, suggest that there were no dramatic changes in the product markets as the ratios are fairy stable. The ratio of current assets to current liabilities too has been stable over the period. The debt to equity ratio rose till 1991–2 after which it dropped in 1992–3 due to greater recourse to shares.

Clearly, the most striking feature has been the dramatic rise in funds channelled through the stock market. Between 1991–2 and 1992–3 there has been a shift from internal sources, borrowings from others, and trade and other current liabilities in favour of shares. This has been possible because of the presence of fairly well-developed stock markets. It is interesting to note that the sharp rise in the share of fixed assets and especially share of plant and machinery has coincided with the substantial increase in the importance of equity shares in the sources of funds. Financial liberalization thus, has not led to a major disruption in investment activity of the private corporate sector. This ability to respond to shocks generated by interest rate deregulation was a consequence of far reaching changes in the primary issues market which opened up a new source of funds. Moreover, the real sector reforms, especially the reduction of legal barriers to entry, opened up new investment opportunities which could be taken advantage of even in the presence of high interest rates.

In an influential paper, Singh (1992) had argued, for reasons which have been discussed in detail in Chapter 3, that '..an important general policy principle for least developed countries should be to attempt to insulate as far as possible the real industrial economy from the influence of the stock market' (p. 44). The data presented suggests that all the negative influences of the stock markets listed by Singh notwithstanding, one great advantage that fairly developed stock markets provide, is the possibility of raising funds through it, when as a result of financial liberalization, other sources have either dried up or are more expensive. Clearly the presence of a fairly well-developed stock market has helped firms to respond rather quickly to shocks brought about by financial liberalization. Moreover, the fall in the debt to equity ratio suggests that firms would in all probability now be in a position to face further increases in the interest rate which future reforms may entail. All the positive features of debt notwithstanding, the higher the debt to equity ratio the lower will be the ability of firms to face the consequences of a higher interest rate.

We present in Table 5.4 some general information concerning public sector enterprises owned by the Central Government. In Table 5.5 the sources of funds of 200 public sector enterprises are presented. This data is available only upto 1991–2. The following observations emerge:

1) The number of loss-making enterprises has risen over the years.

2) The percentage of gross profit to capital employed has been stable. This is likely to be slightly misleading as those enterprises operating in monopolized sectors like petroleum and power are extremely profitable while those in other sectors are much less profitable.

3) The share of budgetary support in total planned investment has dramatically fallen over the years. This is due to the policy followed by the government of steadily reducing budgetary support to these enterprises.

4) Internal sources/retentions have decreased in importance over the years. This again is likely to be more a reflection of poor financial performance of these enterprises rather than a decision on the part of respective managements to depend more on external sources.

5) The importance of shares has been pretty significant, though over the years it has decreased. This source does not refer to funds channelled through the stock market as budgetary support to these enterprises is in many cases routed through an increase in the government's shareholding. However in 1993–4 and 1994–5 some enterprises did raise capital through the stock market.

6) Borrowings as a source of funds has become extremely important especially in 1991–2 with foreign borrowings recording a large increase and borrowings from financial institutions, banks and mutual funds also growing substantially in importance. A part of this borrowing is in the form of public sector bonds which are tax free and a part is in the form of loans. Borrowings from the central government which represent budgetary assistance have decreased dramatically though it rose between 1990–1 and 1991–2.

7) The amount of money raised by these enterprises has fallen after 1989–90 and stagnated thereafter.

Turning to the uses of funds by central government public enterprises (presented in Table 5.6), we see that the percentage of funds invested in fixed assets has risen since 1989–90, but as noted earlier the total amount of funds available to them has declined.

Table 5.4

Profile of Public Sector Enterprises Owned by the Central Government

	1989–90	1990–1	1991–2	1992–3	1993–4
No. of Operating Enterprises	233	236	237	239	240
No. of Loss making enterprises	98	111	102	106	117
Gross Profit to Capital Employed (%)	12.53	10.88	11.59	11.39	11.57
Percentage of Budgetary Support to Total Plan Investment	31.7	24.7	19.1	14.0	14.1

Source: Public Enterprise Survey, Government of India, various issues.

Table 5.5

Sources of Funds of Central Public Sector Enterprises[a]

	1987–8	1988–9	1989–90	1990–1	1991–2
1) Internal Sources/Retentions	41.7	32.7	31.8	29.8	25.0
2) *External Sources*	58.3	67.3	68.2	70.2	75.0
a) Shares:	12.9	21.1	14.6	15.7	10.7
i) Central Govt.	12.8	20.7	14.5	15.4	7.0
ii) State Govt.	neg.	neg.	0.1	0.2	0.3
iii) Foreign Participation	neg.	0.2	neg.	neg.	neg.
iv) Financial Institutions, Banks, Mutual Funds	neg.	neg.	neg.	0.1	3.4
v) Private Participation, Employees	neg.	0.1	neg.	neg.	neg.
b) Borrowings:	51.3	45.2	32.5	38.0	76.8
i) Central Govt.	25.0	4.5	6.0	3.4	9.0
ii) State Govt.	neg.	neg.	neg.	neg.	neg.
iii) Foreign Loans	8.1	17.4	6.9	13.2	40.7
iv) Financial Institutions, Banks, Mutual Funds	2.3	3.7	8.9	–4.4	21.2
v) Others	15.9	19.7	10.7	25.7	6.0
c) Cash Credit	–5.9	1.0	20.9	16.4	–12.5
Total	15,092	21,749	29,102	25,910	25,858

Note: [a] All figures in the table are percentages except the total which is in Rs Crores.

Source: Key financial Data on Central Government Enterprises, Economic Intelligence Service, Centre For Monitoring the Indian Economy, Mumbai, May 1993.

Table 5.6
Uses of Funds of Central Public Sector Enterprises[a]

	1987–8	1988–9	1989–90	1990–1	1991–2
Gross Block	77.4	51.4	51.6	65.2	73.2
Capital Work in Progress	16.2	14.8	6.2	–2.1	21.8
Working Capital	–6.7	20.2	28.8	23.0	17.5
Investments	13.1	13.5	13.4	14.1	–12.5
Total	15,092	21,749	29,102	25,910	25,858

Note: [a] All figures in the table are percentages except the total which is in Rs Crores.

Source: Key financial Data on Central Government Enterprises, Economic Intelligence Service, Centre For Monitoring the Indian Economy, Mumbai, May 1993.

It should be noted that of the amount of resources raised by these enterprises an insignificant portion is routed through the stock markets. This trend of course is slowly being reversed by the hard budget constraint placed on them. The enterprises have responded to financial liberalization by slowing down investments and increasing borrowings. They however, enjoy a privileged position as both the government and RBI advise public sector banks to provide preferential treatment to them in the allocation of credit (Gupta 1988). There is no doubt that as liberalization proceeds this privileged position will be eroded. The government, rightfully, is not taking any hasty steps in this direction because many of these enterprises are not in a position to raise resources from the market. No hard measures in this matter are advisable before a comprehensive policy of restructuring these enterprises is announced. We have had occasion to point out earlier that privatization is not on the government's agenda and strict controls on the investments of these enterprises still remain.

A Bank-Based or Equity-Based System ?

Recent developments in the theory of corporate finance have highlighted the advantages and disadvantages of bank-based and equity-based financial systems in the funding of industry. As Mayer has argued,

> *Prima facie* banking systems would be expected to avoid some of the information deficiencies associated with securities markets. A primary rationale for the existence of banks is that they perform screening and monitoring

> functions that individual investors can only undertake at high cost. Resource allocation, credit availability, and terms of loans may all, therefore, be superior under a bank-based than a market financial system. On the other hand, transactions costs may be lower in the absence of intermediation, and taxation may militate in favour of market-based sources of capital (1990, p. 308).

From the findings of Singh and Hamid (1992) and from our own findings, it appears that external sources of funds (shares, borrowings and trade credit) are the dominant source for developing countries (including India) in sharp contrast to the reality in the developed countries (see Mayer 1990). Thus, the issue of the relative superiority/inferiority of debt versus equity gains is of overwhelming importance in the Indian context. One peculiar feature of the Indian financial system which we have noted at several points in our study is the importance of the developmental finance institutions in the intermediation of funds to industry. Developmental financial institutions such as IDBI and ICICI have traditionally subscribed to the equity of firms, as well as, gave direct loans to them. An interesting feature of the Japanese financial system that Hoshi, Kashyap and Scharfstein (1991) have drawn attention to is the ownership by banks of the equity of firms to whom they lend. These close ties between the banks and firms have, according to the authors, led to a reduction in the cost of capital of such firms. Since banks own a large equity share of these firms and lend considerable capital,

> they have strong incentives to get around the information and incentive problems typically associated with arm's-length capital market transactions... Moreover, because banks are both shareholders and debtholders, firms have less incentive to take action that benefit one class of investors at the expense of another (p. 38).

It can be argued then, that in the Indian context, development finance institutions have a role to play (similar to banks in the oft-discussed Japanese case) in the monitoring and screening of firms. This is particularly relevant in a liberalized environment with the elimination of industrial licensing which, as we have argued in the previous section, in effect acted as a screening mechanism. A reassuring feature of the nature of financial assistance provided by the development financial institutions to firms is that the structure of incentives that motivate the development financial institutions to perform these functions efficiently is in place. The importance of this feature in the evolution of the financial system should not be underestimated. In our view, the debate on the superiority or inferiority of a bank-based versus equity-based system is of limited significance in the light of our discussion on the special role of the development finance institution in the monitoring and screening of firms in India.

III. The Financing of Agriculture in India

While we know that problems of asymmetric information and contract enforcement are characteristic of credit markets, it has been argued by Caprio and Summers (1993) and Besley (1994) among others, that they are particularly severe in the rural credit markets in the developing countries. Besley (1994) identifies two features that make rural credit markets different from other credit markets. Firstly, as Stiglitz and Weiss (1983) have argued, collateral acts as a screening device to separate the good borrowers from the bad. Typically, rural borrowers are not endowed with assets that could act as collateral. Also, with poorly developed property rights in land, appropriating collateral in the event of default is almost impossible. This discourages financial intermediaries from lending to farmers. Secondly, a special feature of agriculture in less developed economies is the risk of income shocks. These shocks (weather shocks being particularly important in India) can lead to a generalized default over a geographical area. This risk is not diversifiable by a financial intermediary whose area of operation is geographically restricted. As a consequence, we may observe, both financial distress among financial intermediaries operating in geographically restricted areas, and 'a failure of funds to flow across regions or groups of individuals even though there are potential gains to do so, as when the needs for credit differ across locations' (Besley 1994, p. 32). The severe enforcement and informational problems in rural credit markets imply that such markets are particularly susceptible to market failure and this provides a strong rationale for government intervention.

Since independence (and especially after the nationalization of banks in 1969) RBI has through active policy initiatives built up an elaborate mechanism for the disbursement of agricultural credit. The approach that has been followed is the setting up of a multi-agency and multi-tiered system. At the bottom of the tier are three sets of institutions, i.e. the co-operative banks, commercial banks, and regional rural banks (RRB).

In the post-nationalization period, the prime role in the provision of rural finance is supposed to be played by the co-operative credit system. According to Gupta (1988), the main reasons for this are as follows:

i) The co-operative banks are best suited to the socio-economic conditions of the Indian villages.

ii) The existence of a vast network of such banks throughout the country.
iii) Intimate knowledge of the local conditions and problems.

The co-operative system consists of Primary Agricultural Credit Societies (PACS), Primary Co-operative Banks (PCB) and Land Development Banks (LDB). PACS are specialized rural credit institutions based in individual villages or groups of villages. They have the most developed network with nearly 95,000 societies and are present in nearly all the villages. The PACS mobilize little resources of their own and their credit outstanding exceeds their deposit mobilization by a factor of 10. Instead they borrow from central and state PCBs which together have nearly 9,000 urban and semi-urban branches, where they mobilize deposits. The state PCBs in turn borrow or are refinanced from NABARD. LDBs are co-operative institutions that lend for long-term purposes. The state LDBs raise resources by issuing debentures to the Government of India, NABARD and various other financial intermediaries. In 1992–3, there were 83 PACSs, 1,399 PCBs and 19 LDBs.

In the case of commercial banks, as we have discussed in Chapter 3, priority sector lending requirements make it mandatory for them to lend to the agricultural sector. Also, as pointed out earlier, commercial banks have significantly extended their credit allocation to this sector.

RRBs are the most recent additions to the rural credit system. These banks were formed in 1976 following the recommendations of a working group set up by the government, which identified the various weaknesses of the co-operative banks and commercial banks and came to the conclusion that they may not be able to fill the regional functional needs in the rural credit system. Therefore, it was recommended that a new type of institution that combined the rural touch and experience of co-operatives with the modernized outlook and deposit mobilization capacity of commercial banks be established. In September 1993, there were 196 RRBs with 14,546 branches covering 405 districts in the country.

In Table 5.7 we present the shares of direct institutional finance to the agricultural sector of the above-mentioned institutions. The co-operatives are the most important followed by commercial banks and RRBs. After 1991–2, there seems to be a small shift in shares in favour of co-operative banks and against commercial banks. Financial liberalization does not seem to have had as yet a significant impact on the institutional mechanism of rural credit.

Table 5.7

Direct Institutional Finance for Agriculture and Allied Activities (loans issued during the year)[a]

	1988–9	1989–90	1990–1	1991–2	1992–3	1993–4
1) Co-operatives	51.7	50.9	47.3	50.3	56.8	56.1
2) State Governments	2.9	2.7	3.5	2.9	2.8	2.5
3) Commercial Banks	40.4	40.3	46.0	41.6	35.4	35.7
4) Regional Rural Banks	5.0	6.1	3.2	5.2	5.0	5.9
Total	9,428.3	10,628.2	10,187.7	11,540.3	14,002.4	15,115.2
a) Short-term loans	62.5	61.1	61.2	64.2	68.8	64.4
b) Long-term loans	37.5	38.9	38.9	35.8	32.2	35.6

Note: [a] Figures are in percentages except for the total which is in Rs Crores.

Source: Report on Currency and Finance, RBI, various issues.

Prior to 1982 the role of overseeing and developing the rural credit system was vested with the RBI. In July 1982, RBI established the National Bank for Agricultural and Rural Development (NABARD) to which it transferred the responsibility for rural credit. The primary function of NABARD is to provide refinancing and make loans and advances to the co-operative banks, RRBs and commercial banks for financing production, marketing and investment activities related to agriculture and allied sectors. It also performs the role of supervising and inspecting co-operative banks and the RRBs.

We present in Table 5.8 the structure of liabilities of NABARD. The following conclusions emerge.

Table 5.8

Liabilities of NABARD[a]

	1980–1	1989–90	1990–1	1991–2	1992–3	1993–4	1994–5
Capital and Reserves	6.9	4.2	4.4	4.7	4.8	5.7	8.7
NRC Fund	21.2	47.7	50.7	50.9	50.4	54.3	48.8
Borrowings from Govt.	50.9	16.3	13.6	11.0	9.3	8.2	6.8
General Line of Credit and Borrowings from RBI	nil.	25.0	24.2	25.7	26.7	23.4	25.9
Market Borrowings	18.5	4.6	5.0	5.0	5.3	5.8	5.6
Others	2.5	2.2	2.1	2.7	3.5	2.6	4.2
Total	1,728	11,846	12,751	14,572	15,787	15,694	17,991
Percentage of Refinance in Total assets	92.0	75.3	71.0	71.0	73.0	79.0	80.5

Note: [a] Figures are in percentages except for the total which is in Rs Crores. The figure for refinance in row no. 9 includes refinance for short-, medium- and long-term loans.

Source: Report on Currency and Finance, RBI, various issues.

i) The main sources of funds are the two National Rural Credit (NRC) Funds which were set up by RBI in 1956 and transferred to NABARD at the time of its establishment, and borrowings from the RBI. The NRC funds have grown over time through contributions of both NABARD and the RBI from their profits. The importance of NRC funds has increased steadily over time and they constituted 48.8 per cent of total liabilities in 1994–5. The importance of borrowings from the RBI has remained more or less stable at about 25 per cent of total liabilities. Thus RBI is an extremely important source of funds to NABARD.

ii) There has been a dramatic decline in borrowings from the Government of India from 50.9 per cent in 1980–1 to 6.8 per cent in 1994–5. This is similar to our findings about the structure of liabilities of development finance institutions. Subsidized credit from government has in general declined across the board for most publicly owned financial institutions.

iii) The small contribution of market borrowings to total liabilities indicate that NABARD has not been forced to tap expensive market sources for funds. It continues to have access to cheap funds from the RBI.

The interest rate deregulation which has been outlined (in the discussion regarding the credit market) has encompassed short-term loans to the agricultural sector. In the process of deregulation of short-term interest rates the agricultural sector was not given preferential treatment. The only benefit provided was indirect because in the smaller slabs which had lower rates of interest (see Table 3.33) the largest number of borrowers were likely to be small farmers. As regards deregulation of the interest rate on long-term loans for the agricultural sector there were distinct attempts to protect the small borrowers from large increases in the interest rate. The interest rate in the highest slab (i.e. above Rs 2 lakhs) was completely deregulated in 1991 with a prescribed minimum lending rate of 15 per cent. Since October 1994, the interest rate on term loans less than Rs 2 lakhs continues to be regulated. Loans less than Rs 25,000 have an interest rate of 12 per cent and loans between Rs 25,000 and Rs 2 lakhs have an interest rate of 14 per cent.

The 'market failure' arguments that we have outlined earlier may justify policy interventions like priority sector lending requirements for commercial banks. Therefore, this policy has an increased relevance in an environment of deregulated interest rates; that is to say, agriculturists may get 'squeezed out' of the market as banks may not be willing to lend to them at *any* interest rate in the absence of such lending requirements. Even though strong reasons exist to retain directed credit programmes to the agricultural sector, the nature of government intervention in the past (e.g. *ad hoc* loan waivers, political interference in the loan allocation process, etc.) may have prevented banks from making loans on sound commercial principles. As a result, overdues (i.e. loans and interest thereon not repaid on due dates) have become an all-pervasive phenomenon in the agricultural credit system (Khusro Committee, RBI 1990).[2]

Given the various problems associated with the operation of the directed credit programmes in India, a possible alternative to them is the creation of institutional mechanisms that can circumvent the problems of asymmetric information and contract enforcement in rural credit markets. Two successful examples of this are group-lending mechanisms in Costa Rica (Wenner 1995), and the use of local agents in rural financial intermediation as in Indonesia (Chaves and Gonzalez-Vega 1996). In the Indian context a renewed emphasis on the co-operative credit system may possibly be successful. While the co-operative credit system has weaknesses in its current stucture and workings, a re-organization of the system along the lines of the Khusro Committee recommendations (RBI, 1990)[3] may be the desired strategy.

IV. Concluding Remarks

One striking feature of the reforms has been the relatively small disruption in production activities in the real sector. This could be in part due to a slow transition to a deregulated environment in both the real and financial sectors. Another important reason why the reforms may not have led to substantial disruption in the industrial sector is that the developments in financial markets allowed firms to substitute relatively easily between different sources of finance. Also, deregulation did not imply a large and persistent contraction of credit to the agricultural sector, thus avoiding a dislocation of agricultural activities on this count. However, both the speed and success of future financial deregulation is going to be constrained by the absence of any real attempts to reform exit and bankruptcy procedures and the public sector enterprises.

[2] For a further discussion of the Indian experience with directed credit programmes in agriculture, see Joshi and Little 1996.

[3] The Khusro Committee report which reviews the functioning of the agricultural credit system in India is an extremely large and comprehensive document and thus a detailed discussion of its recommendations is outside the scope of this study.

6

The Macroeconomic Environment

A stable macroeconomic environment is a prerequisite for successful financial liberalization. The failed liberalizations of the Southern Cone countries (in particular, Argentina, Chile and Uruguay) in the 1970s can be explained in great part by the unstable macroeconomic environment that prevailed in these countries at the time of the liberalization process (McKinnon 1993). In contrast, the success of Korea and Taiwan in reforming their financial sectors can be attributed to the efforts of the policy makers to stabilize the price level and bring about fiscal discipline before liberalizing financial markets (Caprio *et al.* 1994). If the economy is making a transition to market-determined interest rates in the absence of price-level stability, overshooting of the real interest rate above its 'equilibrium' level is a distinct possibility (as is evident from the experiences of the Southern Cone economies, see McKinnon 1993). This can greatly increase the probability of bankruptcies and consequently, bank failures. In this context, a large fiscal deficit financed by domestic borrowing may well make matters worse by putting a further upward pressure on the real interest rate.

The relationship between the macroeconomic environment and financial liberalization is by no means unidirectional; while price-level stability and fiscal discipline are essential preconditions to financial sector reform, the process of financial liberalization itself can lead to further macroeconomic instability. For example, a move to market-determined interest rates in the government bond market in the presence of large fiscal imbalances can lead to an unsustainable growth in public debt in a situation where the real interest rate on government borrowing exceeds the growth rate of the economy. Financial liberalization measures such as the easing of restrictions on foreign capital inflow and bank lending to households and interest rate deregulation can also lead to other undesirable macroeconomic consequences such as an increase in the inflation rate and a decline in private saving and investment rates. Therefore, while financial liberalization undertaken in the context of macroeconomic instability has a high possibility of failure, the process of financial liberalization can itself make an already fragile macroeconomic environment far worse.

In this chapter, we analyse the inter-relationship between the macroeconomic environment and financial liberalization in the context of India's financial sector reforms of the early 1990s. We first provide an overview of the conceptual issues involved. We then trace the evolution of the macroeconomic environment since the beginning of the reform process in 1991. We note that after an initial success in stabilizing the economy in 1991–2, there were signs of a return in macroeconomic instability, as evident by increases in the inflation rate and fiscal deficit to GDP ratio in 1993–4. Further, there had been a significant fall in the gross domestic saving and investment rates in the first three years of the post-reform period. Finally, we examine to what extent the worsening of certain macroeconomic indicators in recent years can be attributed, to the financial liberalization process.

I. The Macroeconomic Environment and Financial Liberalization

Why is macroeconomic stability essential for the success of the financial sector reform? This question can be answered by re-considering the Stiglitz–Weiss (S–W) framework of informational asymmetry in credit markets as discussed in Chapter 1. The S–W model argues that given the 'moral hazard' involved and the adverse selection problems inherent in capital markets, banks often voluntarily limit the increase in the interest rate charged to any one class of borrowers in order to maximize the expected profits. This endogenous credit rationing by banks reduces the possibility of loan defaults since by this mechanism, high-risk (but high-return) borrowers get rationed out. However, as McKinnon (1993) argues, in the context of macro-economic instability, there is no reason to expect that this natural check on adverse selection will necessarily hold. Assuming macroeconomic instability to imply a) higher variance in returns on projects being considered by borrowers, and b) a positive covariance among the expected returns on projects within any one risk class, a higher degree of macroeconomic instability will imply even greater credit rationing by banks. Now with greater variance in bank returns, the (expected) profit maximizing loan rate will decline (assuming risk-averse behaviour on the part of banks). Furthermore, with positive covariances in borrower returns (i.e. the presence of systemic risk), macroeconomic instability means that banks cannot diversify away some of the risks that they face. Again, to guard against unexpected losses, the risk-averse bank will further ration credit.

The above discussion suggests that while macroeconomic instability may lead to more severe credit rationing in the system and consequently, reduce the efficacy of the financial liberalization measures, it may not lead to any serious disruption of the financial intermediation process. However, implicit in the above argument is the assumption that there is no 'moral hazard' problem in the banking system. Once we allow for the presence of deposit insurance, 'moral hazard' on the part of banks is a distinct possibility. Therefore, a bank may be tempted to undertake very risky lending at very high real loan rates on the presumption that favourable outcomes will lead to large profits for its shareholders but unfavourable outcomes that lead to large losses will be borne by the monetary authority. As McKinnon notes,

> When the macroeconomy is stable, a completely diversified bank will be unaffected by such moral hazard because the default rates among the 'large' number of nonbank borrowers are not positively correlated... However, in the presence of macroeconomic instability, which inevitably creates positive covariance in the default rates of the bank's borrowers, moral hazard on the part of the bank itself becomes a very serious problem (p. 90).

As we have argued in Chapter 4, most governments are often impelled to provide deposit insurance—whether explicit or implicit. Clearly then, financial liberalization in the presence of macroeconomic instability is a high-risk venture as it can lead to large-scale bank failures and costly government bail-outs of the failed banks.

How does the process of financial liberalization itself lead to further macroeconomic instability? There are three avenues by which this can happen. Firstly, take the relaxation of controls on foreign capital inflows. The effect that foreign capital inflows may have on the macroeconomic environment and the domestic financial system is best understood by considering the balance of payments indentity:

$$CA + KA + RA \equiv 0,$$

where CA is the current account surplus, KA is the capital account surplus or net capital inflow, and RA is the official reserves account of the balance of payments (if RA is negative, it implies accumulation of reserves by the monetary authorities). Now consider an increase in net private capital inflows. If the central bank does not intervene, then the increase in capital inflow will lead to an increase in domestic absorption. If part of the increased spending is on non-tradable goods, this will in turn lead to a real exchange rate appreciation and consequently, a higher current account deficit. Since a current deficit is equal to the difference between national investment and national savings, in such an instance the foreign capital inflow can be considered to be financing either an increase in investment or in consumption (leading to a fall in savings) or a combination of both. Therefore, in the case of non-intervention by the government, an increase in capital inflows lead to an increase in the current account deficits and are not associated with changes in central banks' holdings of official reserves.

However, in practice, governments in most developing countries do intervene heavily in foreign exchange markets. This is because a real appreciation distorts resource allocation and seriously weakens a country's medium-term objective of increasing its exports. If, in fact, the central bank does intervene and purchase the foreign exchange brought in by the capital inflow, the increase in *KA* is matched, one-to-one, with an increase in official reserves *(RA)* but with no increase in the current account deficit (and hence, in the investment-savings gap).

Central bank intervention in the foreign exchange market can be in two forms. In sterilized interventions, the central bank sells government bonds in exchange for foreign currency (or increases the reserve required ratio) and therefore, insulates the stock of domestic money from variations associated with capital mobility. There are three main difficulties with sterilized interventions. Firstly, sterilization leads to an increase in the differential between the interest rate on domestic government debt and international reserves, thus creating a quasi-fiscal deficit. Secondly, since sterilization may increase the domestic interest rate, it may increase the domestic–foreign interest differential and attract further capital inflows, thereby exacerbating the problem. Thirdly, given the underdeveloped nature of the T bill market in most developing countries, complete sterilization is often not possible.[1]

An alternate way in which the central bank may intervene is by purchasing the foreign exchange brought in by the capital inflow for domestic money. This policy helps avoid nominal exchange rate appreciation but at the cost of the expansion of the monetary base and domestic credit. With the excess liquidity brought into the economy by the foreign capital inflows, this may eventually lead to an increase in the price level and consequently, a real appreciation of the exchange rate. This in turn may well lead to a loss of confidence on the part of

[1] For a further discussion of these issues, see Folkerts-Landau *et al.* (1994); Calvo *et al.* (1995).

economic agents in the capacity of the monetary authorities to maintain a stable nominal exchange rate and precipitate a sudden fall in the external value of the currency along with a reversal of the capital inflow.

A second way in which financial liberalization can affect the macroeconomic environment is by the impact of the market-determination of interest rates on the fiscal deficit. With the market-determination of interest rates in the government securities market, the average interest cost of government borrowing will usually increase (since prior to deregulation, the interest rate on government securities is kept deliberately low). This can lead to a sharp increase in interest payments (and consequently, the government's current expenditures) and make it even more difficult for the government to control the fiscal deficit. In the context of a high initial primary deficit (i.e. the fiscal deficit net of interest payments), the increase in the real interest rate may lead to an unsustainable growth in public debt, particularly in a situation where the real interest rate on government borrowing exceeds the growth rate of real GDP (see Buiter 1983, 1985). Furthermore, if the primary deficit is initially high and mostly financed by domestic borrowing, this will put further upward pressure on the real interest rate.

The above discussion implies that a move to market-determined interest rates on government debt can further worsen the macroeconomic environment, particularly in a situation where the real interest rate exceeds the GDP growth rate. In such a case, bond-financing of the deficit may eventually lead to a monetization of the deficit, when further government borrowing is not possible once the public debt grows to an unsustainable level (Sargent and Wallace 1981). Furthermore, the longer the government postpones the monetization, the higher will be the inflation rate in the long run.[2] Therefore, as Joshi and Little (1994) argue, 'financial liberalization cannot itself solve the problem of growing fiscal deficits, and if deficits are not contained then financial liberalization may well exacerbate the fiscal problem' (p. 256).

A third manner in which financial sector reform can have a negative impact on the macroeconomy is by causing a fall in private savings and investment rates. First consider the saving rate. The lifecycle model of saving states, that individuals smoothen their consumption profile over their lifetimes, borrowing from capital markets when they are young

[2] Studies that have examined the link between public debt and inflation in the Indian context are Rangarajan *et al.* (1989); Bhattacharya (1992); Buiter and Patel (1992, 1993).

and drawing down their savings when they are old (Modigliani and Brumberg 1954). In a financially repressed regime, individuals have limited access to financial intermediaries and consequently, are unable to borrow. As a result, consumers are unable to finance their desired level of consumption when young, with their level of consumption being defined by their level of endowment.

By increasing competition between the providers of financial intermediation, financial liberalization can eliminate the constraint on going into debt. This has a permanent effect on consumption as there is a switch from a partially-constrained consumption path to an unconstrained one (Bayoumi 1993). Consequently, there is an one-time decline in the private saving rate in the economy. As Jappelli and Pagano (1991) show, financial deregulation can account for a significant proportion of the decline in the national saving rate in the 1980s in several OECD countries. With a lower amount of investible funds available to firms, the decline in the saving rate may itself cause a fall in the private investment rate. Moreover, with interest rate deregulation, a sharp rise in the bank lending rate will *ceteris paribus* lead to an increase in the rental cost of capital. This may further depress private investment (Warman and Thirwall 1994).[3]

II. The Evolution of the Macroeconomic Environment, 1991–2 to 1994–5

In the summer of 1991, India was in the middle of a severe balance of payments crisis, with foreign exchange reserves that covered less than two weeks of imports. The immediate cause of the crisis was the increase in world oil prices and the drop in remittances of migrant workers in the Gulf following the annexation of Kuwait in September 1990. The foreign exchange crisis was exacerbated by the drying-up of commercial loans and the outflow of foreign currency non-resident (FCNR) deposits as there was an expectation of default on the part of the Indian government on its external commitments. However, the roots of the crisis were more long-term in nature and lay in the increasing deficits at all levels of government and in particular, in the central government's own deficit. The fiscal deficit to GDP ratio increased steadily over the eighties reaching a peak of 8.3 per cent in 1990–1. The fiscal imbalance spilled over to the external sector with the current

[3] It should be kept in mind that if the financial sector reforms encompass an increase in the real bank deposit rate which has a positive effect on savings, the net effect of financial liberalization on domestic savings and investment is ambiguous.

account deficit to GDP ratio standing at 3.2 per cent in 1990–1. Also, with fiscal deficits being increasingly monetized, the inflation rate increased fairly steadily in this period to about a high of 14 per cent in 1991–2. At the same time, the eighties were a period of strong growth for the Indian economy with real GDP growth rates averaging over 5 per cent. This was mostly the result of a high rate of growth of manufacturing output. We provide a summary of the salient features of the macroeconomic environment in Table 6.1 (for details of the macro-economic crisis and its aftermath, see Agarwal *et al.* 1995).

Table 6.1
Selected Macroeconomic Indicators, 1981–2 to 1994–5

	1981–2 to 1985–6	1986–7 to 1990–1	1991–2	1992–3	1993–4	1994–5
Output and Prices Growth Rates of:						
GDP	5.0	6.3	0.8	5.1	5.0	6.3
GDP, Agriculture	2.7	4.6	–2.6	6.6	3.4	5.1
GDP, Manufacturing	8.1	7.2	–3.7	4.1	4.3	9.0
GDP, Finance[a]	6.1	7.6	10.5	3.0	8.5	4.3
Inflation	6.8	7.8	13.7	10.1	8.4	10.4
Savings and Investment as percentage of GDP:						
Domestic Savings	19.1	21.4	22.8	21.8	21.4	24.4
Real Investment	22.6	24.0	20.4	21.8	20.2	n/a
Monetary Variables Growth Rates of:						
M3	16.4	17.6	18.5	16.4	18.2	19.7
Monetary Base	14.4	18.4	13.4	11.5	24.9	22.4
Net RBI Claims on Govt.	19.1	18.0	5.8	4.7	0.9	2.2
Foreign Currency Assets	2.4	19.7	136.0	20.2	127.1	45.3
Real Bank Credit	10.4	50.6	–5.1	10.0	–0.2	11.4
Fiscal Policy						
CPSD[b] (as percentage of GDP)	–9.8	–11.9	–10.6	–10.2	–11.7	–12.2
Financing (per cent):						
Internal borrowing	76.5	75.1	79.8	74.1	82.1	89.3
External borrowing	8.3	7.3	9.4	8.4	5.6	4.9
Monetization	15.2	17.6	10.8	17.5	12.4	5.8

Contd.

Contd.

	1981–2 to 1985–86	1986–7 to 1990–1	1991–2	1992–3	1993–4	1994–5
As percentage of GDP:						
Fiscal deficit	–6.8	–8.4	–5.7	–5.7	–7.5	–6.5
Primary deficit	–4.3	–4.6	–1.6	–1.3	–2.9	–1.8
Seigniorage	1.8	2.2	1.9	1.2	n/a	n/a
External Debt						
Debt / GNP	16.9[c]	24.1	34.0	37.5	37.3	n/a
Debt Service / Exports	17.7[c]	29.9	30.6	29.4	28.4	n/a
Short Term / Total Debt	7.8[c]	10.4	8.4	7.0	4.0	n/a

Notes: [a] Finance and Real Estate.
[b] Combined Public Sector Deficit (includes public sector enterprises).
[c] Averages for years 1982–3 to 1985–6.

Source: Economic Survey, Ministry of Finance, various issues; *Report on Currency and Finance,* RBI, various issues; World Debt Tables, World Bank, various issues; Easterly *et al.* (1994); Buiter and Patel (1993).

The new government that came to power in 1991 undertook a comprehensive stabilization programme in that year. This involved a drastic cut in the fiscal deficit, a devaluation of about 18 per cent in nominal terms and constraints on monetary growth. The measures seem to have had an almost immediate impact with the inflation rate falling to around 10 per cent by the next fiscal year. Foreign exchange reserves increased from a low of 5,479 million US dollars in 1990–1 to 9,220 million US dollars in 1991–2. With the easing of restrictions on foreign portfolio investment, there was a large inflow of the same in 1993–4 leading to a further build-up of reserves to 19,254 million US dollars in the same year. As expected, the austerity measures led to a slowdown in the growth rate of real output in the initial year of the stabilization programme. By 1992–3, the GDP growth rate was showing signs of recovery, in most part due to strong growth in agricultural output. The growth in output was maintained in 1993–4 and 1994–5, with the manufacturing sector now stepping up its rate of growth.

However, there were indications of a return to macroeconomic instability by the end of the fiscal year 1993. This was evident on two fronts—a resurgence in the inflation rate which had once again crossed double digits by mid-1994, and an increase in the fiscal deficit from 5.7 per cent of GDP in 1992–3 to 7.5 per cent in 1993–4. Furthermore, the savings and investment rates which had shown a steady increase all through the eighties decreased significantly in the post-reform period.

The last was particularly worrying to policy makers as this signalled a possible return to the external imbalances of the late eighties and early nineties. Can the deterioration in the macroeconomic environment—in particular, the increases in the inflation rate and the fiscal deficit to GDP ratio and the decline in the savings and investment rates be considered to be an unintended consequence of financial liberalization? We examine these issues in the next section.

III. The Macroeconomic Consequences of Financial Liberalization

Foreign Capital Inflows and Inflation

The easing of restrictions on private capital inflow has led to a significant increase in both foreign direct and portfolio investment since 1991–2. The initial surge in private capital inflow came in the form of portfolio investment which increased from 92 million US dollars in 1992–3 to 3,490 million US dollars in 1993–4, comprising 85 per cent of total foreign investment inflow in that year (Table 6.2). Most of the increase in portfolio investment in 1993–4 came from an increase in foreign borrowing by domestic firms (in the form of GDRs) and FII investment in the Indian stock market. However, in 1994–5, the share of portfolio investment in total foreign investment inflows decreased to 73 per cent as there was an increase in foreign direct investment from 620 million US dollars in 1993–4 to 1,314 million US dollars in 1994–5. The surge in private capital inflow in 1993–4 led to a sharp increase in India's total capital inflows from 2,966 US million dollars (1.7 per cent of GDP) in 1992–3 to 8,992 US million dollars (3.5 per cent of GDP) in 1993–4 (Table 6.3). Foreign investment which comprised 20 per cent of total capital inflows in 1992–3 increased its share to 46 per cent in 1993–4.

The increase in total capital inflow in 1993–4 did not lead to any significant widening of the current account deficit in that year, which in fact improved from –1.8 per cent of GDP in 1992–3 to –0.1 per cent of GDP in 1993–4 (Table 6.4). Instead, there was a sharp increase in official reserves which went up from –560 million US dollars (0.1 per cent of GDP) in 1992–3 to 8,677 million US dollars (3.4 per cent of GDP) in 1993–4. This indicated that the capital inflow was met with a rather heavy degree of foreign exchange intervention by RBI as it attempted to limit the effect of the capital inflows on the exchange rate. To sterilize the impact of the foreign capital inflow, the RBI undertook large scale open market operations during this period which were equivalent to a 2.8 per cent increase in the cash reserve ratio. Also, after initially reducing the CRR from 15 per cent to 14 per cent in April–May 1993, the RBI raised it back again in three phases from 14 per cent to 15 per cent in June–August 1994. While these steps may have mitigated the increase in money stock, clearly the thinness of the T bill market and the already high level of the CRR acted as a constraint to any further sterilization of the capital inflow. Therefore, a large proportion of RBI intervention in the foreign exchange market during this period was in the form of purchase of foreign currency for domestic currency. Consequently, the growth rate of net foreign assets went up from 17.7 per cent in 1992–3 to 110.9 per cent in 1993–4. This led to a sharp increase in reserve money and M1 during this period (Figure 6.1). As Figure 6.2 makes clear, among the sources of reserve money growth, net RBI claims on government (mobilization of the deficit) did not show any discernible upward trend during this period as the government consciously limited the extent of monetization of the deficit. On the other hand, there was a sharp rise in net foreign exchange assets from about mid-1993.

Table 6.2

Foreign Investment Inflows, 1991–2 to 1994–5 (US $ million)

Type of Investment	1991–2	1992–3	1993–4	1994–5
Direct Investment	150	341	620	1,314
Portfolio Investment:	8	92	3,490	3,581
GDRs	...	86	1,460	1,839
FIIs	...	1	1,665	1,503
NRIs	8	5	15	n/a
Offshore Funds and others	...	...	350	239
Total	158	433	4,110	4895

Source: Report on Currency and Finance, 1994–5, RBI.

Table 6.3

India's Capital Account, 1990–1 to 1994–5 (US $ million)

Item	1990–1	1991–2	1992–3	1993–4	1994–5
External Assistance (net)	2,210	3,037	1,859	1,700	1,250
Commercial Borrowings (net)	2,249	1,456	–358	1,252	1,029
Short Term Credit (net)	1,074	–515	–1079	–800	330
NRI Deposits (net)	1,536	290	2,001	940	847
Foreign Investment	68	154	585	4,110	4,895
Rupee Debt Service	–1,193	–1,240	–878	–745	–1,050
Other Capital (net)	1,244	786	836	2,535	917
Total Capital Account	7,188	3,968	2,966	8,992	8,218

Source: Report on Currency and Finance, 1994–5, RBI.

Table 6.4
India's Balance of Payments, 1990–1 to 1994–5

Item	1990–1	1991–2	1992–3	1993–4	1994–5
Balance on Current Account:					
US $ Million	–9,680	–1,178	–3,526	–315	–2,315
As percentage of GDP	–3.2	–0.4	–1.8	–0.1	–0.8
Balance on Capital Account:					
US $ Million	7,188	3,968	2,966	8,992	8,218
As percentage of GDP	2.4	1.6	1.7	3.5	2.7
Overall Balance:					
US $ Million	–2,492	2,790	–560	8,677	5,903
As percentage of GDP	–0.8	1.2	0.1	3.4	1.9

Source: Report on Currency and Finance, 1994–5, RBI.

The sharp increase in domestic liquidity in the latter half of the fiscal year 1993 had an immediate and perceptible effect on the domestic price level. As is clear from Figure 6.3, the inflation rate had shown a steady decline since September 1991. However, this was reversed in mid-1993 as the rate of inflation climbed back to double digits by mid-1994. Since then, the rate of inflation has shown no discernible trend hovering in the range of 8 to 12 per cent. The high inflation rate in 1993–4 and 1994–5 was the major factor behind the sustained real appreciation of the rupee in this period, with RBI maintaining a more or less stable nominal exchange rate during this period (Figure 6.4). While an increase in the fiscal deficit was an important contributing factor in the resurgence of inflation, the sharp increase in foreign capital inflows that led to a significant growth in base money can be taken to be the primary cause of the high rates of inflation in 1993–4 and 1994–5. In 1994–5, with private capital inflows still continuing unabated, there were indications of a lesser degree of intervention by the RBI in the foreign exchange market. Now, part of the capital inflow was met by a higher current account deficit (and consequently, a larger investment-savings gap), which increased from 0.1 per cent of GDP in 1993–4 to 0.8 per cent of GDP in 1994–5. Reflecting the lower amount of RBI intervention in the foreign exchange market, the growth rate of net foreign assets declined to 44.3 per cent in 1994–5. The increase in the current account deficit during this period could be attributed to a sharp increase in aggregate investment from 21.6 per cent of GDP in 1993–4 to 25.3 per cent of GDP in 1994–5, and not to any stagnation or decline in the private saving rate, which in fact increased from 20.9 per cent of GDP in 1993–4 to 22.7 per cent in 1994–5. We will discuss issues relating to savings and investment in the post-reform period in greater detail later in this chapter.

Table 6.5
Growth Rates of Net Domestic Assets (NDA) and Net Foreign Assets (NFA), 1990–1 to 1994–5

Variable	1990–1	1991–2	1992–3	1993–4	1994–5
NDA	16.0	11.0	14.2	11.4	15.9
NFA	59.1	100.4	17.7	110.9	44.3

Source: Report on Currency and Finance, RBI, various issues.

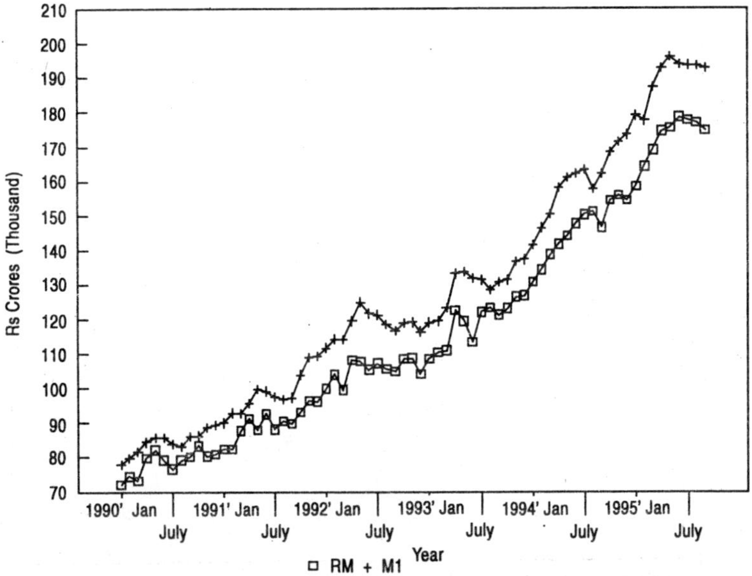

Figure 6.1 Reserve Money and M1, January 1990 to September 1995

Source: RBI Bulletin, various issues.

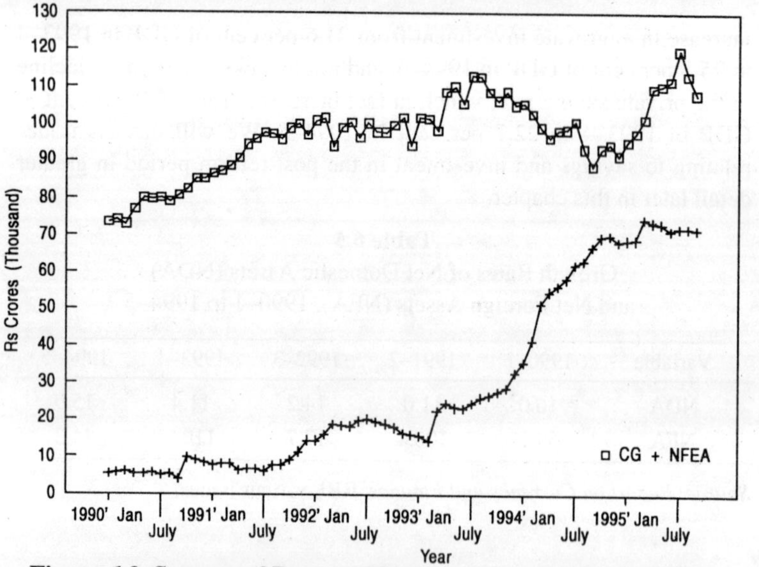

Figure 6.2 Sources of Reserve Money—Claims on Government (CG) and Net Foreign Exchange Assets (NFEA), January 1990 to September 1995

Source: RBI Bulletin, various issues.

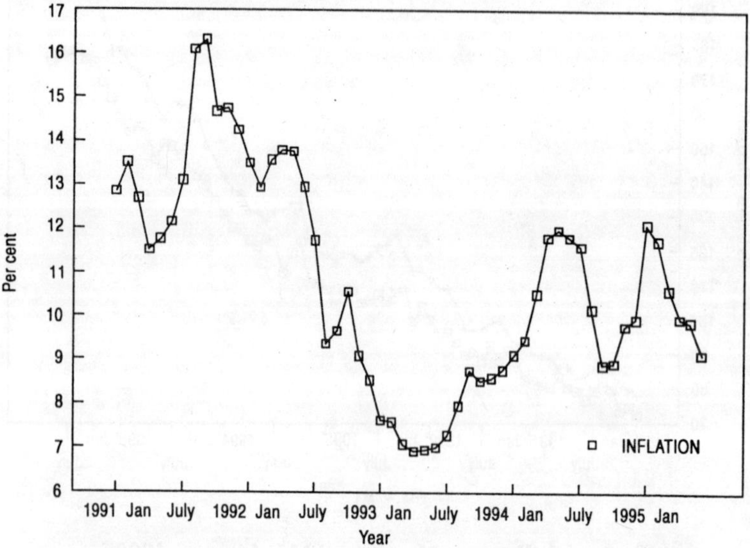

Figure 6.3 Inflation Rate,[a] January 1991 to June 1995

Note: [a] Point to Point.

Source: RBI Bulletin, various issues.

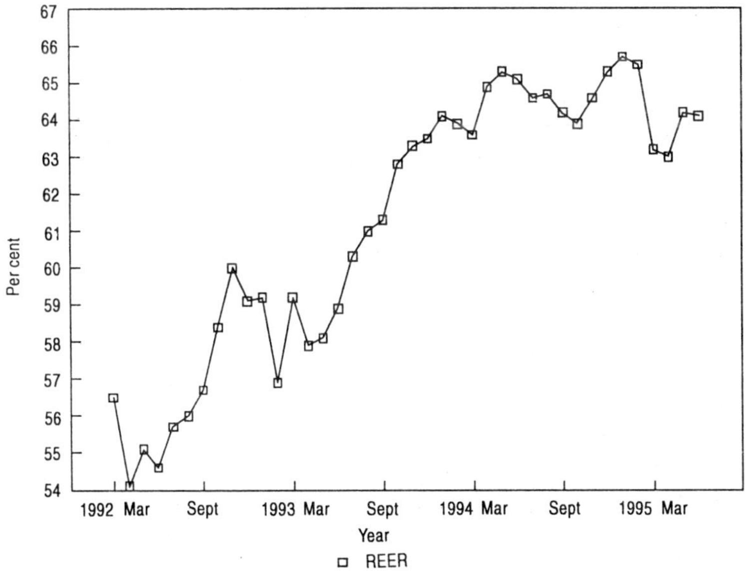

Figure 6.4 Real Effective Exchange Rate—Trade-weighted (REER), March 1992 to June 1995

Source: RBI Bulletin, various issues.

INTEREST RATES AND THE FISCAL DEFICIT

We have discussed in Chapter 3 the move to market-determined interest rates in the government securities market since the late eighties. This was one important outcome of the Chakravarty Committee Report which recommended that the government finance its deficit directly from the market at market-related rates rather than through automatic monetization by RBI. Yet a weakness of this particular recommendation was its focus on the monetization of the deficit as the main cause of macroeconomic disequilibrium. Clearly the mode of financing the deficit is not as important a cause of macroeconomic disequilibrium as the deficit itself. Moreover, behind the Chakravarty Committee's recommendation was the assumption that as the government faced a higher cost of borrowing in the market, it would attempt to curtail its expenditures (that is to say the government's demand for funds in the bond market is interest-sensitive). Given that political factors have become increasingly important over the years in determining expenditure patterns of central and state governments in India (Rao and Sen 1993), the assumption of interest-sensitivity of government expenditures could not be considered to be realistic.

After two years of fiscal adjustment in 1991–2 and 1992–3, the fiscal deficit to GDP ratio shot up to 7.4 per cent of GDP in 1993–4. With monetization of the deficit in check (due to the government's agreement with the RBI not to issue *ad hoc* T bills, see Chapter 7), the government borrowed heavily from the domestic capital market in 1992–3 and 1993–4. Market borrowings as a share of total financing of the deficit increased from 21.3 in 1990–1 to 51.1 per cent in 1993–4, then declined to 35.6 per cent in 1994–5. With a reduction in the SLR, conventional market borrowing (which includes SLR investments by banks) decreased as a percentage of total market borrowing from 96 per cent in 1990–1 to 15.4 per cent in 1994–5. Since 1992–3, market borrowing by the central government was done mostly in the form of 182–364 day T bills and auctioned government securities which increased from 0.8 per cent of total capital receipts in 1990–1 to 30.1 per cent in 1994–5 (Table 6.6). With respect to T bills, the usual government practice here was to 'fund' maturing T bills—i.e. to convert them to dated government stock when they became due. Sale of public enterprise shares also became an important source of capital receipts.

Table 6.6

Capital Receipts of the Central Government, 1990–1 to 1994–5

As per cent of Total Capital Receipts	1990–1	1991–2	1992–3	1993–4	1994–5[a]
Conventional Market Borrowing	20.5	19.5	10.2	6.3	5.5
Short-term Borrowing	0.8	7.6	13.2	–0.7	4.9
Medium and Long-term Borrowing	...	...	...	45.5	25.2
External Loans	8.2	14.1	14.7	6.5	5.8
Disinvestment of PSE shares	0.0	7.9	5.4	4.3	8.5
Small Savings	21.3	14.7	12.1	7.6	17.4
Public Provident Fund	2.0	2.5	3.7	2.6	3.3
Other Receipts	47.2	33.8	40.7	27.9	29.4
Memo Item:					
Capital Receipts/GDP (percentage)	7.3	6.3	5.1	7.5	7.9

Note: [a] Revised Estimates.

Source: Report on Currency and Finance, 1993–4 and 1994–5, RBI.

The increasing reliance on non-conventional market borrowings led to an increase in the average interest rate on both internal and external debt over the period 1990–1 to 1994–5 (Table 6.7). As we have described in Chapter 3, the interest rates on 182-day and 364-day T bills have been market determined since their introduction into the government bond market in November 1986 and April 1992 respectively, while dated government securities were sold on an auction basis from April 1992. With increased government borrowing in Indian capital markets in recent years, there has been a gradual increase in the real interest rate on Government of India securities (Figure 6.5). While difficult to quantify, there can be no doubt that the upward pressure on the real interest rate may have contributed in some degree to the crowding out of private corporate investment in recent years.

Table 6.7

Average Rate of Interest on Outstanding Liabilities of the Central Government, 1990–1 to 1994–5

Average Rate of Interest	1990–1	1991–2	1992–3	1993–4	1994–5
1. Internal Liabilities:	8.2	8.4	8.6	9.2	9.3
a) Internal Debt:	7.4	7.4	7.8	7.8	7.9
i) Market Borrowing	10.2	10.2	10.4	11.3	10.7
ii) Others	4.9	4.9	5.7	5.4	5.6
b) Other Internal Liabilities	9.2	9.2	9.6	10.9	11.1
2. External Debt	6.5	6.5	9.6	8.8	8.7
3. Total Liabilities	8.0	8.0	8.7	9.1	9.2

Source: RBI Bulletin, various issues.

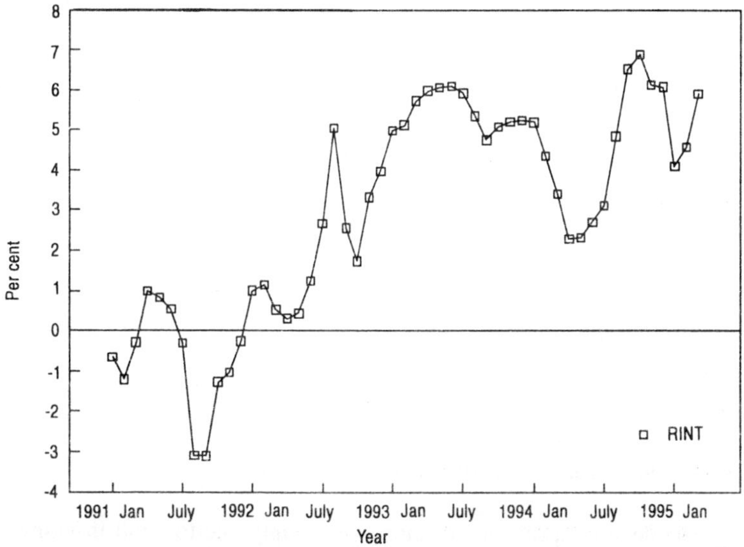

Figure 6.5 Real Interest Rate on Government of India Securities,[a] January 1991 to March 1995

Note: [a] Redemption Yield minus inflation rate.

Source: Economic Survey, 1994–5, Ministry of Finance.

There was clearly a need for the government to control the deficit on a more permanent basis before making the transition to market-determined interest rates in the government securities market. Certainly the problems that the government faced in 1993–4 and 1994–5 —with a large proportion of its current expenditures being in the form of interest payments—were in some part due to the high real interest rates that prevailed during that time. Yet it should be pointed out, that if the fiscal adjustment process that was initiated in 1991–2 had stayed its course, the 'fiscal problem' might not have been so severe. As can be observed from Table 6.1, the increase in the fiscal deficit in 1993–4 was in great part due to the increase in the central government's primary deficit. The increase in the latter was itself due to an increase in revenue expenditures from 13.2 per cent of GDP in 1992–3 to 13.5 per cent of GDP in 1993–4 and a fall in revenue receipts from 10.5 per cent of GDP in 1992–3 to 9.4 per cent of GDP in 1993–4. This brought about an increase in the revenue deficit from 2.6 per cent of GDP in 1992–3 to 4.3 per cent of GDP in 1993–4 (Table 6.8). However, the revenue deficit declined to 3.6 per cent of GDP in 1994–5 (approximately the same level that it was in 1990–1) due to a cut in revenue expenditures by half a percentage point of GDP in the same year.

Table 6.8

Receipts and Expenditures of the Central Government, 1990–1 to 1994–5

As per cent of GDP	1990–1	1991–2	1992–3	1993–4	1994–5[a]
Revenue Receipts	10.3	10.7	10.5	9.4	9.4
Revenue Expenditure	13.7	13.4	13.2	13.5	13.0
Of which: interest payments	4.0	4.3	4.4	4.6	4.7
Revenue Deficit	3.5	2.6	2.6	4.1	3.6
Capital Expenditures	5.9	4.7	4.3	4.2	4.2
Fiscal Deficit	8.3	5.9	5.7	7.5	6.5

Note: [a] Revised Estimates.
Source: Economic Survey, 1995–6, Ministry of Finance.

The decline in revenue receipts was mainly due to a fall in indirect taxes from 8.5 per cent of GDP in 1990–1 to 6.8 per cent of GDP in 1993–4 (direct taxes, on the other hand, increased from 2.1 per cent of GDP in 1990–1, to 2.5 per cent of GDP in 1993–4). Part of the decrease in indirect taxes was due to the substantial cuts in import duties that occurred in the post-1991 period (revenue from import duties decreased as a percentage of GDP from 3.9 per cent of GDP in 1990–1 to 2.8 per cent of GDP in 1993–4). Interestingly, while there were no significant cuts in excise duties (though there was a rationalization of the excise duty structure), excise duties as a percentage of GDP decreased from 4.6 per cent of GDP in 1990–1 to 4.0 per cent of GDP in 1993–4. Given the imperatives of the structural adjustment programme which necessitated the reduction in import duties (so that an initial decline in tax revenues was perhaps inevitable) there was a pressing need for the central government to curtail its consumption expenditures. Yet there was only a marginal fall in central government expenditures as a percentage of GDP from 4.2 per cent of GDP in 1990–1 to 4.0 per cent of GDP in 1993–4. Clearly then, as in the late eighties, inability to control its own consumption expenditures has been a key factor behind the government's deteriorating fiscal accounts. It should be noted here that a key objective of the financial sector reforms was to allow the private sector greater access to funds for investment from the financial sector and at competitive rates. To this purpose, the government has been systematically reducing the SLR since 1991. However, the large fiscal deficits in the post-1991 period and their mode of financing—large-scale borrowing at market rates from domestic financial markets—have significantly diminished the possible benefits that the private sector may have obtained from the reforms.

Savings and Investment

There has been a significant decline in the gross domestic savings and investment rate in the first three years of the post-reform period. The savings rate (gross domestic savings as a per cent of GDP in current prices) fell from a peak of 23.6 per cent in 1990–1 to 21.4 per cent in 1993–4 and then recovered to 24.4 per cent in 1994–5. The gross real investment rate (gross domestic capital formation to GDP in constant prices) fell from 23.9 per cent in 1990–1 to 20.2 per cent in 1993–4, recovering to 22.9 per cent in 1994–5. This initial decline could be seen as a reversal of the steady increase in the savings and investment rates all through the eighties. To what extent can the fall in the savings and investment rates in 1991–2 to 1993–4 be seen as an unintended consequence of the financial liberalization process (either by itself or in combination with other reforms)?

First consider the savings rate. As Table 6.9 indicates, the fall in the savings rate since 1991 has been mostly due to the fall in the total household savings rate. The household savings rate has fallen from a peak of 19.8 per cent in 1990–1 to 17.4 per cent in 1993–4. Public sector savings rate has also shown a negative trend over much of the eighties and nineties. The corporate savings rate, on the other hand, has increased steadily over time. The table clearly indicates that the decline in the total household savings rate has been due to a corresponding decline in the rate of household physical savings. There has been a significant fall in the latter from a peak of 11.3 per cent (of GDP) in 1990–1 to 6.6 per cent in 1993–4—that is a drop in the household physical savings rate by about 5 percentage points of GDP in a space of three years. Household financial savings as a percentage of GDP has, on the other hand, increased over time to a peak of 10.8 per cent in 1993–4. Since household savings in physical assets contributed approximately half of the total domestic savings in the entire economy in the late eighties, clearly the sharp decrease in the household physical savings rate is the most important factor behind the recent decline in the savings rate. Before we analyse the reasons for the fall in the household physical savings rate, it is necessary to gain a clear understanding of the way household physical savings is measured in CSO savings/investment estimates.

Table 6.9

Gross Domestic Savings by Sectors, 1981–2 to 1994–5
(as a percentage of GDP)

Year	Household			Private corporate	Public	Total
	Financial	Physical	Total			
1981–2	6.0	7.7	13.7	1.6	4.5	19.8
1982–3	7.2	5.8	12.9	1.6	4.4	19.0
1983–4	6.4	7.7	14.1	1.5	3.3	18.9
1984–5	7.7	6.0	13.7	1.7	2.8	18.2
1985–6	7.1	7.5	14.6	2.0	3.2	19.8
1986–7	8.0	6.2	14.2	1.8	2.7	18.7
1987–8	8.0	8.9	17.0	1.7	2.2	20.9
1988–9	6.9	10.4	17.3	2.2	2.0	21.5
1989–90	8.1	10.0	18.1	2.6	1.6	22.3
1990–1	8.7	11.3	19.8	2.8	1.0	23.6
1991–2	10.1	7.7	17.7	3.2	1.9	22.8
1992–3	8.4	8.4	16.8	2.8	1.5	21.2
1993–4	10.8	6.6	17.4	3.5	0.5	21.4
1994–5	11.1	7.8	18.9	3.8	1.7	24.4

Source: National Accounts Statistics, CSO, various issues.

The starting point of the procedure for estimating household physical savings is the estimation of gross domestic capital formation

(GDCF) using the commodity flow method. Household physical savings is then derived as a residual by subtracting the public sector's and private corporate sector's capital formation from GDCF. The component of household physical savings (savings in total physical assets) in Indian saving data is, therefore, identical to the component of household investment in physical assets in domestic investment data. In the case of the public and the private corporate sectors, the CSO estimates capital formation of these two sectors directly by the expenditure approach using government budget documents and the annual reports of private corporate enterprises. While investment estimates for the public sector and corporate sector may be considered reasonably reliable, estimates of total investment are subject to significant biases and errors arising from the nature of the commodity flow method used in estimating that aggregate (see RBI 1982; Rakshit 1983; Srinivasan 1994). Since household physical savings is obtained as a residual, any biases and errors in the measurement of GDCF would be reflected in the estimation of household physical savings.

The capital formation data (Table 6.10) also indicates that the decline in the investment rate has been predominantly due to the fall in the rate of household physical savings (=investment) rate (along with a slight decline in public investment). Furthermore, this significant fall in household investment rate has occurred in a context where the private corporate investment rate has recorded an impressive increase, going up from 5 per cent of GDP in 1990–1 to 7.6 per cent of GDP in 1993–4. It should be noted here that the term 'households' as used in national accounts is a misnomer. The household sector includes not only individuals but also non-government unincorporated enterprises such as proprietorship and partnership firms and the unregistered small-scale industrial sector and is to a large extent synonymous with the unorganized sector. In theory, the same set of economic factors should drive investment decisions in the private sector, whether they be private corporate firms or unincorporated enterprises. The negative relationship between the two sectoral investment rates in the recent past is, therefore, difficult to explain in terms of economic behaviour.

As Athukorala and Sen (1995) argue, there is reason to believe then that the decline in the household physical savings rate (and consequently, the aggregate savings and investment rates) may be a 'statistical artefact' owing to an underestimation of GDCF in recent years. There are two reasons that can be given for the systematic downward bias in the measurement of GDCF in the post-1991 period. Firstly, with the new trade liberalization and industrial delicensing

Table 6.10

Real Gross Domestic Capital Formation by Sectors, 1981–2 to 1994–5
(as a percentage of GDP—in constant prices)

Year	Household Sector	Private Corporate Sector	Public Sector	Total	Gross Fixed Capital Formation			
					Household	Private Corporate	Public	Total
1981–2	8.4	5.9	10.5	24.8	6.6	3.7	9.1	19.4
1982–3	5.5	6.1	11.1	22.6	5.0	4.4	10.1	19.5
1983–4	6.9	3.4	9.6	20.0	5.4	3.3	9.6	18.3
1984–5	4.7	4.6	10.5	19.9	4.9	3.7	9.8	18.4
1985–6	6.3	5.7	10.3	22.3	5.1	3.9	9.7	18.7
1986–7	5.5	5.5	10.6	21.6	4.8	4.2	10.4	19.4
1987–8	8.4	4.0	9.3	21.7	7.6	3.4	9.6	20.6
1988–9	10.3	4.5	9.1	23.9	7.7	3.2	9.2	20.1
1989–90	8.7	4.6	9.1	22.4	8.3	3.5	8.6	20.5
1990–1	9.8	5.0	9.1	23.9	8.3	4.1	8.7	21.1
1991–2	7.1	4.9	8.4	20.4	6.9	4.5	8.7	20.1
1992–3	6.4	7.3	8.1	21.8	5.6	6.4	7.7	19.7
1993–4	4.2	7.6	8.4	20.2	3.9	8.1	7.8	19.8
1994–5	6.7	7.5	8.6	22.9	5.8	7.9	8.4	22.2

Source: National Accounts Statistics, CSO, various issues.

policies, the incentive structures seem to have changed in favour of manufacturing sectors suited for the profitable operation of small-scale units. Quantitative restrictions on imports of consumer goods (which is chiefly the domain of small scale activity) have remained in place while there have been significant tariff cuts on capital goods imports. In a context where the relative contribution of informal sector production units continues to grow at a rapid rate, estimates based on the commodity flow mehod which does not take into account small scale activity are likely to understate domestic capital formation. Secondly, there has been a rapid growth of capital (and intermediate) goods imports as a result of import liberalization initiatives since 1991. Given the time-lag involved in the compilation of trade data, it is likely that the estimates of total fixed capital formation obtained by using a historical ratio of imported to total available capital goods understate increases in capital formation based on imported capital goods in the post-reform economy.

One important feature of India's post-reform investment performance that we have noted is the sharp increase in real private corporate capital formation as a percentage of GDP. This has happened in spite of an increase in the bank real lending rate by about two percentage points in the post-1991 period. Two reasons can be given for the rise in the private corporate investment rate. Firstly, some elements of the reform package such as liberalization of capital and intermediate goods imports, relaxation of restrictions on industrial licensing and the new emphasis on the role of the private sector in economic growth may have been instrumental in bringing about favourable changes in business perception leading to higher investment. Secondly, one important component of the trade liberalization measures was the significant cut in tariffs of capital goods. This led to a sharp decline in the rental cost of capital in 1991–2 to 1993–4 (as the relative price of capital goods fell with the tariff cuts) by about 24 per cent from its level in 1986–7 to 1990–1 (Athukorala and Sen 1996). The reforms then seem to have had a significant positive effect on private corporate investment in the short and medium term.

The experiences of other countries undertaking structural reforms (such as Chile in the 1970s and Mexico in the 1990s) indicate that financial sector reforms that have eased restrictions on bank lending to households for the purchase of consumer goods (along with the easing of restrictions on the import of consumer goods) can lead to a 'consumption boom' and hence, a decline in the private savings rate

(McKinnon and Pill 1995). While lack of data does not allow us to examine whether there has indeed been a significant increase in consumer credit in the post-reform period, such an explanation does not suffice to explain the recent savings decline in India. Firstly, as noted, there has been virtually no elimination of quantitative restrictions on the import of consumer goods. Secondly, as can be seen in Figure 6.6, bank lending to households (as a percentage of GDP) does not show any increase in the post-1991 period. Figure 6.6 also shows an increase in the household financial savings rate in 1991–2 to 1994–5; this rate would arguably be the one that would decline if there had been a tendency for households to substitute savings for current consumption.

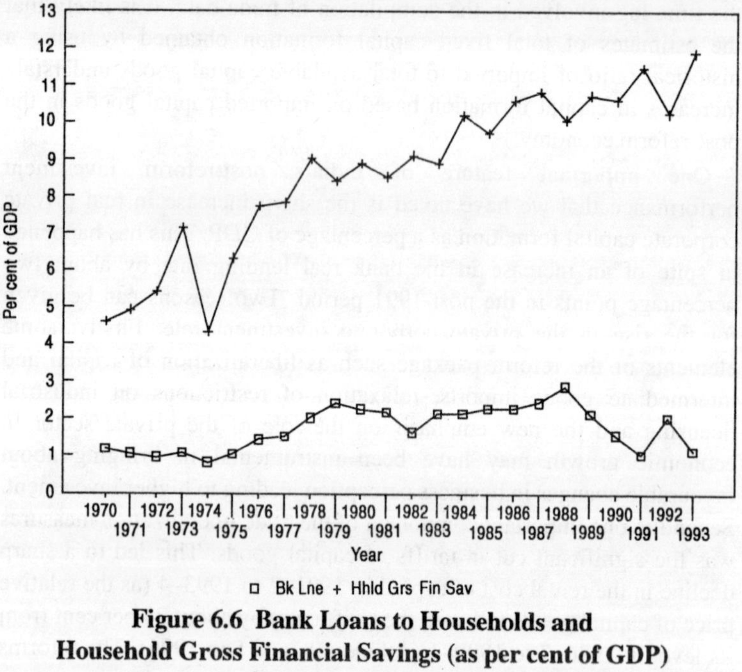

Figure 6.6 Bank Loans to Households and Household Gross Financial Savings (as per cent of GDP)

Source: Report on Currency and Finance, RBI, various issues.

IV. Concluding Remarks

It would be fair to argue that not all of the instability in the macroeconomic environment that prevailed in the period 1991–2 to 1994–5 was a direct outcome of the financial liberalization process. The relatively high level of real interest rates prevailing during this period was an outcome of the large fiscal imbalances financed by domestic borrowing. In the case of the observed initial decline in the savings and investment rates in the post-reform period there is reason to believe that the decline may well be a statistical artefact rather than a real consequence of the reform process. However, an unanticipated surge in capital inflows brought about by financial liberalization contributed to macroeconomic instability. The success of reforms in the future depends critically on the ability of the government to control its deficits and a better management of foreign capital inflows.

7

Financial Liberalization and Monetary Policy

It is difficult to envisage a process of financial liberalization without the active participation of the central bank. The decontrol of interest rates, the dismantling of entry barriers into the banking sector, the easing of restrictions regarding whom banks can lend to, and how much, all of which form the standard ingredients of a financial liberalization package, are usually implemented under the guidance and initiative of the central bank. At the same time, as the financial sector of the economy gets more and more deregulated, it becomes progressively difficult for the central bank to conduct monetary policy. Monetary control procedures such as monetary base targeting (or components thereof) or changes in the required reserve ratio become increasingly redundant as the money multiplier becomes unpredictable with the growing sophistication of the financial sector. Simultaneously, with the creation of new assets that are close substitutes to money and the development of cash management techniques, money demand becomes increasingly unstable. Therefore, financial liberalization can have a significant impact on the conduct of the monetary policy both by altering the process of money supply creation and by leading to fundamental changes in the relationship between money demand, incomes and interest rates. As we discussed in Chapter 3, there has been considerable deregulation and development in commercial bank asset and liability markets, and household asset markets since the late eighties. In this chapter, we undertake an econometric investigation of the money multiplier and the money demand function to determine whether they show any evidence of instability during the process of financial liberalization. This we do in Sections I and II, respectively.

In a deregulated financial environment, two other issues in monetary policy are also of importance. The first relates to the debate on what should be the desirable 'target' of the central bank and the appropriate 'instrument' to achieve this target. A target here is defined to be the variable that the central bank wishes to have control over. For example, if price stability is the ultimate goal of the central bank, then it could target prices directly (using whatever means it has at its disposal). However, if it believes that the price level has a determinate and predictable relationship with some other variable over which it has more direct control (such as the monetary base), then it may wish to target that variable instead. The 'instrument' problem relates to the choice of the operating procedure. By an operating procedure, we mean the price or quantity that the central bank can directly and immediately control. The choice of an operating procedure becomes relevant in an environment where open market operations become the primary focus of the monetary policy function and, therefore, where there is a need to specify how the central bank will conduct such operations. Since open market operations are essentially a trading activity, the operating procedure must either be a price or a quantity. Simply put, the central bank must decide which variable to control in the short-term—the interest rate or bank reserves. In Section III, we address the instruments and targets issue. As we will find when we discuss this issue, the stability of money demand and money supply functions is an important consideration in the choice of the appropriate 'instrument' and 'target' for RBI in the context of the financial sector reforms.

A second issue which is of relevance in the context of the current efforts to delink monetary policy from fiscal policy in India is whether it is desirable for the central bank to be independent of the government. There has been considerable debate both within the Indian central bank and outside on this issue since the reforms. In Section IV, we discuss the literature on central bank independence and trace some of its implications for the current debate in India.

I. The Money Supply Process

The standard approach to money stock determination is that of the money multiplier approach. If money stock is taken to be $M1$, then it comprises two components—currency (C) and demand deposits (D) held by the non-bank public, i.e. $M1 = C + D$. The monetary base (H), on the other hand, is defined as currency with the public and banks' cash and balances with the central bank (R), i.e. $H = C + R$. By algebraic manipulation of these two identities, we get a third identity: $M1 = mH$, where m, the money multiplier, equals $[1 + C/D]/[R/D + C/D]$. It is important to distinguish between required reserves (RR) which are policy-determined and excess reserves (*ER*) which is determined by banks' portfolio behaviour. In India, required reserves are maintained as a ratio of total (net) demand and time liabilities. Denoting the ratios of currency to demand deposits, time deposits to demand deposits, required reserves to demand plus time deposits and excess reserves to demand plus time deposits as *c*, *k*, *r* and *e* respectively, we can write the money multiplier as:

$$m = [1 + c]/[(r + e)(1 + k) + c]$$

The money multiplier for *M3* needs to be modified somewhat by adding *k* to the numerator in the above expression.

Two critical assumptions form the basis of the money multiplier approach: firstly, that banks and the non-bank public maintain stable reserve and cash to deposit ratios, and secondly, that the monetary base is usually treated as exogenous (Cobham 1991). Considering the first, the assumption of stable reserve and cash to deposit ratios implicitly assumes that either the portfolios of commercial banks and households are invariant to interest rates or that portfolio decisions of these two sets of economic agents, have a fairly stable and predictable relationship with relative rates of return.

Either of these assumptions may be tenable in a financially repressed system. Firstly, in such a system, the lack of depth in the financial markets usually implies that there are few assets that are close substitutes to non-interest bearing reserves and deposits (assuming that cash is held primarily for transactions purposes). Secondly, in a financially repressed system, interest rates are administered by the government and usually kept fixed for long periods of time. Since the government attempts to maintain parity between interest rates regardless of the riskiness or liquidity premium of assets, changes in such rates are made ensuring that their differentials stay intact. Also, in the case of commercial banks, there is little freedom to adjust their portfolios as the government controls the direction and magnitude of banks' uses of funds to a large extent. Under these conditions, one can argue that the assumption of stable reserve and cash to deposit ratios may not be unrealistic and that one should not expect great variation or instability in the money multiplier in a financially repressed economy.

Consider now an economy which is liberalizing its financial sector. Key features of the liberalization are the withdrawal of government controls on bank lending, especially to the private corporate sector, and the introduction/creation of new assets (or old assets with 'new' characteristics) that could be considered close substitutes to non-interest bearing reserves and deposits such as auctioned government securities and money market mutual funds. Therefore, as the financial sector becomes more market-oriented and sophisticated over time, there is less reason to believe that the reserve and cash to deposit ratios will remain stable over time. For example, while the non-bank public's demand for currency would be largely unaffected by financial deregulation, banks' holding of excess reserves and households' demand for bank deposits would vary with changes in relative rates of return. Therefore, the currency and reserves to deposit ratios would now need to be embedded in a general equilibrium theory of portfolio determination, where banks' and households' portfolios would depend on the relative yields of various assets (Goodhart 1984, 1989). Since the portfolio choice of banks and households would be based on a variety of disparate expectations of relative yields, there would be little reason to expect that there would be a *stable* relationship between reserve and cash to deposit ratios and interest rates, at least in the immediate post-deregulation period (Dow and Earl 1982).

Now consider the assumption of an exogenous monetary base. Clearly, in a financial repressed economy, the monetary base cannot be considered as exogenous to the economic system. This is because of the government's seigniorage needs—an important characteristic of a financially repressed economy is the high rate of money creation to finance the government's large and ever-widening budget deficits. It should be pointed out here that *money financing of the deficit is not a necessary implication of financial repression.* However, it is usually those governments not having access to other means of financing their expenditures (say, because of a weak tax collection system) and in great need of financing the deficit via the inflation tax that would prefer to keep the financial system of the economy repressed (Roubini and Sala-i-Martin 1992, 1995). As the government liberalizes the financial sector of the economy in question and simultaneously reduces the fiscal deficit (so that its seigniorage needs decline), the link between the budget deficit and the monetary base tends to weaken. Does this imply that with financial liberalization, the monetary base becomes truly exogenous to the economic system?

There are two important reasons why the above may not be true. Firstly, as the government opens up its capital markets to foreign portfolio investment, the rush of foreign funds that usually accompanies such a decision (especially if the country in question is perceived as an 'emerging market') can potentially lead to significant increases in the monetary base if the central bank is unable to either sterilize the inflow of funds or let the exchange rate appreciate. The first may not occur if the T bills market is not developed enough for the central bank to conduct open market operations. The second is not a strong possibility if the government is interested in making sure that the growth in exports does not slow down because of the appreciation of the currency. Here, changes in current income which lead to changes in expectations of future income growth can produce movements in portfolio investment either in or out of the country and cause corresponding changes in the monetary base.[1]

There is a second (and perhaps more fundamental) reason why the monetary base cannot be considered to be exogenous in an economy which has liberalized its financial sector. With a more sophisticated financial sector and market-determination of prices of most financial assets, it is in the central bank's interest to adjust bank reserves so as to keep the prices of financial assets stable. That is, under most circumstances, the central bank lets the supply of bank reserves meet its demand in order to prevent wide and unpredictable fluctuations in interest rates. Therefore, even if the central bank could keep the monetary base at a pre-determined level, it will choose not to do so to ensure the stability of financial markets and in its role as lender of last resort.

As bank asset and liability markets develop, one important structural change that occurs in the banking system is the shift from *'asset management to liability management'* (Goodhart 1984, p. 148, emphasis ours). Liability management is the technique of bidding for wholesale deposits at negotiated rates and is an outcome of the development of wholesale money markets such as the CD market. In a system of asset management, when the central bank wishes to slow down the growth of money supply, it could simply increase reserve requirements. Given restrictions on other uses of funds, banks would perforce have to curtail loans to the corporate sector, the one segment of their portfolio where they had some flexibility. In a system of liability management, this would no longer be the case. As Chick (1988) argues, liability management fundamentally alters bank behaviour; 'instead of the willingness to lend being dependent on the liquid assets and/or reserve component of their balance sheet, banks could now decide on a target expansion of lending and fund the result by competing for wholesale deposits' (p. 39). With the development of money markets, an increase in the reserve requirement would lead banks to bid for more wholesale deposits; for example, by issuing more CDs. Parallel to this is the increasing use of the call money market by banks for short-term funds.

[1] In the limit, with full capital convertibility and a *de facto* fixed exchange rate regime (with nominal exchange rate targeting), Mundell-Fleming results will hold; that is to say, the central bank will have no control over the monetary base (Frenkel and Mussa 1985).

As a consequence, with liability management, banks could always 'find' the funds to meet the demand for bank loans, albeit at higher costs of borrowing for bank customers. The control over the size of the banks' books would depend increasingly on the interest elasticity of bank loans, 'an interest elasticity which is always somewhat uncertain and low in the short-term' (Goodhart 1984 p.154). Therefore, in a deregulated financial system, 'strict control of the monetary base ... would continually threaten frequent and potentially massive movements in interest rates, if not complete instability' (Ibid, p. 212).

From the above arguments, it is clear that an assumption of monetary base exogeneity would be valid only if the central bank were willing to tolerate large and unpredictable movements in interest rates with possibly severe macroeconomic consequences. The maintenance of monetary base exogeneity may compel the central bank to throw on to the financial markets the burden of adjustment that it would otherwise share with the financial system in its role as lender of last resort, in its open market operations, in its foreign exchange interventions, and in the permitted short-term variability in the level of balances held by individual banks with the central bank.[2]

In our discussion of Indian money markets in Section III of Chapter 3, we have had occasion to point out that there has been significant deregulation and development in these markets since the late eighties. In particular, developments relevant to our analysis of the money supply process is the lifting of the ceiling rate in the call money market in May 1989 and the introduction of the CD as a new source of funds for commercial banks in 1988–9. In the rest of this section, we examine if these changes in the money markets (along with decontrol of bank lending rates) have led to an increasing instability in the money multiplier over the period 1982–4.[3]

An issue that we need to address before delving into the details of the 'stability' issue is the appropriate empirical methodology. The problem of spurious regressions has been well-documented in the

[2] This is the reason why Post-Keynesians such as Davidson (1988) and Moore (1988) argue that, for all practical purposes, money supply is endogenously determined in advanced market economies. For a less developed economy, the relevant question is to ask: when is the assumption of money supply endogeneity a reasonable one to make? As we have argued, the answer greatly depends on the state of development of the financial markets.

[3] Most studies on the money multiplier have focussed on predictability of the money multiplier, e.g. Hafer and Hein (1984), Bomhoff (1977) and Johannes and Rasche (1979, 1981), for other countries and Nachane and Ray (1989) for India. Note that evidence that the multiplier is unpredictable in the short-run does not preclude the possibility of a long-run stable relationship between money stock and the monetary base. A recent paper that examines stability issues in India is Nachane (1992); also see Chitre (1986) and Rangarajan and Singh (1984).

literature (for example, Granger and Newbold 1974). Such possibilities arise because most economic time-series exhibit non-stationary tendencies. This could be particularly likely when the R^2 is greater than the DW statistic. High R^2 may arise due to correlated trends and not through economic relationships. Low DWs may arise due to non-stationary residuals. The standard method of overcoming this problem is to see whether the relationship discovered in levels persists after first differencing. The problem with such an approach is that it involves the loss of low frequency (long-run) information. Co-integration and error correction modelling (ECM) allows the identification of non-spurious relationships without forcing the loss of long-run information (Engle and Granger 1987). Moreover, ECMs allow for suitable economic interpretations since they incorporate equilibrium relationships as suggested by economic theory along with the possibility of variables responding to short-run disequilibrium as favoured by time-series econometricians.

A common test for co-integration is the Engle and Granger (1987) two-step procedure. The steps involved are as follows.

Before testing for co-integration, in the multivariate case, one needs to ensure that the order of integration of the dependent variable is not higher than the order of integration of any of the independent variables. To do this, the standard Dickey-Fuller (DF) and Augmented Dickey-Fuller (ADF) tests are generally used. Following this, the first step in the Engle-Granger two-step procedure involves running a least squares regression on the levels of the variables in question and testing the hypothesis of co-integration by determining the order of integration of the residuals of this regression. If the hypothesis of co-integration is to be accepted then the residuals must be integrated of order zero (i.e., stationary). Usually the tests to determine the order of integration of the residuals are the DF and the ADF tests.

The equation estimated at step one is generally referred to as the 'static regression'. The coefficients of this regression are called the 'co-integrating parameters'. These parameters can be interpreted as defining the long-run or equilibrium relationship between the variables in question. After the presence of co-integration has been established the second step requires the construction of an error correction model. This involves regressing the first difference of each variable in the co-integration equation onto lagged values of the first differences of all the variables plus the lagged value of the error correction term (that is, the error term from the co-integration regression).

The first step of the Engle-Granger procedure provides an intuitively compelling method of testing for stability. If in fact the money multiplier is stable, then there must be a long-run relationship (co-integration) between money stock and the monetary base (MB). This relationship should be independent of the period of analysis. We test for stability over the period April 1980 to December 1994 and the sub-period April 1980 to March 1986. Since the deregulation in the money markets occurred in the late eighties we should expect the money multiplier to be stable in the sub-period considered but not over the entire period. We test for co-integration between money stock measures (M1 and M3) and MB for each of the sub periods and for the entire period.

STABILITY OF THE MONEY MULTIPLIER

We first deseasonalized the three series [i.e. M1, M3, MB] using the multiplicative filter. For the period under consideration we found the three series to be I(1) using the DF and ADF tests.

The co-integrating regression was :

$$M1 = 0.70 + 0.94\ MB$$

$$R^2 = 0.99,\ DW = 0.68,\ ADF\ (8\ lags) = -1.40\ (-3.37)$$

$$M3 = 0.94 + 1.02\ MB$$

$$R^2 = 0.99,\ DW = 1.09,\ ADF\ (5\ lags) = -2.02\ (-3.38)$$

Critical Values are in parenthesis.

The ADF tests suggest that there is an absence of co-integration between M1 and MB, and M3 and MB. This suggests that over this period the money multipliers have not been stable.

To investigate whether this finding is robust across an alternate time period we considered the sub-sample April 1980 to March 1986. We obtain the following results. All three series were found to be I(1).

The co-integrating regression was :

$$M1 = 0.82 + 0.94\ MB$$

$$R^2 = 0.99,\ DW = 1.56,\ ADF\ (2\ lags) = -5.38\ (-3.43)$$

$$M3 = 0.43 + 1.07\ MB$$

$$R^2 = 0.99,\ DW = 1.28,\ ADF\ (2\ lags) = -3.82\ (-3.43)$$

In this case we find that both M1 and M3 are co-integrated with MB. This indicates that the money multipliers have been stable for the period April 1980 to March 1986.[4]

[4] To see whether the seasonal filter used made any difference to our results we have repeated the entire analysis with unseasonalized data. The results indicate that no revision of the above reported conclusions was warranted. Due to constraints of space we do not report the results here.

In our earlier discussion, we had drawn attention to two theoretical predictions on the implications of financial liberalization on the money multiplier. The first of these related to the possibility of instability in the money multiplier relation with the onset of financial sector reforms. The second prediction relates to the endogeneity of the monetary base as commercial banks take recourse to liability management and the central bank gradually abandons a strict control of the monetary base (if it had followed such a policy to begin with) in the interests of financial stability. We find that the first prediction is borne out in the Indian context by our findings on the instability of the multipliers for M1 and M3 over the period 1980–94. While the second prediction is difficult to establish empirically, in our discussion of the call money market (Section III, Chapter 3), we have already drawn attention to increasing intervention by RBI in the call money market after December 1994 in response to the volatility in the call money rate. This indicates that the central bank is increasingly willing to share with financial markets the burden of adjustment that is inevitable in any move to the market determination of interest rates. Thus, it can be argued that in the current context, the money multiplier approach to money supply determination is of limited applicability in India. The implications of this for the conduct of monetary policy will be discussed later in this chapter.

III. Money Demand

There are two conceptually distinct reasons for holding money; first, the transactions motive, where money is held as a medium of exchange; and second, the asset motive, where money is one of several possible assets in which wealth may be held. The transactions demand theory of money is based on the need for money to even out the differences between income and expenditure streams. The Baumol–Tobin model forms the basis for this theory of money demand (Baumol 1952, Tobin 1956). In this model, real money balances—that is, nominal money balances divided by an appropriate price level—is a positive function of the volume of real transactions. Money demand is inversely related to the opportunity cost of holding money, approximated by the interest rate on a highly liquid asset. Also, money demand declines with a decrease in transactions cost, i.e. the costs in converting the liquid asset into money.[5] In semi log-linear form (with all variables except the

[5] Transactions cost could either be implicit costs or explicit costs. In the former would be the amount of time it takes to make a standard financial transaction; e.g. withdrawing cash from a savings account. In the latter would be brokerage costs. It can be argued both types of costs would be higher in a financially repressed economy due to the higher degree of inefficiency among financial intermediaries and the relatively underdeveloped nature of the payments technology in such an economy.

interest rate being in natural logarithms), the transactions demand for money function could be written as:

$$(1)\ M^{d}_{t}/P_t = a_0 - a_1 r_t + a_2 T_t + a_3 c_t$$

where M is nominal money balances, *P* is the price level, *r* is the short-term interest rate, *T* is the volume of real transactions, and *c* is a measure of transaction cost. In practice, it is often difficult to find an empirical measure of transactions cost; the standard procedure here is to assume either that there is no change in payments technology in the time-period under consideration, or that there is a secular decline in the transactions cost over time (as the payments technology continually improves). In the former case, the transactions cost variable is subsumed in the constant term; in the latter case, it is approximated as a time trend. One other modification that needs to be made to the Baumol–Tobin model is to permit the possibility of durable goods to be held as a substitute for money or near-money assets. In this case, the yield on durable goods is given by the expected inflation rate (π^e).[6] Subsuming the transactions cost variable into the constant, we reformulate the transactions demand for money equation as follows,

$$(1')\ M^{d}_{t}/P_t = a_0 - a_1 r_t + a_2 T_t + a_3 \pi^{e}_{t}$$

The asset demand theory of money, argues that money is one of many different forms of holding wealth and each form has its own explicit return (i.e. interest and capital gains) and implicit return (i.e. non-pecuniary). For money, transaction services would be included in the latter. Individuals choose the composition of their portfolio of assets so as to maximize the returns they expect from that portfolio. The theory predicts that individuals will choose their portfolio by balancing more certain but lower returns with higher but riskier ones (Tobin 1958). The resulting money demand function would be similar to (1′) but with two important differences. First, wealth rather than the volume of transactions demand would be the relevant 'scale' variable. Second, some measure of the volatility of returns pertaining to alternative assets would enter into the function in addition to expected returns.[7]

From the above discussion, it follows that in the Indian context the transactions demand for money is more applicable to the demand for

[6] We abstract from storage costs and depreciation.

[7] One issue of contention here is whether money will be held at all as a portfolio asset. Ando and Shell (1975) argue that T bills will dominate money as a portfolio asset since the former has the same risk characteristics as money but yields a positive return. Baba, Hendry and Starr (1992) contend, on the other hand, that with capital market imperfections (modelled as a divergence between borrowing and lending rates), money will have both a transactions and a portfolio function.

real M1 (which includes currency with the public and non-interest-bearing demand deposits), while the asset demand for money is possibly more applicable to real M3 (which also includes interest-bearing time deposits). We now trace the implications of financial liberalization on both the transactions demand and the asset demand for money. Consider the former: with a more competitive financial system, the possible introduction of new near-money assets (e.g. money market mutual funds) and innovations in payments technology (e.g. automated teller machines), one can expect a significant decline in the cost of converting liquid assets into money. This would lead to a decline in the transactions demand for money. In terms of the money demand function as in (1′), the decrease in transactions cost would result in a one-time downward shift of the intercept term. A likely fall in income-elasticity of money demand can also be expected as deposits will be held as interest-bearing liquid assets, rather than simply to facilitate transactions (Davis and Lewis 1992). Further, with the introduction of savings accounts with limited transactions characteristics such as money market mutual funds and money market deposit accounts, there will be an increase in the interest-elasticity of narrow money (Thornton and Stone 1992).[8]

A similar argument can be made in the case of the demand for money as an asset; that is, the demand for M3. The introduction of new assets with risk characteristics similar to savings and time deposits but with higher returns may also lead to an increase in the degree of responsiveness of the demand for money to rates of return on alternative assets. The final outcome of financial liberalization on interest-elasticity of M3 is unclear. It is conceivable that if banks are given greater flexibility in the setting of deposit rates, there may well be a decrease in the interest-elasticity of money demand, as bank deposit rates become more responsive to market rates. Also, if interest rates on bank deposits become market-determined, there could be a re-intermediation into bank time deposits as the latter become higher yielding. Finally, if financial liberalization leads to a higher volatility in interest rates, this could also contribute to the increased preference to hold M3 as a safe asset (Baba, Hendry and Starr 1992).

The above discussion makes it clear that while it would be difficult to predict the direction and magnitude of change of the coefficients that link the demand for real M1 and M3 to their determinants in an episode of financial deregulation, the relationship between money demand and

[8] Other things being the same, the elasticity of demand for any good increases with the number and the closeness of its substitutes.

its determinants will become increasingly volatile and unreliable during this period. However, the extent of instability of money demand in the post-liberalization period will depend on the nature of the liberalization process; that is, have new assets been created with similar characteristics to M1 and M3, and have banks been given the freedom to set interest rates on their liabilities? In the rest of this section, we examine the evidence of money demand instability in India (both M1 and M3) since the reforms. It should be recalled that, as compared to bank asset and liability (CD) markets, developments in household asset markets have been relatively more recent. Most of the deregulation and the development of household asset markets have occurred in the early nineties with the decontrol of interest rates on corporate bonds and the introduction of new assets in the capital market. However, bank deposit rates continue to be regulated. We have already noted in Chapter 3 that there is clear evidence of a shift in the portfolio of households from bank deposits to corporate securities in 1991–2 to 1994–5. To see whether this has led to instability in money demand, we undertake an econometric estimation of the money demand function using annual data.[9]

We take the period of analysis to be from 1955–93. The sub-periods considered are 1955–85 and 1955–90. Our discussion earlier suggests (1′) as the appropriate specification for the money demand function. The independent variables (the dependent variable obviously being real M1 and M3) are the interest rate (the one-year interest rate on time deposits), real GDP (as a measure of the volume of real transactions), and the current inflation rate (as a proxy for expected inflation). While examining the time series properties of the variables in question, we find that real M1 (RM1), real M3 (RM3), real GDP (RY) and the interest rate (ID) are I(1), while the inflation rate (INF) is I(0). We also find that RM1 and RM3 are not co-integrated with ID and RY.[10] This implies that the variables suggested by (1′) are not co-integrated. The fact that there does not exist a co-integrating vector among the variables and that four out of the five variables are I(1) suggests that an appropriate estimation procedure is to estimate the money demand

[9] Recent studies that have examined the stability of money demand for other countries are Johansen and Juselius (1990), Hafer and Jansen (1991), Hendry and Ericsson (1991), Miller (1991), and Mehra (1993). Jadhav (1995) has studied the stability of money demand for India. Studies which examine the consequences of financial deregulation on money demand are Baba, Hendry and Starr (1992), Orden and Fisher (1993) and Arrau *et al.* (1995). Goldfield and Sichel (1990) provide an useful and up-to-date survey of the empirical literature on money demand.

[10] Results are available on request and are excluded for brevity.

equation in first differences. We present in Table 7.1 a summary of the results with real M1 as the dependent variable.

Table 7.1

Results for Real M1[a]

	1955–85	1955–90
Constant	0.05	0.05
	(3.99)	(4.67)
Dummy variable for 1974	–0.20	–0.20
	(–3,72)	(–3.93)
Dummy variable for 1979	–0.25	–0.26
	(–4.29)	(–4.56)
Real GDP (one lag)	0.15	0.16
	(1.14)	(1.26)
Interest rate (one lag)	–3.29	–3.16
	(–2.80)	(–2.78)
Inflation rate	–0.31	–0.29
	(–2.04)	(–2.00)
R^2	0.71	0.68
Predictive failure test (chi-square)	3.54	4.76
	(0.62)	(0.19)

Note: [a] T-ratios in brackets.

The estimation procedure adopted begins with the most general specification of (1′) with two lags for each independent variable and the dependent variable. The results reported correspond to the most parsimonious specification possible and satisfy all standard diagnostic tests. We find that as expected the interest rate and the inflation rate (the opportunity cost variables) have a negative influence on real money demand. Dummy variables for the oil shock years (1974 and 1979) are also significant. Testing for predictive failure for the two sub-periods indicate that the real M1 demand equation has been stable in the period of analysis.[11]

Turning to the estimation of the equation for real M3 (and using the same estimation procedure as outlined above), we find that the dummy variable for the oil shock year of 1979 and the interest rate (which is now the own rate of return on real M3) are not significant (Table 7.2). In the Indian context, constructing a satisfactory variable for the opportunity cost of holding real M3 is not possible for the entire period under consideration. Given the attractiveness of holding durable goods

[11] For the first sub-period, i.e. 1955–85, we tested for predictive failure over the next five years. For the second sub-period, i.e. 1955–90, we tested for predictive failure over the next three years.

as assets in India, we can take the inflation rate as a proxy for the rate of return on alternative assets. Also, with lack of satisfactory data on wealth in India, we use real GDP instead.

Table 7.2
Results for Real M3[a]

	1955–85	1955–90	1955–93
Constant	0.05 (4.37)	0.06 (5.13)	0.06 (5.44)
Dummy variable for 1974	–0.17 (–2.85)	–0.18 (–3.10)	–0.18 (–3.12)
Real GDP (one lag)	0.22 (1.51)	0.22 (1.66)	0.23 (1.70)
Inflation rate	–0.35 (–2.26)	–0.34 (–2.39)	–0.34 (–2.37)
Dummy variable 1991 to 1993	...	...	–0.01 (–0.25)
Slope dummy on Real GDP 1991 to 1993	...	...	–0.37 (–0.25)
Slope dummy on inflation 1991 to 1993	...	...	4.18 (3.00)
R^2	0.40	0.39	0.46
Predictive failure test (chi-square)	1.47 (0.92)	11.62 (0.01)	...

Note: [a] T-ratios in brackets.

Here we find a clear evidence of instability in the money demand function in the post-1991 period as indicated by the predictive failure test. To investigate the source of instability we use intercept and slope dummies for the period 1991–3. We find that the reason for instability is an increase in the elasticity of real money to the inflation rate. The lack of stability of demand for real M3 on the one hand, and the stability of demand for real M1 on the other, in the post-1991 period, is consistent with the received theories of money demand behaviour in the context of financial deregulation.

Consider M1 first. It is clear that in the Indian context there has been little change in the payments technology (even credit cards or ATMs are not commonly used), nor has there been any creation of new assets with limited transactions characteristics. Therefore, it is hardly surprising that the demand for real M1 has been stable in the post-reform period. On the other hand, as we have observed in Chapter 3, there has been a proliferation of new assets with characteristics that are close to time deposits, particularly since 1991. This seems to have led to an increase in the elasticity of money demand with respect to alternative rates of return (as evident by the significant and positive slope dummy on the inflation rate in the real M3 equation for the post-1991 period).[12] Therefore, our finding of instability in the demand for M3 but not that for M1 in India can be related to the implications of the nature of the financial liberalization process in its current form for the demand for money as an asset rather than as a medium of exchange.

III. Targets and Instruments of Monetary Policy

TARGETS

The use of any given intermediate target variable for monetary policy can be considered to be a two-step procedure (Friedman 1990). In the first stage, the central bank determines the value of the intermediate target which would be consistent with the desired ultimate policy objective under a variety of *ex ante* assumptions. At the second stage, the central bank proceeds to achieve this value of the intermediate target as if doing so were the objective governing policy. Since price stability is the ultimate objective of most central banks, the intermediate target *par excellence* is money, given its apparent determinate relationship with the price-level in the long run. It is well known that the relationship between money and the price-level remains a contentious one in the literature. This is particularly true in the Indian context where inflation is often considered to be caused by supply-side factors rather than excessive monetary growth (Balakrishnan 1991). It could be argued that the relationship between money and prices is even more tenuous during the process of financial liberalization. As Thornton and Stone (1992) argue, with financial innovation, the interest elasticity of money increases. Therefore, with velocity now responsive to interest rates, it becomes difficult to determine the precise monetary policy response required to achieve a specific nominal income or price-level target. In that case, the first step of the targeting procedure becomes redundant. Hence, Goodhart (1994) argues that it may be better for the central bank to target the price-level directly rather than use an intermediate target such as money which has little information content in a deregulated financial environment with regard to the future path of inflation. Our finding that M3 demand has become unstable

[12] Also, the higher volatility of the inflation rate (which, as we have argued, can be considered to be a proxy for the interest rate on alternative financial assets) in the early nineties may have led to an increased preference by households for real M3.

since the onset of the reforms, but not M1, provides some justification for using M1 as the intermediate target rather than M3. However, with changes in the payments technology and greater deregulation, the observed stability in the M1 demand function may be short-lived. We would argue that in order to achieve the desired policy objective of price stability, the central bank should target a wider set of variables (such as credit aggregates, exchange rates and interest rates) rather than pin its hopes on one or two variables.

INSTRUMENTS

The 'instrument problem'—that is, the selection of the specific price or quantity which the central bank directly and immediately controls—began with the seminal contribution of Poole (1970) who compared the relative merits of targeting interest rates or monetary aggregates. Poole showed that the choice between the interest rate and money stock as the appropriate operating procedure was determined by the relative magnitudes of the unpredictable elements of the non-bank public's behaviour in the market for goods and services and the market for financial assets. Fixing the interest rate—that is, supplying money elastically, shields income from disturbances to portfolio behaviour but 'provides no protection against disturbances to spending behaviour' (Friedman, 1990, p. 1191). On the other hand, inelastically fixing the money stock will reduce the impact of disturbances to spending but only at the cost of exposing income to disturbances to portfolio behaviour.[13]

One limitation of Poole's analysis was the assumption that the central bank can set the money stock exogenously. In most economies where a large proportion of the money with the public represents the liabilities of private depository institutions, the money-creating activities of these institutions can be considered to be outside the immediate control of the central bank. Here, what the central bank can directly set is some measure of its own liabilities—that is, bank reserves or the monetary base. The instrument problem now becomes an issue of targeting bank reserves (or the monetary base) *versus* interest rate. The treatment of the portfolio behaviour of banks *separately* from that of the non-bank public provides an additional dimension to the instrument

[13] Obviously, under the assumption of short-run money neutrality and rational expectations, the choice of the appropriate operating procedure becomes a non-issue since monetary policy has no real effects, whatever be the operating procedure. In fact, as Sargent and Wallace (1975) have argued, the price-level becomes indeterminate under an interest rate instrument. It should be noted, however, that once one allows for a non-trivial aggregate supply behaviour (that is less than perfectly flexible prices and wages), the basic insight of Poole's analysis with respect to the choice of the appropriate instrument remains, even under the rational expectations assumption.

problem. Friedman (1990) extended the Poole model by introducing a demand function for reserves by banks (along the lines of Brunner and Meltzer 1972), where the demand for reserves is positively related to the interest rate. Friedman showed that as before under interest rate targeting, income is exposed to effects due to disturbances in aggregate spending behaviour. However, under bank reserve targeting, income is exposed to the effects of disturbances in both money demand and money supply behaviour.

As we have found, the process of financial liberalization in India has led to a higher variance in money and bank reserve demand. In this case, an interest rate peg may be considered to be the desirable operating procedure. This is for two reasons. Firstly, an interest rate peg minimizes the variability of output in a period of unstable money supply and money demand.[14] Secondly the volatility of interest rates can often lead to reduced trade in financial assets and thereby, act as a possible constraint to the success of the reform process. This has been most clearly seen in the Indian context when the volatility in the call money market in the second half of 1994, led several firms and financial institutions to hold back on their proposals to issue floating rate bonds in the Indian capital market (see *EPW* Money Market Review, 15 October, 1994).

As yet, no serious consideration seems to have been given to the instrument problem by RBI, which stills appears to follow a *de facto* base targeting procedure (though the latter has come under severe pressure with the turbulence in the call money market). However, an explicit interest rate peg can only be successful with greater integration of the different short-term financial markets than is the case currently and with the ability of the RBI to monitor these markets more closely.

IV. Central Bank Independence

We have had occasion to point out (Chapter 6) that there were certain indications of macroeconomic instability by the end of 1993. The inflation rate was approaching the two-digit mark and the fiscal deficit to GDP ratio had risen to 7.4 per cent in 1993. Though a large part of the increase in inflation can be linked to increased foreign inflows and

[14] It is interesting to note that the central banks of six industrial countries—the United States, Japan, Germany, the United Kingdom, Canada, and Switzerland—use interest rate operating objectives to guide their daily activities (Kasman 1992). One reason for this is that 'the relationship between reserves and economic activity generally has been viewed as too volatile to function as an effective short-run guide to policy' (Ibid, p. 5), particularly in the context of the deregulation of the financial sector in several of these countries in the late seventies and early eighties.

a consequent rise in liquidity, and though the growth in fiscal deficit was not accompanied by an increase in the extent of monetization, the fact that both inflation and the deficit had risen was a matter of concern.

The success or failure in curtailment of the deficit (and its mode of financing) has a lot to do with political factors. The literature on political budget cycles argues that political parties in power would use the policy instruments at their command in their attempts to increase the probability of being re-elected. Recent models that incorporate rational expectations and forward-looking voter behaviour (e.g. Rogoff and Sibert 1988; Rogoff 1990) predict opportunistic electoral cycles in policy variables like taxes, government consumption and investment expenditures, deficits and inflation, with little or no cycles in real variables like output and employment. Sen and Vaidya (1996) attempt to test the validity of these predictions. They find strong evidence of an increase in the budget deficit and its monetization in the years leading up to an election. Weak evidence was also found of electoral cycles in government investment expenditures and taxes. No such cycles were discernible in output. Therefore, the predictions of the recent theories of political budget cycles appear to be valid in the Indian context.

Another strand of the literature focuses on the dynamic inconsistency problem of monetary control (see Blackburn and Christensen 1989 for an excellent survey). The basic argument here is that pledges by the monetary authorities to control inflation, lack credibility, because the public at large realizes that policy makers have an incentive to allow for temporary increases in monetary expansion, so as to achieve an increase in output. The Public Choice theorists (e.g. Brennan and Buchanan 1981; Sheffrin 1989) have argued that unless there exist constitutional or institutional constraints, a democratically elected government always has a bias towards deficit financing. However, McCallum (1995) argues that constitutional or institutional arrangements which constrain the central bank to follow a non-inflationary monetary policy would be unnecessary, provided the central bank is able to recognize the futility of continually exploiting expectations, and that its objectives will be more fully achieved if it were to abstain from such short-sighted attempts to exploit these temporarily given expectations. Here it can be argued that only a central bank that is functionally independent (in the sense of the absence of an arm of the government, which is empowered to supersede the policy decisions of the central bank) would be likely to behave in such a fashion.

The curtailment of the deficit and especially its mode of financing is vital to the success of financial liberalization. A mechanism that has been suggested by various authors to mitigate inherent inflationary pressure is that of greater central bank independence. In operational terms this would imply that the central bank would be granted the power to refuse to monetize the deficit. At an empirical level, several studies (e.g. Haverilsky and Granato 1993) have demonstrated that greater central bank independence is associated with lower inflation rates.

In the Indian context there is no real move towards complete central bank autonomy. A step that has in fact been initiated is with regard to the extent of monetization of the deficit. In September 1994 an agreement was signed between the Government of India and RBI which stipulated that at the end of the financial year 1994–5 the net issue of *ad hoc* treasury bills should not exceed Rs 6,000 crores and the net issue of *ad hoc* treasury bills should not exceed Rs 9,000 crores for more than ten continuous working days. If the limit was to be exceeded, the RBI would auction Government of India dated securities to the extent of the excess. In effect, this implies that RBI credit to the government is curtailed and that RBI does possess limited power to refuse to fund the deficit. In such a scenario, if the deficit is not curtailed, the internal public debt of the government would automatically rise. As we have observed in Chapter 6, there are clear indications that this is in fact happening in the Indian context.

Whether this limited independence is likely to overcome the problem of dynamic inconsistency is a debatable issue. McCallum (1995) has pointed out that central bank independence does not overcome the problem of dynamic inconsistency but merely relocates it to the government's own policy horizon. Assuming opportunistic behaviour on the part of parties in power (following the political budget cycles literature) and the fact that typically governments have limited terms in office (five years in the Indian context), even this limited independence is unlikely to survive, especially in the years leading up to an election. It remains to be seen whether the independence that has been conferred on the RBI continues in the face of political compulsions.

V. Concluding Remarks

We have found in this chapter that the financial liberalization process has had a significant impact on the conduct of the monetary policy both by altering the process of money supply creation and by causing changes in the money demand function. We saw that the money multipliers pertaining to M1 and M3 were unstable in the late eighties and early nineties. In the case of money demand, real M1 was found to be stable; however there is evidence of instability in real M3 demand in the post-1991 period. We have also discussed some of implications of the literature on the targets and instruments of monetary policy and central bank independence for India.

8

Conclusions

It is now over four years since the initiation of financial sector reforms in India. Though enough time has not passed to arrive at any firm conclusions about its success or failure, clear patterns are emerging which indicate the possible course and likely implications of the reform process. It should be remembered that the reforms were undertaken at a time when the economy was in the midst of a severe macroeconomic crisis. That the reforms have not led to serious disruptions in economic activity can be attributed both to the initial conditions and the 'gradualist' approach followed.

Important among the initial conditions was the presence of a diversified financial sector with institutions that had a long history in the intermediation of funds. Three sets of institutions of which special mention needs to be made (in contrast to other liberalizing economies) were the commercial banks, that had already contributed significantly to the financial deepening in the economy, the development finance institutions, who over a period of time had built strong links with the corporate sector, and the stock market which, though underdeveloped in many respects, had a fairly important position in the mobilization of funds. Another favourable initial condition was that the reform process in the real sector had already begun well before the financial sector reforms. As a consequence, the market mechanism already had a significant role to play in the allocation of resources across various industries.

The gradualist approach followed involved the cushioning of certain sectors from the possible adverse consequences of deregulation. This is particularly evident in the case of commercial banks, in whose case mandatory lending requirements were kept intact to ensure that the flow of credit to the agricultural sector and the small scale industries was not disrupted. While the reform process has led to a decline in subsidized and captive sources of credit for developmental finance institutions in general, NABARD and SIDBI continued to have access to them. Another important component of the gradualist approach was the phased deregulation of interest rates, both on short- and long-term credit.

With two decades of 'social control', commercial banks have been arguably the weakest of the financial institutions at the beginning of the reform process. Significant steps have been taken to make banks capable of operating in a more competitive environment. These involved the lifting of several restrictions on uses of funds by banks, interest rate deregulation, recapitalization of banks, and the adoption of a uniform accounting norm. However, certain features of the earlier era still remain: in particular, branch licensing policies which were maintained, though in a slightly weaker form and priority sector lending restrictions. This reflects a reluctance on the part of policy makers to shift to a truly deregulated and competitive banking system. In this instance, policy makers face a dilemma regarding the continued need for the presence of financial institutions in rural areas and the need to ensure that bank operations are guided increasingly by the profit motive.

A noteworthy feature of the intermediation process has been the increasingly important role of other financial institutions (especially the development finance institutions who both make long-term loans to and hold equity of corporate firms) in the intermediation of funds to the private corporate sector. Reforms of the development finance institutions involved the contraction of captive and subsidized sources of funds and deregulation of lending rates. It is important to note that the very fact that these institutions had a fairly long history of operations allowed them to make the transition from captive and subsidized sources of funds to the market within a relatively short period. We have found that the links between corporate firms and these institutions have strengthened in recent years. We have argued that the role of these institutions in the monitoring and screening of firms can lead to a better allocation of resources.

The deregulation of financial markets has followed a sequence, with short-term markets such as the money and T bills markets being deregulated first. This was followed by the deregulation of credit markets (both short-term and long-term), the stock market (especially the primary issues market) and the market for dated securities. In all these markets, reforms have transformed the primary markets in a significant manner. In comparison relatively less progress has been made in the development and reform of secondary markets. This implies that an efficient pricing mechanism for financial assets is still not in place (this may be less true of the stock market as compared to the market for government securities).

The timing of deregulation of interest rates on long-term loans (which led to an immediate and significant rise in the interest rate) and the primary issues markets (which led to a substantial decrease in the cost of raising funds because of free pricing of new issues) enabled the corporate sector to shift from the relatively costlier source to the cheaper source within a year. Though the investment climate was uncertain for about a year after deregulation of interest rates, within about two years the tempo was revived, with the primary issues market playing a far larger role than ever before. An important characteristic of the way Indian firms (and firms in other underdeveloped countries) finance their operations is the greater reliance on external sources of funds. This dependence on external sources has increased after the onset of reforms.

One feature of the intermediation of funds in the past (due to policies that led to financial repression) has been the dominant position of the government among ultimate borrowers. With financial sector reforms, while it is clear that the nature of government borrowing has fundamentally changed, there is no evidence, yet, of a decrease in the dependence of the government on the financial markets for financing its expenditures. This has acted as a constraint on the flow of full benefits of reforms to the productive sectors, in terms of both availability and cost of funds. There are no indications that the situation is going to change in the short- to medium-term.

Inertia on the part of the government, to curtail its reliance on market borrowings to finance its expenditures, created difficulties for RBI in following a monetary policy consistent with both price and financial stability. The conduct of monetary policy became even more problematic with the instability in the money multiplier and money (M3) demand function with the onset of the reforms. This in turn meant that strict control of the monetary base on the part of RBI could lead to frequent and potentially massive movements in interest rates (signs of which were already evident in the call money market). There was, therefore, a need for the RBI to share with the financial markets the burden of adjustment that is an inevitable consequence of financial liberalization. This implied that RBI needed to shift its operating procedures to an explicit interest rate peg, a move that was desirable in the interests of financial stability. However, a shift to an explicit interest rate peg was not feasible in the context of the absence of well-developed secondary markets for treasury bills.

Another impediment to the success of financial sector reforms is the public ownership of commercial banks and certain financial institutions. This ownership pattern is unlikely to change in the immediate future. While the monitoring of managers is a problem with public sector enterprises in general, it is of particular significance in the case of financial intermediaries (especially banks) due to the problem of 'moral hazard' that is so much a feature of financial markets. While the literature on financial sector reform has emphasized the negative effects that public ownership of banks may have on the efficiency of financial intermediation, we would argue that, owing to the externalities that are evident with bank insolvency, public ownership of banks may have potentially more adverse implications on the stability and solvency of the financial system in a deregulated environment.

Perhaps the most complex issue in the process of financial liberalization is the sequencing of steps in the various markets and sectors. Experiences of other countries have shown that the appropriate ordering of the steps involved has often been the key determinant of the success of the reforms. Two aspects of the sequencing issue are of particular relevance for India. These are: i) the sequencing of microeconomic and macroeconomic reforms; and ii) the sequencing of real and financial sector reforms. With regard to the first, it can be argued that the ordering of steps left a lot to be desired. In particular, the liberalization of controls on foreign portfolio investment without having adequately developed the treasury bills market led to problems of macroeconomic management two years into the reforms. Here, given that the need of the hour was macroeconomic stability, in the wake of the 1991 crisis a more cautious opening up of the Indian capital market to foreign portfolio investment along with a greater use of quantitative controls on the inflow of short-term capital was called for.[1] As Devlin *et al.* (1994) have argued, 'the more pressing the need for management, and the more underdeveloped fiscal and monetary policy is, the more likely it is that the use of direct regulations on certain types of capital flow will be warranted, even if temporarily' (p. 41). Therefore, while regulation of capital inflows can have possible microeconomic costs, it could be argued that in the Indian context, the costs would perhaps

[1] The Latin American experience with foreign portfolio investment in the nineties is particularly revealing. Chile employed a wide range of quantitative controls on short-term capital inflow and was able to manage capital flows fairly effectively till late 1995. Mexico, on the other hand, suffered a run on its international reserves in early 1995 in part due to a more 'laissez-faire' attitude to short-term capital inflows (on this, see Devlin *et al.* 1994; McKinnon and Pill 1995).

have been offset by the benefits obtained from macroeconomic stability.

Another important aspect of the micro/macro sequencing issue was the move to the market-determination of interest rates that occurred in the presence of large fiscal deficits. By putting an upward pressure on domestic interest rates, this further worsened an already fragile macroeconomic environment. The inappropriate sequencing of partial capital account liberalization before putting the fiscal house in order also greatly constrained the ability of policy makers to co-ordinate fiscal and monetary policies in an appropriate manner. Thus, in the face of the large fiscal deficits of 1993–4 and the already high real interest rates that prevailed during that time, a greater recourse to money-financing of the deficit was called for. With the monetization of the foreign capital inflows and the consequent upward pressure on the price level, this was clearly not a feasible policy action for RBI under the given circumstances.

However, it can be argued that given the greater market-determination of the allocation of resources in the industrial sector, deregulation of interest rates was a logical policy step in the reform process. Furthermore, in such an environment, the improvement of the financial health of commercial banks and other financial institutions was vital. Interest rate deregulation (with the safeguards mentioned earlier being incorporated) along with the recapitalization of banks was intended to achieve this. For the policy makers then, there was little flexibility available with respect to the timing of interest rate deregulation.

With regard to the pace of financial sector reforms in the future, two important constraints are likely to arise from the real sector. Firstly, there has been no real attempt to streamline the operations of bankruptcy laws and exit procedures. The inefficient functioning of the exit process leads to the existence of far too many firms that may have otherwise shut down and affects the financial health of intermediaries who may have made loans to loss-making enterprises. Secondly, the reluctance of the government to privatize public sector enterprises is a major hindrance to restructuring of the industrial sector. The investments of public sector enterprises are still under direct supervision of the government and thus these investments are not necessarily market-driven.

The costs that a transition from financial repression to financial liberalization imposes on the economy may be large and immediate. In a democracy, it is important to safeguard certain sectors of the economy from bearing these costs. It can be argued that this has been fairly successfully achieved in the Indian context. The expected benefit of financial liberalization is a better allocation of resources and a more efficient intermediation of funds. The realization of expected benefits may take time and would depend on the regulatory regime, the pace of other reforms, the macroeconomic environment and the conduct of monetary policy.

References

Agarwal, P., S. Gokarn, V. Mishra, K.S. Parikh and K. Sen (1995), *Economic Restructuring in East Asia and India: Perspectives on Policy Reform,* Basingtoke, UK: Macmillan.

Anant, T.S. Gangopadhyay and O. Goswami (1992), *Industrial Sickness in India: Initial Findings,* Paper No. 2, Studies in Industrial Development, Ministry of Industries, Government of India.

Ando, A. and K. Shell (1975), 'Demand for Money in a General Portfolio Model in the Presence of an Asset that Dominates Money', in G. Fromm and L. Klein (eds), *The Brookings Model: Perspectives and Recent Developments,* New York: North Holland.

Arrau, P., *et al.* (1995), 'The Demand for Money in Developing Countries: Assessing the Role of Financial Innovation', *Journal of Development Economics,* vol. 46, pp. 317–40.

Athukorala, P. (1995), 'Interest Rates, Saving and Investment in India', *Australia South Asia Research Centre,* Australian National University, mimeo.

Athukorala, P. and K. Sen (1995), 'Economic Reforms and the Rate of Saving in India', *Economic and Political Weekly,* vol. 30(35), September 2, pp. 2184–90.

——(1996), 'Reforms and Investment in India', *Australia South Asia Research Centre,* Australian National University, mimeo.

Baba, Y., D.F. Hendry and R.M. Starr (1992), 'The Demand for M1 in the USA, 1960–1988', *Review of Economic Studies,* vol. 59, pp. 25–61.

Balakrishnan, P. (1991), *Pricing and Inflation in the Indian Economy,* New Delhi: Oxford University Press.

Barua, S.K., V. Raghunathan and J.R. Varma (1994) 'Research on Indian Capital Markets: A review', *Vikalpa,* vol. 19(1), pp. 15–31.

Baumol. W. (1952), 'The Transactions Demand for Money: An Inventory Theoretic Approach', *Quarterly Journal of Economics,* vol. 66, pp. 545–56.

——(1959), *Business Behaviour and Growth,* New York: Macmillan.

Bayoumi, T. (1993), 'Financial Deregulation and Household Saving', *Economic Journal,* vol. 103, pp. 1432–43.

Bernanke, B. (1983), 'Non-Monetary Effects of the Financial Crisis in the Propagation of the Great Depression', *American Economic Review,* vol. 73, pp. 257–76.

Besley, T. (1994), 'How do Market Failures Justify Interventions in Rural Credit Markets?', *World Bank Research Observer,* vol. 9(1), pp. 27–47.

Bhattacharya, B.B. (1992), 'Behaviour of Public Debt in India', *Journal of Quantitative Economics,* vol. 8(1), pp. 29–50.

Bhaumik, S. and J. Sarkar (1996), 'Entry Deregulation and Banking Market Competition: The Indian Experience', Indira Gandhi *Institute of Development Research,* Discussion Paper No. 131, Mumbai.

Black, F. (1970), 'Banking and Interest Rates in a World without Money: The Effects of Uncontrolled Money', reprinted in Fisher Black, *Business Cycles and Equilibrium,* New York: Basil Blackwell.

Blackburn, K. and M. Christensen (1989), 'Monetary Policy and Policy Credibility: Theory and Evidence', *Journal of Economic Literature,* vol. 27, pp. 1–45.

Bombay Stock Exchange (BSE, 1995), *The Stock Exchange Official Directory.*

Bomhoff, E. (1977), 'Predicting the Money Multiplier: A Case-Study of the U.S. and the Netherlands', *Journal of Monetary Economics,* vol. 3, pp. 325–46.

Brennan, G.H. and J.M. Buchanan (1981), 'Monopoly in Money and Inflation', in J.M. Buchanan (ed.), *Constitutional Economics,* Oxford: Basil Blackwell.

Brunner, K. and A. Meltzer, (1972), 'Money, Debt and Economic Activity', *Journal of Political Economy,* vol. 80, pp. 951–77.

Buiter, W. (1983), 'Measurement of the Public Sector Deficit and Its Implications for Policy Evaluation and Design', *International Monetary Fund Staff Papers,* vol. 30, pp. 306–49.

——(1985), 'A Guide to Public Sector Debt and Deficits', *Economic Policy,* pp. 13–79.

Buiter, W. and U. Patel (1992), 'Debt, Deficits and Inflation: An Application to the Public Finances of India', *Journal of Public Economics,* vol. 47, pp. 172–205.

——(1993), 'Indian Public Finances in the 1990s: Challenges and Prospects', *Economic Growth Center,* Yale University, mimeo.

Calomiris, C. and G. Gorton (1991), 'The Origins of Banking Panics: Models, Facts and Bank Regulation', in R.G. Hubbard (ed.),

Financial Markets and Financial Crisis, Chicago: University of Chicago Press.

Calvo, G., L. Leiderman and C. Reinhart (1995), 'Capital Inflows to Latin America with reference to the Asian Experience', in S. Edwards (ed.), *Capital Controls, Exchange Rates and Monetary Policy in the World Economy,* Cambridge: Cambridge University Press.

Caprio, G., I. Atiyas and J. Hanson (1994), *Financial Reform: Theory and Experience,* New York: Cambridge University Press.

Caprio, G. and L. Summers (1993), 'Finance and its Reform: Beyond Laissez-Faire', Working Paper No. 1171, Washington DC: World Bank.

Centre for Monitoring the Indian Economy (1993), *Key Financial Data on Central Government Enterprises,* Economic Intelligence Service, Mumbai.

Chakravarty, S. (1987), *Development Planning: The Indian Experience,* New Delhi: Oxford University Press.

Chaves, R.A. and C. Gonzalez-Vega (1996), 'The Design of Rural Financial Intermediaries: Evidence from Indonesia', *World Development,* vol. 24(1), pp. 65–78.

Chick, V. (1988), 'Sources of Finance, Recent Changes in Bank Behaviour and the Theory of Investment and Interest', in P. Arestis (ed.), *Contemporary Issues in Money and Banking,* London: Macmillan.

Chitre, V.S. (1986), 'Quarterly Predictions of Reserve Money Multiplier and Money Stock in India', *Arthavijnana,* vol. 28, pp. 1–123.

Cho, Y.J. (1986), 'Inefficiencies from Financial Liberalization in the Absence of Well-Functioning Capital Markets', *Journal of Money, Credit and Banking,* vol. 18(2), pp. 191–9.

Chou, T-C. (1995), 'Taiwan', in C.H. Lee and S. Haggard (eds), *Financial Systems and Economic Policy in Developing Countries,* Ithaca: Cornell University Press.

Cobham, D. (1991), 'The Money Supply Process', in C.J. Green and D.T. Llewellyn (eds), *Surveys in Monetary Economics,* vol. II, Oxford: Basil Blackwell.

Damme, E. Van (1994), 'Banking: A Survey of Recent Microeconomic Theory', *Oxford Review of Economic Policy,* vol. 10(4), pp. 14–33.

Davidson, P. (1988), 'Endogenous money, the production process and inflation analysis', *Economic Applique,* vol. 56(1), pp. 151–69.

Davis, K.T. and M.K. Lewis (1992), 'Deregulation and Monetary Policy', in K. Dowd adn M.K. Lewis (eds), *Current Issues in Financial and Monetary Policy,* London: Macmillan.

Devlin, R., *et al.* (1994), 'Surges in Capital Flows and Development: An Overview of Policy Issues', in R. Ffrench-Davies and S. Griffith-Jones (eds), *Coping with Capital Surges: Latin American Macroeconomics and Investment,* Boulder: Lynne Rienner.

Dewatripont, M. and J. Tirole (1994), *The Prudential Regulation of Banks,* Cambridge, US: The MIT Press.

Diamond, D. (1984), 'Financial Intermediation and Delegated Monitoring', *Review of Economic Studies,* vol. 51, pp. 393–414.

——(1991), 'Monitoring and Reputation: The Choice between Bank Loan and Directly Placed Debt', *Journal of Political Economy,* vol. 99, pp. 689–721.

Diamond, D. and P. Dybig (1983), 'Bank Runs, Deposit Insurance and Liquidity', *Journal of Political Economy,* vol. 91, pp. 401–19.

Diaz Alejandro, C. (1985), 'Goodbye Financial Repression, Hello Financial Crash', *Journal of Development Economics,* vol. 19, pp. 1–24.

Dow, S. and P. Earl (1982), *Money Matters: A Keynesian Approach to Monetary Economics,* Oxford: Martin Robertson.

Easterly, W., *et al.* (1994), *Public Sector Deficits and Macroeconomic Performance,* New York: Oxford University Press.

Economic and Political Weekly, Money Market Reviews, 15 October, 1994; 14 January, 1995; 11 February, 1995; 11 March, 1995; and 8 April, 1995.

Edwards, J. and K. Fischer (1994), *Banks, Finance and Investment in Germany,* Cambridge: Cambridge University Press.

Engle, R. and C.W.J. Granger (1987), 'Cointegration and Error Correction: Representation, Estimation and Testing', *Econometrica,* vol. 55, pp. 251–76.

Fama, E. (1980), 'Banking in the Theory of Finance', *Journal of Monetary Economics,* vol. 6(1), pp. 39–57.

——(1985), 'What's Different About Banks?', *Journal of Monetary Economics,* vol. 15, pp. 29–39.

Fazzari, S.M., R.G. Hubbard and B. Petersen (1988), 'Financing Constraints and Corporate Investment', *Brookings Papers on Economic Activity,* vol. 1, pp. 141–95.

Folkerts-Landau, D., *et al.* (1994), *The Effect of Capital Inflows on the Domestic Financial Sectors in Developing Countries,* Washington DC: IMF.

Frenkel, J. and M. Mussa (1985), 'Asset Markets, Exchange Rates and the Balance of Payments', in R.W. Jones and P. Kenen (eds), *Handbook of International Economics,* vol. II. Amsterdam: North Holland.

Friedman, B. (1990), 'Targets and Instruments of Monetary Policy', in B. Friedman and F.H. Hahn (eds), *Handbook of Monetary Economics:* vol. II. Elsevier Science Publishers.

Frowen, S. and S. Kath (eds) (1992), *Monetary Policy and Financial Innovation in Five Industrial Countries,* London: Macmillan.

Gertler, M. and A. Rose (1994), 'Finance, Public Policy and Growth', in G. Caprio, I. Atiyas and J. Hanson (eds), *Financial Reform: Theory and Experience,* New York: Cambridge University Press.

Gokarn, S. (1995), 'Regulation of the Indian Stock Market: An Assessment of Recent Reforms', *Indira Gandhi Institute of Development Research,* Mumbai, mimeo.

Goldfield, S., and D.E. Sichel (1990), 'The Demand for Money', in B. Friedman and F.H. Hahn (eds), *Handbook of Monetary Economics,* Amsterdam: North Holland.

Goldsmith, R.W. (1969), *Financial Structure and Development,* New Haven: Yale University Press.

Goodhart, C.A.E. (1984), *Monetary Theory and Practice: the UK Experience,* London: Macmillan.

——(1989), *Money, Information and Uncertainty,* London: Macmillan.

——(1993), 'Can We Improve the Structure of Financial Systems?', *European Economic Review,* vol. 37(2–3), pp. 269–91.

——(1994), 'What should Central Banks do? What should be their Macroeconomic Objectives and Operations?', *Economic Journal,* vol. 104, pp. 1424–36.

Goodhart, C.A.E. and D. Schoenmaker (1995), 'Should the Functions of Monetary Policy and Banking Supervision be Separated?', *Oxford Economic Papers,* vol. 47, pp. 539–60.

Gopalsamy, N. (1994), *Capital Issues and SEBI Guidelines,* New Delhi: South Asia Publications.

Gorton, G. (1994), 'Bank Regulations when "Banks" and "Banking" are not the same', *Oxford Review of Economic Policy,* vol. 10(4), pp. 106–19.

Gorton, G. and D. Mullineaux (1987), 'The Joint Production of Confidence: Endogenous Regulation and 19th Century Commercial Bank Clearing-houses', *Journal of Money, Credit and Banking,* vol. 19(4), pp. 458–68.

Goyal, R. (1995), 'Volatility in Stock Market Returns' *RBI Occasional Papers,* vol. 16(3), pp. 175–95.

Granger, C.W.J. and P. Newbold (1974), 'Spurious Regression in Econometrics', *Journal of Econometrics,* vol. 26, pp. 1045–66.

Greenwald, B. and J. Stiglitz (1992), 'Information, Finance and Markets: The Architecture of Allocative Mechanisms', *Journal of Industrial and Corporate Change,* vol. 1(1), pp. 37–63.

Greenwald, B., J. Stiglitz and A. Weiss (1984), 'Informational Imperfections in the Capital Market and Macroeconomic Fluctuations', *American Economic Review,* vol. 74, pp. 194–99.

Gupta, S.B. (1988), *Monetary Economics: Institutions, Theory and Policy,* New Delhi: S. Chand and Co.

Hafer, R.W. and S.E. Hein (1984), 'Predicting the Money Multiplier', *Journal of Monetary Economics,* vol. 14, pp. 375–84.

Hafer, R.W. and D.W. Jansen (1991), 'The Demand for Money in the United States: Evidence from Cointegration Tests', *Journal of Money, Credit and Banking,* vol. 23(2), pp. 155–68.

Hart, O. (1995), *Firms, Contracts and Financial Structure,* New York: Oxford University Press.

Haverilsky, T. and J. Granato (1993), 'Determinants of Inflationary Performance: Corporatist Strategy Vs Central Bank Autonomy', *Public Choice,* vol. 76, pp. 249–61.

Hendry, D.F. and N.R. Ericsson (1991), 'Modelling the Demand for Narrow Money in the UK and the US', *European Economic Review,* vol. 35, pp. 833–66.

Hoshi, T., A. Kashyap and D. Scharfstein (1991), 'Corporate Structure, Liquidity and Investment: Evidence from Japanese Industrial Groups', *Quarterly Journal of Economics,* vol. 106, pp. 33–60.

Ignatius, R. (1992), 'The Bombay Stock Exchange: Seasonalities and Investment Opportunities', *Indian Economic Review,* vol. 27, pp. 223–27.

Indian Banks Association (IBA, 1994), *Indian Banking Yearbook 1994,* Mumbai.

Jadhav, N. (1995), *Monetary Economics for India,* New Delhi: Macmillan.

Jappelli, T. and M. Pagano (1991), 'Saving, Growth and Liquidity Constraints', *Istituto Universitario Navale,* Napoli, mimeo.

Johannes, J.M. and R.H. Rasche, (1979), 'Predicting the Money Multiplier', *Journal of Monetary Economics,* vol. 5, pp. 301–25.

——(1981), 'Can the Reserves Approach to Monetary Control really work?' *Journal of Money, Credit and Banking,* vol. 13, pp. 298–313.

Johansen, S. and K. Juselius (1990), 'Maximum Likelihood Estimation and Inference on Cointegration—With Applications to the Demand for Money', *Oxford Bulletin of Economics and Statistics,* vol. 52(2), pp. 169–210.

Joshi, V. and I.M.D. Little (1994), *India: Macroeconomics and Political Economy,* 1964–1991, New Delhi: Oxford University Press.

——(1996), *India's Economic Reforms, 1991–2001,* New Delhi: Oxford University Press.

Kasman, B. (1992), 'A Comparison of Monetary Policy Operating Procedures in Six Industrial Countries', *Federal Reserve Bulletin of New York Quarterly Review,* Summer, pp. 5–24.

King, R. and R. Levine (1993), 'Finance, Entrepreneurship and Growth', *Journal of Monetary Economics,* vol, 32, pp. 513–42.

Krishnaswamy, K.S., K. Krishnamurty and P.D. Sharma (1987), *Improving Domestic Resource Mobilisation Through Financial Development: India,* Manila: Asian Development Bank.

Krueger, A. (1995), *Political Economy of Policy Reform in Developing Countries,* Cambridge, MA.: The MIT Press.

Marris, R. (1964), *The Economic Theory of Managerial Capitalism,* Glencoe, Illinois: Free Press of Glencoe.

Mayer, C. (1988), 'New Issues in Corporate Finance', *European Economic Review,* vol. 32, pp. 1167–89.

——(1990), 'Financial Systems, Corporate Finance and Economic Development', in R.G. Hubbard (ed.) *Asymetric Information, Corporate Finance and Investment,* Chicago: University of Chicago Press.

McCallum, B. (1995), 'Two Fallacies concerning Central Bank Independence', *NBER Working Paper,* Cambridge, MA.

McKinnon, R. (1973), *Money and Capital in Economic Development,* Washington DC: The Brookings Institute.

——(1993), *The Order of Economic Liberalisation: Financial Control in the Transition to a Market Economy,* London: John Hopkins University Press.

McKinnon, R. and H. Pill (1995), 'Credible Liberalisations and International Capital Flows: The "Over-borrowing" Syndrome', *Department of Economics,* Stanford University, mimeo.

Meek, P. (1991), 'Central Bank Liquidity Management and the Money Market', in G. Caprio and P. Honohan (eds), *Monetary Policy Instruments for Developing Countries,* Washington DC: The World Bank.

Mehra, Y.P. (1993), 'The Stability of the M2 Demand Function:

Evidence from an Error-Correction Model', *Journal of Money, Credit and Banking,* vol. 25(3), pp. 455–60.

Miller, S.M. (1991), 'Monetary Dynamics: An Application of Cointegration and Error-Correction Modelling', *Journal of Money, Credit and Banking,* vol. 23(2), pp. 139–54.

Ministry of Industry (MOI, 1993), *Report of the Committee on Industrial Sickness and Corporate Restructuring* (Goswami Committee Report), New Delhi.

Modigliani, F. and R. Brumberg (1954), 'Utility Analysis and the Consumption Function: An Interpretation of Cross-section Data', in K.K. Kurihara (ed.), *Post-Keynesian Economics,* New Brunswick, N.J.: Rutgers University Press.

Modigliani, F. and E. Perotti (1991), 'The Rules of the Game and the Development of Security Markets', in S. Rhee and R.P. Chang (eds), *Pacific-Basin Capital Markets Research,* vol. II, Amsterdam: North Holland.

Moore, B.J. (1988), *Horizontalists and Verticalists: the Macroeconomics of Credit Money,* Cambridge: Cambridge University Press.

Myers, S. and N. Majluf (1984), 'Corporate Financing and Investment Decisions when Firms have Information that Investors do not have', *Journal of Financial Economics,* vol. 13, pp. 187–221.

Nachane, D. and D. Ray (1989), 'The Money Multiplier: A Re-examination of the Indian Evidence', *Indian Economic Journal,* vol. 37(1), pp. 56–73.

Nachane, D. (1992), 'The Money Multiplier in India: Short-run and Long-run Concepts', *Journal of Quantitative Economics,* vol. 8(1), pp. 51–66.

Nam, S-W. and C.H. Lee (1995), 'Korea', in C.H. Lee and S. Haggard (eds), *Financial Systems and Economic Policy in Developing Countries,* Ithaca: Cornell University Press.

Orden, D. and L.A. Fisher (1993), 'Financial Deregulation and the Dynamics of Money, Prices and Output in New Zealand and Australia', *Journal of Money, Credit and Banking,* vol. 25(2), pp. 273–92.

Patrick, H. and Y.C. Park (1994, eds), *The Financial Development of Japan, Korea and Taiwan: Growth, Repression and Liberalization,* New York: Oxford University Press.

Poole, W. (1970), 'Optimal Choice of Monetary Policy Instrument in a Simple Stochastic Macro Model', *Quarterly Journal of Economics,* vol. 84, pp. 197–216.

Rakshit, M. (1983), 'On Assessment and Interpretation of Saving-Investment Estimates in India', *Economic and Political Weekly,* April, pp. 753–76.

Ramchandran, J. (1985), *Behaviour of Stock Prices, Trading Rules, Information and Market Efficiency,* Doctoral Dissertation, Indian Institute of Management, Ahmedabad.

Rangarajan, C. (1994), 'Developing the Money and Securities Markets in India', *Reserve Bnk of India Bulletin,* April, pp. 481–90.

Rangarajan, C. and A. Singh (1984), 'Reserve Money: Concepts and Policy Implications for India', *RBI Occasional Papers,* vol. 5(1), pp. 1–26.

Rangarajan, C., A. Basu and N. Jadhav (1989), 'Dynamics of Interaction between Government Deficit and Domestic Debt in India', *RBI Occasional Papers,* vol. 10(3), pp. 163–220.

Rao, M.G. and T. Sen (1993), 'Government Expenditure in India: Level, Growth and Composition', *National Institute of Public Finance and Policy,* mimeo.

RBI (1982), 'Capital Formation and Saving in India: 1950–1 to 1979–80', *Report of the Working Group on Saving: Raj Committee Report,* Mumbai.

——(1983), *The Reserve Bank of India: Functions and Working,* Mumbai.

——(1985), *Report of the Committee to Review the Working of the Money Market* (Chakravarty Committee Report), Mumbai.

——(1987), *Report of the Working Group on the Money Market* (Vaghul Committee Report), Mumbai.

——(1990), *Report of the Agricultural Credit Review Committee* (Khusro Committee Report), Mumbai.

——(1992), *Review of the Committee on Financial Companies* (Shah Committee Report), Mumbai.

——*Annual Reports,* Mumbai, various issues.

——*Banking Statistics,* Mumbai, various issues.

——*Report on Currency and Finance,* Mumbai, various issues.

——*Report on Trend and Progress in Banking,* Mumbai, various issues.

——*Reserve Bank of India Bulletin,* Mumbai, various issues.

Rogoff, K. (1990), 'Equilibrium Political Budget Cycles', *American Economic Review,* vol. 55, pp. 21–36.

Rogoff, K. and A. Silbert (1988), 'Equilibrium Political Business Cycles', *Review of Economic Studies,* vol. 55, pp. 1–16.

Roubini, N. and X. Sala-i-Martin (1992), 'Financial Repression and

Economic Growth', *Journal of Development Economics,* vol. 39(1), pp. 5–30.

——(1995), 'A Growth Model of Inflation, Tax Evasion and Financial Repression', *Journal of Monetary Economics,* vol. 35, pp. 275–31.

Saha, B. (1995), 'Forming or Reforming the Exit Policy', in K.S. Parikh (ed.), *Mid-year review of the Economy 1994–95,* New Delhi: Konark Publishers.

Sargent, T. and N. Wallace (1975), '"Rational Expectations", the optimal monetary instrument and the optimal money supply rule', *Journal of Political Economy,* vol. 83, pp. 241–54.

——(1981), 'Some Unpleasant Monetarist Arithmetic', *Federal Reserve Bank of Minneapolis Quarterly Review,* vol. 5(3), pp. 1–17.

Sen, K. and R.R. Vaidya (1995), 'The Determination of Industrial Prices in India: A Post Keynesian Approach', *Journal of Post Keynesian Economics,* vol. 18(1), pp. 29–51.

——(1996), 'Political Budget Cycles in India', *Economic and Political Weekly,* vol. 31(30), July 27, pp. 2023–27.

Shah, A. (1995), 'The Indian IPO Market: Empirical Facts', *Centre for Monitoring the Indian Economy,* Mumbai, mimeo.

Shaw, E. (1973), *Financial Factors in Economic Development,* New York: Oxford University Press.

Sheffrin, J. (1989), *The Making of Economic Policy,* Cambridge, MA.: Basil Blackwell.

Singh, A. (1992), 'The Stock Market and Economic Development: Should Developing Countries Encourage Stock Markets?', *UNCTAD/OSG Discussion Paper No. 49,* Geneva.

Singh, A. and J. Hamid (1992), 'Corporate Financial Structures in Developing Countries', *International Finance Corporation, Technical Paper No. 1,* Washington DC.

Srinivasan, R. (1993), *Security Prices Behaviour Associated with Rights Issue Related Events,* Doctoral Dissertation, Indian Institute of Management, Ahmedabad.

Srinivasan, T.N. (1994), 'Database for Development Analysis', *Journal of Development Economics,* vol. 44(1), pp. 3–27.

Stiglitz, J. (1993), 'The Role of the State in Financial Markets', *World Bank Economic Review,* Proceedings of the Annual Conference on Development Economics, pp. 19–52.

Stiglitz, J. and A. Weiss (1983), 'Credit Rationing in Markets with Imperfect Information', *American Economic Review,* vol. 71(3), pp. 393–410.

Subrahmanyam, G. (1993), 'Productivity Growth in India's Public

Sector Banks', *Journal of Quantitative Economics,* vol. 9(2), pp. 209–24.

Subramaniam, S. (1989), *The Impact of Political and Economic Events on Stock Behaviour,* Doctoral Dissertation, Indian Institute of Management, Ahmedabad.

Taylor, L. (1983), *Structuralist Macroeconomics,* New York: Basic Books.

Thomas, S. (1995), 'Hetroskedasticity Models on the Bombay Stock Exchange', *Centre for Monitoring Indian Economy,* Mumbai, mimeo.

Thornton, D.L. and C.C. Stone (1992), 'Financial Innovation: Causes and Consequences', in K. Dowd and M.K. Lewis (eds), *Current Issues in Financial and Monetary Policy.*

Tobin, J. (1956), 'The Interest Elasticity of Transactions Demand for Cash', *Review of Economics and Statistics,* vol. 38, pp. 241–7.

——(1958), 'Liquidity Preference as Behaviour Towards Risk', *Review of Economic Studies,* vol. 25, pp. 65–86.

Tseng, W, and R. Corker (1991), 'Financial Liberalisation, Money Demand and Monetary Policy in Asian Countries', *IMF Occasional Paper No. 84,* Washington DC.

Vaidya, R.R. (1994), 'Disinvestment of Public Sector Enterprise Shares', in K.S. Parikh (ed.), *Mid-year review of the Economy 1994–95,* New Delhi: Konark Publishers

Warman, F. and A.P. Thirwall (1994), 'Interest Rates, Saving, Investment and Growth in Mexico 1960–90: Tests of the Financial Liberalisation Hypothesis', *Journal of Development Studies,* vol. 30(3), pp. 629–49.

Wenner, M.D. (1995), 'Group Credit: A Means to Improve Information Transfer and Loan Repayment Performance', *Journal of Development Studies,* vol. 32(2), pp. 263–81.

White, M.J. (1989), 'The Corporate Bankruptcy Decision', *Journal of Economic Perspectives,* pp. 129–51.

Wijnbergen, S. Van (1983), 'Interest Rate Management in LDCs', *Journal of Development Economics,* vol. 12, pp. 433–52.

The World Bank (1993), *The East Asian Miracle: Economic Growth and Public Policy,* New York: Oxford University Press.

——*World Debt Tables,* Washington DC.

Index